JN 40 WHI

Palgrave Studies in European Union Politics

Edited by: **Michelle Egan**, American University USA, **Neill Nugent**, Manchester Metropolitan University, UK and **William Paterson OBE**, University of Aston, UK.

Editorial Board: **Christopher Hill**, Cambridge, UK, **Simon Hix**, London School of Economics, UK, **Mark Pollack**, Temple University, USA, **Kalypso Nicolaïdis**, Oxford UK, **Morten Egeberg**, University of Oslo, Norway, **Amy Verdun**, University of Victoria, Canada, **Claudio M. Radaelli**, University of Exeter, UK, **Frank Schimmelfennig**, Swiss Federal Institute of Technology, Switzerland.

Following on the sustained success of the acclaimed *European Union Series*, which essentially publishes research-based textbooks, *Palgrave Studies in European Union Politics* publishes cutting edge research-driven monographs.

The remit of the series is broadly defined, both in terms of subject and academic discipline. All topics of significance concerning the nature and operation of the European Union potentially fall within the scope of the series. The series is multidisciplinary to reflect the growing importance of the EU as a political, economic and social phenomenon.

Titles include:

Ian Bache and Andrew Jordan (*editors*)
THE EUROPEANIZATION OF BRITISH POLITICS

Richard Balme and Brian Bridges (*editors*)
EUROPE-ASIA RELATIONS
Building Multilateralisms

Thierry Balzacq (*editor*)
THE EXTERNAL DIMENSION OF EU JUSTICE AND HOME AFFAIRS
Governance, Neighbours, Security

Michael Baun and Dan Marek (*editors*)
EU COHESION POLICY AFTER ENLARGEMENT

Derek Beach and Colette Mazzucelli (*editors*)
LEADERSHIP IN THE BIG BANGS OF EUROPEAN INTEGRATION

Chris J. Bickerton
EUROPEAN UNION FOREIGN POLICY
From Effectiveness to Functionality

Tanja A. Börzel (*editor*)
COPING WITH ACCESSION TO THE EUROPEAN UNION
New Modes of Environmental Governance

Milena Büchs
NEW GOVERNANCE IN EUROPEAN SOCIAL POLICY
The Open Method of Coordination

Joan DeBardeleben, and Achim Hurrelmann (*editors*)
TRANSNATIONAL EUROPE
Promise, Paradox, Limits

Kenneth Dyson and Angelos Sepos (*editors*)
WHICH EUROPE?
The Politics of Differentiated Integration

Michelle Egan, Neill Nugent, William E. Paterson (*editors*)
RESEARCH AGENDAS IN EU STUDIES
Stalking the Elephant

Kevin Featherstone and Dimitris Papadimitriou
THE LIMITS OF EUROPEANIZATION
Reform Capacity and Policy Conflict in Greece

Stefan Gänzle and Allen G. Sens (*editors*)
THE CHANGING POLITICS OF EUROPEAN SECURITY
Europe Alone?

Heather Grabbe
THE EU'S TRANSFORMATIVE POWER

Eva Gross
THE EUROPEANIZATION OF NATIONAL FOREIGN POLICY
Continuity and Change in European Crisis Management

Adrienne Héritier and Martin Rhodes (*editors*)
NEW MODES OF GOVERNANCE IN EUROPE
Governing in the Shadow of Hierarchy

Wolfram Kaiser, Brigitte Leucht, Michael Gehler
TRANSNATIONAL NETWORKS IN REGIONAL INTEGRATION
Governing Europe 1945–83

Hussein Kassim and Handley Stevens
AIR TRANSPORT AND THE EUROPEAN UNION
Europeanization and its Limits

Robert Kissack
PURSUING EFFECTIVE MULTILATERALISM
The European Union, International Organizations and the Politics of Decision Making

Katie Verlin Laatikainen and Karen E. Smith (*editors*)
THE EUROPEAN UNION AND THE UNITED NATIONS
Intersecting Multilateralisms

Esra LaGro and Knud Erik Jørgensen (*editors*)
TURKEY AND THE EUROPEAN UNION
Prospects for a Difficult Encounter

Ingo Linsenmann, Christoph O. Meyer and Wolfgang T. Wessels (*editors*)
ECONOMIC GOVERNMENT OF THE EU
A Balance Sheet of New Modes of Policy Coordination

Hartmut Mayer and Henri Vogt (*editors*)
A RESPONSIBLE EUROPE?
Ethical Foundations of EU External Affairs

Philomena Murray (*editor*)
EUROPE AND ASIA
Regions in Flux

Costanza Musu
EUROPEAN UNION POLICY TOWARDS THE ARAB-ISRAELI PEACE PROCESS
The Quicksands of Politics

Daniel Naurin and Helen Wallace (*editors*)
UNVEILING THE COUNCIL OF THE EUROPEAN UNION
Games Governments Play in Brussels

David Phinnemore and Alex Warleigh-Lack
REFLECTIONS ON EUROPEAN INTEGRATION
50 Years of the Treaty of Rome

Sebastiaan Princen
AGENDA-SETTING IN THE EUROPEAN UNION

Emmanuelle Schon-Quinlivan
REFORMING THE EUROPEAN COMMISSION

Roger Scully and Richard Wyn Jones (*editors*)
EUROPE, REGIONS AND EUROPEAN REGIONALISM

Asle Toje
AFTER THE POST-COLD WAR
The European Union as a Small Power

Jonathan White
POLITICAL ALLEGIANCE AFTER EUROPEAN INTEGRATION

Richard G. Whitman and Stefan Wolff (*editors*)
THE EUROPEAN NEIGHBOURHOOD POLICY IN PERSPECTIVE
Context, Implementation and Impact

Palgrave Studies in European Union Politics
Series Standing Order ISBN 978–1–4039–9511–7 (hardback)
and ISBN 978–1–4039–9512–4 (paperback)

You can receive future titles in this series as they are published by placing a standing order. Please contact your bookseller or, in case of difficulty, write to us at the address below with your name and address, the title of the series and one of the ISBNs quoted above.

Customer Services Department, Macmillan Distribution Ltd, Houndmills, Basingstoke, Hampshire RG21 6XS, UK.

Political Allegiance After European Integration

Jonathan White

Lecturer in European Politics, European Institute, London School of Economics and Political Science, UK

First published 2011 by
PALGRAVE MACMILLAN

Palgrave Macmillan in the UK is an imprint of Macmillan Publishers Limited, registered in England, company number 785998, of Houndmills, Basingstoke, Hampshire RG21 6XS.

Palgrave Macmillan in the US is a division of St Martin's Press LLC, 175 Fifth Avenue, New York, NY 10010.

Palgrave Macmillan is the global academic imprint of the above companies and has companies and representatives throughout the world.

Palgrave® and Macmillan® are registered trademarks in the United States, the United Kingdom, Europe and other countries

ISBN 978-0-230-27978-0   hardback

This book is printed on paper suitable for recycling and made from fully managed and sustained forest sources. Logging, pulping and manufacturing processes are expected to conform to the environmental regulations of the country of origin.

A catalogue record for this book is available from the British Library.

Library of Congress Cataloging-in-Publication Data

White, Jonathan, 1973–
    Political allegiance after European integration / Jonathan White.
        p. cm.
    Includes index.
    ISBN 978–0–230–27978–0 (hardback)
    1. Allegiance–European Union countries. 2. European federation. I. Title.

JN40.W45 2011
323.6'5094–dc22   2011004877

10   9   8   7   6   5   4   3   2   1
20   19   18   17   16   15   14   13   12   11

Printed and bound in Great Britain by
CPI Antony Rowe, Chippenham and Eastbourne

Contents

Acknowledgements

A fair proportion of the text that follows was supplied to the author in conversation. A great deal of thanks goes to all the participating taxi-drivers who turned off their meters for a couple of hours and lent me their words on a range of topics. Their paragraphs are undoubtedly the most readable. For help in turning these resources into a book, I am deeply grateful to many at the European University Institute in Florence. Peter Wagner was a humane source of guidance and encouragement throughout. Donatella della Porta, Michael Keating and Stefano Bartolini read earlier texts and suggested a number of very useful leads. Volker Balli, Cesare Cuttica, Koen Jonkers, Rüdiger von Krosigk, Christine Reh, Herwig Reiter, Jakob Skovgaard, Kristina Stoeckl and Michael Voříšek were good enough to discuss my ideas, improve my German and Czech, and eat, drink or live with me. In Prague, Barbora Tichá expertly assisted preparation of the Czech topic guide and transcripts, while Pavel Barša and Andrea Baršová were the source of many enjoyable discussions and hospitality. Much of the study's textual analysis was conducted in Boston during a fellowship at Harvard's Kennedy School of Government: I especially thank Michèle Lamont for arranging the stay and reacting to my research on several occasions. Rainer Bauböck, Richard Bellamy, Damian Chalmers, Thomas Christiansen, Sophie Duchesne, Klaus Eder, Niilo Kauppi, Claudia Schrag, Neil Walker and several anonymous reviewers have also read parts of the manuscript or its entirety, commenting incisively and generously. Amber Stone-Galilee and Steven Kennedy have been supportive editors.

Some sections of the following draw on text I have published elsewhere. Selected paragraphs from Chapters 5 and 6 first appeared in 'Europe in the Political Imagination', *Journal of Common Market Studies*, 48 (4) 2010; Chapter 3 contains text from 'Thematization and Collective Positioning in Everyday Political Talk', *British Journal of Political Science*, 39 (4) 2009, while material from Chapter 1 has appeared in 'Europe and the Common', *Political Studies*, 58 (1) 2010. I gratefully acknowledge Cambridge University Press and Wiley-Blackwell Publishing for permission to reproduce.

The greatest impact on my work in recent years has been from Lea Ypi. She has immeasurably enriched my intellectual experiences as well as my life in general, and I am particularly indebted to her. I would also like to make special mention of my parents, for consistent support at all stages. The book is dedicated to them.

Introduction

The years around the turn of the millennium witnessed growing interest amongst scholars of the EU in the democratic basis of this political arrangement. Questions such as 'Does Europe need a constitution?' and 'Is there, or can there be, a European society?' were being asked, and proposals put forward on 'How to democratise the European Union and why bother'. In some ways this was remarkable, since for most of the period of post-war integration, issues of democracy had been rather marginal. Integration was widely conceived to be an elite-driven process in which broader societal concerns played a limited role, and the degree to which institutions were insulated from direct popular pressure seemed justifiable due to the control enjoyed by the representatives of national government. Yet from the early 1990s, it seemed, neither the empirical nor the normative argument could so readily be accepted. 'Non-elites' were clearly liable to have a strong influence on the course of the integration process, as the referenda results on the Maastricht Treaty in France and Denmark seemed to demonstrate, while the terms of this treaty suggested the emergence of something more than an intergovernmental forum for solving problems of a technical kind. Hence the scholarship on the EU developed a new concern for questions of democracy and political community: the responsiveness of institutions on the one hand, and the significance of culture, ideas and notions of peoplehood as preconditions for the acceptance of these institutions on the other. A debate emerged concerning the existence or possibility of a European 'demos', with this latter often understood in terms of socio-cultural regularities.

At the same time as scholars of the EU were discovering democracy, scholars of democracy were going through a period of revaluation themselves. In Anglo-Saxon political science and theory, it had become common to conceptualise the legitimacy of political association according to two, perhaps competing, principles: the principle of democracy (or collective self-rule) and the principle of constitutionalism (or the rule of law). While such a distinction is traceable in much of modern political thought, where the need to balance the expression of popular will with safeguards against a tyranny of the majority has been a familiar theme, what was perhaps new was the tendency to emphasise the latter at the expense of the former. The rule of law, it seemed, was being treated as more fundamental to democracy than the principle of democracy itself. A redefinition seemed to be taking place, such that certain changes in the world of practice could be more easily accommodated. Processes of juridification, of the weakening of political authority, and the decline of democratic deliberation in the representative institutions of the nation-state and amongst the broader public, were coming to be seen not as deviations from democracy but as patterns which could be accepted and even celebrated (Tully 2002; Mair 2006). The study and theorising of democracy was evolving rapidly.

Today, while Europe's political and economic climate has profoundly changed, both these trends continue. On the one hand, in EU studies, the 2005 referenda defeats for the proposed EU constitution slowed somewhat the flow of scholarship on 'constitutional moments' and the active founding of a polity, but questions to do with the viability of the EU and with its democratic credentials have if anything become more salient. On the other hand, in political science and thought, a small literature has begun to emerge on the dangers of depoliticisation, but in general the subordination of questions to do with 'the people' and the democratic principle has continued. Indeed, some of this has fed back into the debate concerning the democratic status of the EU: these redefinitions of democracy have been used to argue that the EU already satisfies the criteria of democratic legitimacy, not because it is no more than an interstate organisation (though this argument is sometimes heard), but because the kinds of policy-making it engages in are those which in modern democracies are properly put beyond majority control.

It may be possible to set these two bodies of concerns, to do with democracy and the EU, side by side without concluding that the EU must subordinate collective self-rule to the rule of law. One way to read debates about the possibility of a European demos is to see them as expressing a renewed concern about the conditions under which ideas of collective self-rule can be meaningfully realised. Yet to focus on socio-cultural regularities and treat these as the prerequisites of a viable democratic polity, as much of this literature has done, is to claim strong limits to the options available for political co-existence. While it may well be that individuals must hold something 'in common' if they are to regulate their lives through the same institutions, it may be appropriate to conceptualise this in ways less prone to determinism and to the devaluing of political adversarialism. The challenge would be to develop a less restrictive understanding of the possibilities for political association, *without* falling into the kind of voluntarism which blinds one to the existence of very real obstacles to democracy in the European context and prevents one acknowledging the weakness with which it is currently pursued.

Conversely, regarding the significance of the EU for democracy more generally, it may be that the EU experience encourages us to rethink the nature of political community, not so as to reduce it to a bare constitutionalism but so as to find ways of uncoupling it from the nationality principle which has been its underpinning in the context of the nation-state. If one understands the period of 'organised modernity' as being characterised by a fairly high degree of congruence between socio-economic practices, practices of social-cultural identification and the boundaries of the polity, and if one understands by contrast the contemporary world as one in which such closure can no longer be taken for granted (and on this there seems to be some consensus), then it may be that new concepts are needed that can better render conditions of boundary irregularity (Wagner 1996; Benhabib et al. 2007). Indeed, it may be that there are normative reasons to welcome these changed conditions. But even if there were not, the political constellation of contemporary Europe, characterised by a high degree of plurality, would seem to be a good place in which to explore the kinds of perspective with which one might try to substitute older, problematic notions of identity.

Two things seem to follow, if this reasoning is secure. It seems one may want ways of continuing the discussion about democracy in the EU, and the allegiances needed to support it, with a particular sensitivity to the idea that the principle of democratic control is being subordinated to the principle of constitutionalism. Likewise, it seems one may want ways of continuing the discussion about the nature of democracy more generally in ways that alert one to the possibility of a multiplication in points of reference and sources of identification, and of a diminishing coherence between these. These are the points of departure for the following project, which elaborates a perspective addressed to both concerns. It advances a conception of citizen allegiances which can be defended on normative grounds, as conducive to a meaningful and robust form of democracy, yet which is of sufficient empirical relevance that it can draw out some of the salient features of citizen self-understanding and political appraisal as they can be found in contemporary Europe.

The book's focus is in some ways prosaic: on the shared political problems which people describe themselves as facing, and the interpretative resources they use when talking about them. It is suggested that the sense of shared predicament before common problems may be a promising way to conceptualise the collective bond necessary for political community. The study opens out how such problems are routinely perceived amongst a chosen set of citizens, the patterns of alliance and opposition which they inspire, and the assumptions one finds concerning whether and how they might be susceptible to organised address.

By taking this problem-oriented approach, the intention is to stick closely to some of the basic issues to do with political association and the exercise of democratic voice. It is an approach different from much of what one finds in EU studies, where a common technique for studying the foundations of the EU amongst 'the people' is to ask a sample of people what they think of it. This is an expression of what one might call the 'EU-centrism' of EU studies: those who wish to study the EU have a natural tendency to put it centre-stage in their research design, leading to the collection of data which, while undeniably tied closely to the research topic, may rather inflate the EU's significance for respondents. The approach taken here, as will become clear, consists not in polling 'opinions' about the institutional architecture of contemporary Europe, nor in discerning abstract loyalties to one cultural world over another, but in examining the reference-points which are invoked spontaneously when people talk about the problems they see themselves, and people like themselves, as facing. The contours of political allegiance should be sought, it is suggested, not so much at the level of conscious beliefs and opinions about 'Europe', but in the taken-for-granted, common-sense understandings people express when talking about substantive issues. These understandings, though always revisable, structure the meanings that EU politics acquires. Rather than as a distinct object of affect, the EU is approached as a context of action, one evoked more readily or less so by its citizens. Such an approach allows one both to avoid an embedded EU-centrism and to comment more generally on questions to do with the health of democracy.

While the book begins in a theoretical mode, it soon takes an empirical turn by looking at the material generated in ten group discussions held with taxi-drivers in Britain, Germany and the Czech Republic. Theoretical ideas, unless one wishes to shelter them from all criticism except that to do with their internal logic, must be explored and developed outdoors. In this sense there is a political-sociological move to the work. But the purpose, it will be understood, is not that of the natural scientist: the empirical work is guided by the goals of concept-formation and critical diagnosis. By probing a small amount of data in considerable depth, one can refine one's concepts and show what they mean in practice. Rather than to test them, the primary goal is to unfold them – something for which a small but varied sample is ideal. A hermeneutic rationale of this sort does not exclude the possibility of generalising from the material and making claims of a falsifiable kind. A secondary aim of the study, beyond elaborating a theoretical approach, is to give an empirical reading of some of the ideational factors conditioning political attachments in the contemporary EU, supported where this is possible with cross-reference to existing data and research. With a detailed description of the research method in the Appendix, the study is in principle reproducible and extendable. Even a strongly interpretative study would undermine its purpose if it were not rigorous in its methods and methodology. But ultimately the guiding concerns here are those of the applied theorist, not those of the collector of facts.

A project such as this has a clearly cross-disciplinary character. It draws on political theory, social theory and political sociology, as well as on the relevant debates in EU studies and political science. It also involves the use of a relatively new qualitative research method – the 'focus group', or group discussion. While this breadth of resources is a positive feature, multidisciplinarity should never be the cause of easy celebration, for there are genuine tensions involved. Perhaps the most notable and most general is that between political and social theorising – a tension which too frequently leads them to be pursued in isolation. In this work, we shall be drawn towards political theory which is especially sensitive to the importance of historical context, and which does not pursue abstract and universal truths. At the same time, inspiration is taken not from classical sociology but from more recent approaches which combine attention to patterns with an emphasis on interpretation, choices, and the possibility of change.

There are six main chapters to the work that follows. Chapter 1 sets out the basic problem, which concerns how best to conceptualise the collective bond that may be necessary for a viable democratic polity. This matter is explored with a particular focus on how political community may be conceived in the EU context, where contemporary processes towards the separation of political authority from the underpinning of nationhood are widely considered advanced, and where a rich debate has unfolded on how to conceptualise social and political ties beyond the nation-state. Arguing that many of the existing approaches are adverse in their implications for contestatory politics and the possibility of collective self-rule, and therefore of a depoliticising tendency, this chapter lays out the contours of an alternative conceptualisation referred to as a *political bond*. It is suggested that if the political allegiances associated with such a bond could be discerned amongst Europeans, in place would be not only the sense of belonging needed for citizens to endorse membership of the EU, but also the popular expectations needed to drive efforts to reform and fully democratise it. Conversely, should these allegiances be absent or partially formed, that stimulus would likewise be weak. Seeking the traces of a political bond is therefore about seeking the basis for a *politically desirable* form of social integration. The political bond is presented as an ideal to be developed further in empirical study, and a sensitising concept with which to orient the empirical analysis.

Chapter 2 looks at the methodological basis on which such a bond may be studied. It assesses some of the empirical approaches which have been taken to the study of mass politics in the European context, and discusses the kinds of social theory appropriate to the concerns of this work, gravitating towards that which places an emphasis on routinised discursive practice. It then presents the strategy and specifics of the exploratory study that follows (on which further details are provided in the Appendix).

From this point onwards, the narrative voice is enriched by the voices of taxi-drivers. Chapters 3, 4 and 5 each explore one of the three key ideas associated with a political bond: the existence and nature of shared political problems constituting a 'political common', the collective positioning one finds with regard to these problems, and the perceived credibility of political projects designed to address them. The study's participants were given considerable scope to foreground whichever political problems they wished to, allowing the analyst to map out and analyse the discursive patterns of political significance which accompany these. Chapter 3 identifies the most salient problems emerging in discussion, and shows how speakers construct these as issues of common concern and dissatisfaction for which remedy of some kind should be sought. Here one encounters many of the 'bread-and-butter' issues of everyday politics, and one sees them richly articulated and discussed with engagement. Political apathy or confusion are little in evidence, and one sees few grounds to suggest a political bond must flounder on political withdrawal. Three bodies of salient problems are identified – *Economics, Society and the Law*, and *Relations between Peoples* – and these become the units of analysis for the remainder of the study.

The next two chapters investigate the context within which speakers locate these problems, and how far this includes a transnational dimension. Chapter 4 examines what kinds of social grouping they inspire. It shows how 'political identities', as they are conventionally called, may vary markedly from one domain of problems to another, be it in their conception of the self, of the nature of opponents, and the scope of those with whom comparisons may appropriately be drawn. Patterns of identification are domain-specific, itself a potentially valuable resource for political community, and only sometimes are they based on national or regional categories. With an eye to the possibility of transnational political ties, the chapter investigates how social groupings in other countries are drawn into these discussions: the extent to which speakers evoke counterparts to themselves abroad – people who share in their predicaments, and perhaps have common adversaries – or treat these places as alien, undifferentiated wholes. The chapter shows how this varies markedly according to the nature of the problems in question, some prompting a much wider horizon of awareness than others. Speakers are willing to assert the relevance of the experiences of other Europeans – but only on some kinds of issue.

If interpersonal ties are the focus of Chapter 4, Chapter 5 deals with ties to institutions, in particular as these are grounded not in perceptions of the competence and trustworthiness of office-holders – a standard focus of survey research – but in perceptions of how far matters of everyday concern are susceptible to organised address. It is suggested that one of the stand-out features of the empirical material is a sense of *fatalism* regarding what political agency of any kind can be expected to achieve. This fatalism is all the stronger for those political issues cast as global in their origins and extension, and of the kind that transnational political structures might be expected to deal with. A political world believed to consist largely of problems without solutions, of difficulties attributed to far-away causes, is one that subverts the plausibility of collective self-rule, and represents a challenge for political authority at all levels. On the basis of these discussions, fatalism rather than political apathy appears the major challenge to political allegiance.

Chapter 6 connects these observations directly to the question of a European polity. It looks at how matters European are drawn into these discussions, and the extent to which the views traced are consistent with a political bond in Europe. It argues that the way problems of everyday concern tend to be understood, combined with expectations concerning their susceptibility to address, generally rules out common action at the European level as a convincing proposition. Rather than contributing to the EU's political credibility, these patterns of understanding invite it to be seen as largely irrelevant to certain sets of problem, while powerless to control, perhaps liable to exacerbate, others. Under such conditions, the EU appears less as an augmentation than a curtailment of the democratic principle of collective self-rule. Some may conclude this is reason to relax such principles, or to call for their realisation in a world composed exclusively of nation-states. But it can equally be the spur to conceiving new repertoires of political understanding, of the kind that give more meaning to the EU as it is, or – less conservatively – that create the expectations conducive to its evolution in a desirable way. The chapter concludes therefore by critically examining in what respects things might need to change in order for stronger political allegiances to take shape.

The discussions with taxi-drivers at the core of this work were conducted in 2004–5. It was an interesting time to be talking: the price of petrol was sharply on the rise, the war on Iraq was becoming the war *in* Iraq, and new waves of migration within Europe were beginning. Bombs went off on the London Tube, and personal debt was quietly growing. The rich were getting richer, though it was not always clear how. In the background, someone somewhere was trying to tie up a constitutional treaty, one that could systematise, even dramatise, the accomplishments of European integration. Democratic concerns were by no means absent from this exercise – they were surely one source of inspiration. But for many amongst the broader public, such tinkerings seemed a peripheral matter, something whose relevance was at most indirect. This book follows the same ordering of priorities. Squarely, though not uncritically, it is in the everyday concerns of ordinary citizens that it roots its political and sociological concerns.

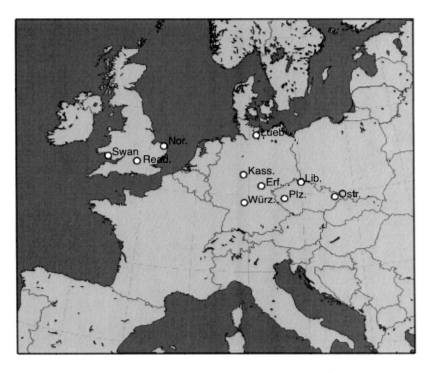

Locations of interviews: Swansea, Reading, Norwich, Kassel, Würzburg, Lübeck, Erfurt, Plzeň, Liberec and Ostrava

1
Political Community and the Bonds of Collectivity

'The people'

What must be common to a set of people such that they may be ruled through the same institutions? While there may be no eternal or inescapable problems in political philosophy, there are some which are of enduring relevance, and which reappear under certain conditions in particular. The question raised here, central to recent debates about the prospects for a European polity, has not been permanently salient in the history of political thought. Few authors have made it the focus of their attention. But a more general concern for issues of democracy and political order has often led thinkers to indicate a position on it. Wherever the foundations, functioning or composition of a political community have been matters of interest or doubt, a position on this question is discernible.[1] In this sense, with some caution, one may suggest that the current debates have been revisiting an older question.

What it is that must be held in common is likely to be considered important under two conditions in particular. The first is if the authority to which people are subject relies on a principle of legitimacy grounded in a concept of 'the people'. Where this is the case, the theoretical question of who the people are naturally arises as a basic constitutional matter. The second is if that set of people, as individuals, have the power to make themselves heard by the institutions which rule

---

[1]A note on terminology: both 'political community' and 'polity' are terms which can be used in multiple ways, from which derives some of their usefulness. Generally, the latter will be used as an umbrella term to refer to an organised arrangement of political power, while the former will be used when intending to emphasise the human and subjective dimensions thereof.

them, and to engage or challenge their coercive authority. Where this is the case, it becomes of some practical importance what kinds of institution make sense to them, and with whom they are willing to engage in government.

One sees immediately that the word 'people' can be used in at least two ways: to refer to an abstraction, the sovereign 'people in reserve' as it has been called, and to refer more empirically to a collective agent or series of agents, 'the people in action' (Canovan 2005).[2] For much of the Middle Ages, with the principal exception of those city-states on the Italian peninsula that carried forward the Roman republican tradition, this double aspect of 'the people' was of little note. Dynastic rule was the norm, and while kings – if pushed – might claim to have been authorised by 'the people' (as an abstraction) to rule over them, the set of people who happened to be alive at any given moment generally had little control over the institutions which governed them. The authority of the power-centre was little challenged, and could be strengthened in moments of crisis by notions of divine legitimacy. While such arguments came under strain in the sixteenth century, when the Protestant-Catholic division meant rebels against the king's authority could invoke divine support for themselves and claim to be acting for the spiritual good of 'the people', the model of dynastic rule survived for some time. In these circumstances, the question of what must be common to a set of people such that they may be ruled together generally did not arise.

It came to the fore with the English Civil War and the French and American Revolutions. With the problematisation and then partial renunciation of monarchical rule, the concept of the people as sovereign was recoupled with the idea of popular rule and the practical ability of the masses to affect the course of government. Article III of the French Declaration of the Rights of Man asserted that 'the principle of all sovereignty resides in the Nation', while the US Constitution declared itself in the name of 'We the People of the United States'. These were assertions of the principle of self-government, and they reopened the question of the identity of 'the people' (the self) who/which were/was constituting the polity and ruling and being ruled

---

[2]One can trace the dual sense of the term back to ancient Rome, where the notion of the 'populus' was used on the one hand to refer to the citizenry and sovereign body of the Roman Empire, and on the other hand to the common masses engaged in popular government, to the 'plebs' who made their political voice heard in the context of the Roman Republic.

together. As Claude Lefort has put it, before the revolutions 'power was embodied in the prince, and it therefore gave society a body. Because of this, a latent but effective knowledge of what *one* meant to the *other* existed throughout the social.' With the arrival of democracy, 'the locus of power becomes *an empty place.*' The commonality of the people, what it is that defines them and holds them together as a political community, becomes no longer obvious but in need of answer, and something to which all answers are contestable (Lefort 1988: 17–18).

One reason these issues became pressing was that the principle of self-government was being established under conditions which, unlike the classical context, did not permit the direct participation of all citizens in the mechanisms of decision-making – even when full citizenship was restricted to a limited number of males. Organs of representation and electoral ballot were required, making necessary the conceptualisation of who constituted the population of voters. Self-government without direct participation also required giving a sense of normative purpose to the polity, justification for obedience to state authority, to the suppression of immediate interests, and to the acts of redistribution the state might engage in. These issues acquired further urgency as a result of the socio-economic developments associated with the Industrial Revolution: as capitalism advanced, wealth inequal-ities and functional specialisation increased. Diversity and fragment-ation heightened the concern with common bonds, the investigation of which would become the task of the emerging social sciences (Wagner 2001). There were also practical issues to do with political association which arose once the unifying figure of the monarch was removed. In the case of territorial disputes, principles would be needed by which to decide whether a certain group of people belonged to one polity or to another. Individual entitlements to political and welfare rights would also need to be granted or withheld.

Not long after the democratic revolutions, a third conception of 'the people' started to emerge, one promising an answer to aporias such as these. This was the idea of the people as a pre-political unity or 'nation'. The nationalist movements of the nineteenth and early twen-tieth century can be read as attempts to bring meaning to the radical declaration of 'rule by the people' (Yack 2001). The model of the nation-state posited – and could be used to call for – a congruence of boundaries between the political unit (the state) and a unit of socio-cultural identification (the nation) (Gellner 1983; Hobsbawm 1991). Thinkers such as J. S. Mill developed sophisticated arguments for seeing the ties of nationhood as indispensable to the democratic state (Mill

1975: Chapter 16, 'Of Nationality'). Yet the linkage of nation and state ran deeper than its explicit theorisation or rhetorical deployment, for arguably it became part of the tacit understanding of a significant portion of social and political thought. That adjacent concepts such as 'society' were, from their point of emergence, premised on the assumptions of the nation-state model – notably the image of internally-homogeneous and externally-bounded units coextensive with state structures – has been the argument developed by Ulrich Beck and others in a critique of 'methodological nationalism' in social theory (Beck 2007; Chernilo 2006). Political philosophy too has a sizeable tradition which takes clearly defined political communities on the nation-state model as given (Benhabib et al. 2007). Contemporary political developments, in Europe especially but not alone, have caused the enduring suitability of such assumptions to be questioned.

One of the distinctive features of the nation-state model is that it joins together two matters which can in fact be considered separately. What we may call the question of 'the common' can be formulated in two ways. One is to pose it as a *membership* or *boundary* question, a question of who is to be included in the political community and who may be properly excluded. Both the territorial extension of the polity and the granting of citizenship rights to temporary and long-term residents are matters to the fore here. In a second formulation, it is as a question of the cohesiveness of a unit one takes as given. In this perspective, the precise extension of polity boundaries is bracketed, but it is assumed that – wherever they fall – they need the support of some kind of integrative force so as to ensure the stability of the polity and the endorsement of its citizens. A *collective bond* is required in order to conjure the unity of 'the people' such that they are suited to rule through the same institutions, and such that those institutions are democratically viable.

Phrasing the matter as a *boundary* question has proved objectionable to many on normative grounds, since to accept that there may be legitimate reasons to draw boundaries of membership to a political community is always close to adopting a position of ethical particularism. Universalistic perspectives in all periods, from contemporary liberal cosmopolitanism back to Marxism, the humanism of Erasmus or the Christianity of St. Augustine, have all been inclined to see the drawing of political boundaries as morally arbitrary, and have therefore had little reason to place emphasis on the kinds of principle one might invoke to do so. Yet there is also a theoretical reason why the problem of boundaries may be one to avoid: it is rather resistant to logical reasoning (Dahl 1990; Singer 1996; Yack 2001; R. M. Smith 2003). Clearly it cannot be resolved by a straightforward appeal to democratic decision-making, to an aggregation of individual votes, since as Robert Goodin puts it, 'that is like saying the winning lottery ticket will be pulled out of the hat by the winner of that selfsame lottery' (Goodin 2007: 43). Nor do appeals to the principle of 'all affected interests', or 'all probably affected interests', suggest a solution, since then there are problems of who can authoritatively judge such questions. Appeals to cultural markers or geographical features simply beg the question of which should properly be invoked.[3]

The difficulty with formulating the question of the common as a boundary question is that it may imply membership is something to be settled definitively rather than a matter of ongoing interpretation. It may suggest 'the people' can be captured in a single representation, and that this can correspond neatly with the material world. On the contrary, as Lefort's notion that power in a democracy is an 'empty place' makes clear, 'the people' will always be the site of contested representations. If rules, as Wittgenstein reminds, do not contain the rules for their own application, then there is an inescapably practical basis to all moves to create, extend and withhold the rights of citizenship. No doubt this is why the few thinkers who have tackled this formulation of the question have generally concluded it is a matter more for historians than theorists and philosophers (Dahl 1990: 45; Whelan 1983: 16; Loriaux 2008).

Thus while both renditions of the question of the common raise issues of political importance, any answer to the second (concerning the collective bond) need not depend for its validity on the clarity of answer it provides to the first (concerning membership). The membership question is never fully resolved, and for this reason one may find value in conceptualisations of the collective bond which remain open on the question of boundaries.

How best to characterise the *collective bond* necessary for a viable democratic polity is at the centre of the project that follows. It is by no means simply a descriptive problem. That multiple representations of 'the people' are possible means that this collective bond can be

---

[3]Sociologists have also had difficulties with the appraisal of boundaries, not least due to their frequent reliance on empirical data produced by national governments (censi being the paradigmatic case) which presume a social space coextensive with the political.

conceptualised in different ways, and the best way to do so can be a matter for extensive debate. Importantly, different conceptualisations, as well as varying in the degree to which they are theoretically coherent and empirically plausible, vary in their normative implications. They are laden with consequences for how one understands the purpose of the polity and the nature of citizenship, and how one understands the challenges which a particular polity or polities in general may face. Different conceptualisations of the common suggest different positions on why citizens should accept decision-making when it runs counter to their perceptions of self-interest. They may shape what citizens understand by the common good, or whether they doubt the existence of such a thing, and the extent to which they seek participation in the political process. Towards whom solidarity should be shown will depend substantially on how one makes sense of the collective. Also, while no conceptualisation can provide a settled answer to the question of boundaries, some may serve to naturalise certain boundaries while problematising others. Why it is logical for 'us' to share a certain political arrangement depends crucially on how that 'we' is elaborated.

The bonds of collectivity are of relevance to political community on all scales. The matter has clear relevance to polities on the scale of the Westphalian state, all the more as commentators increasingly question whether the *nation*-state can be regarded an empirical reality – if this was ever possible. Processes associated with globalisation, notably increased cross-border flows of information, goods and people, have questioned this model, and while some regard it as an ideal to be restored, many treat this as unfeasible and undesirable. One alternative line of thought has been to develop new images of the collective bond for polities on the existing scale, developing for instance notions of 'patriotism' instead of nationhood – arguments we shall touch on in this chapter. Another response has been the call for a *cosmopolitan* perspective. Amongst political philosophers, this is generally understood in explicitly normative terms, and a debate has emerged on the nature, demands and possible forms of democratic politics on a global scale (Archibugi 2008; Held 2003). Amongst social theorists, the move is understood not so much as a desirable option as a conceptual and empirical imperative – 'reality itself has become cosmopolitan' (Beck 2007: 287). Then there is a third, intermediary option, which is to focus on the global-regional level, i.e. on a scale larger than the Westphalian state but considerably less than the global. In this context, the study of the European Union (EU) has proved to be a rich site for re-engaging with questions to do with the bonds of collectivity and their political significance.[4]

While EU studies has traditionally been restricted to a fairly narrow range of institutional questions, chiefly to do with how best to explain the process of regional integration, the last two decades have witnessed a broadening of the literature. Many researchers have shifted from seeking to *explain* integration to exploring the nature of its outcome. Rather than as a highly developed form of inter-state organisation, such perspectives see the EU as a self-standing entity worthy of study in its own right. For those accepting this shift, the amount and scope of legislation produced in Brussels, and the extent to which this is beyond the immediate control of any single member-state government, point towards the need to see the EU as a polity *of some sort*. Some scholars are resolutely sceptical of such a perspective (Moravcsik 2002), yet arguably it is deeply embedded: indeed, all those who speak of the 'European Union', rather than itemising a set of inter-state treaties, are on a set course to granting its status as an independent political entity. Under modern conditions, where political authority is held to derive its legitimacy from the consent of 'the people' and where popular discontent may severely challenge this authority, this opens the question of the common as posed. A range of enquiries has followed, sometimes characterised as part of a 'normative turn' in the discipline (Bellamy and Castiglione 1998; Offe 2000; Føllesdal 2006; Karolewski 2009; Kraus 2008; Risse 2010). If democracy requires a demos, to what extent does one exist on a scale coextensive with the Union? What kind of collective bond should a demos be understood to imply, and what are the preconditions thereof? The prospect of enlarging the Union to include states on its periphery, and thereby to increase the diversity within it, adds to the force of such questions.

---

[4]Note that these different points of focus need not be exclusive. As Goodin, a cosmopolitan political philosopher, acknowledges, 'even the most dewy-eyed cosmopolitans rarely envisage a centralized, unitary government issuing world-wide diktats from some Capital of the World. The proposal is almost always for a "world government, federal in form"' (Goodin 2007: 65). Once one reverts to a federal model, taking territorial states as given and exploring the possible relations between them, the question of the common quickly returns at a sub-global level, for even in a global federation the viability of the federal units is crucial. See also Beck's assertion of the EU's significance: 'the unit of political action in the cosmopolitan era is no longer the nation but the region' (http://www.guardian.co.uk/commentisfree/2009/apr/13/european-union-economic-crisis).

Acknowledging these questions' import certainly does not depend on seeing the EU as a 'polity' in the fullest sense of the term – as an emergent superstate, centralised and hierarchical in the Westphalian image. Even much looser forms of association in which authoritative decision-making spans multiple actors whose relations mix coercion and consent, as pictured in 'neo-medieval' accounts of the EU (Zielonka 2006), raise practical questions of cohesiveness and normative ones concerning the responsiveness of institutions to pressures formed outside them. Indeed, even if one interprets 'polity' in the weakest sense, to include all international regimes with sufficiently regularised scripts of action to be considered one step removed from any single state's control, these questions are likely to carry weight. As theorists of globalisation convincingly argue (Archibugi 2008; Held 2003), even such looser structures of association are not immune to interrogation for their consistency with the democratic principle. If the EU were no more than one of those, it would still be an appropriate site for a critical re-examination of collective ties.

But while political cosmopolitanism remains a distant project, political restructuring at the European level is well advanced. This alone is justification for examining the European case more closely, even while affirming the desirability of moral cosmopolitanism. A European focus also offers advantages over a focus on existing state structures, for it offers opportunities for developing new conceptions of the collective bond. For the very fact that a multinational polity cannot rest on a national bond, these conditions act as a spur to the development of images of the collective which avoid some of the shortcomings of the national idea. Also, precisely because the EU's popular endorsement is uncertain, the case is a useful reminder that political authority on its own, at least in its less repressive forms, is unlikely to be sufficient in itself to bind together its citizens and thus autonomously to solve the question of the common.

Of course, taking seriously this question's relevance to a European polity is not necessarily to argue *against* a cosmopolitan perspective, nor perhaps against a reversion to the Westphalian state. To make an exclusive claim for the importance of the one political setting would be to conflate once again the question of social cohesiveness with that of where the boundaries of the collective should lie. The arguments pursued in this work are developed in particular awareness of the European debate, and are premised on the view that a European polity, correctly conceived, has some desirable implications. Such a polity facilitates making a wide range of socio-economic and environmental challenges responsive to human agency, developing ties of mutual awareness and concern across a wide social space, and giving individuals a rich sense of the context in which their life experiences unfold. The existing EU may do some of these things, others may remain possibilities to be developed. That this study addresses itself to the contemporary European context does not mean though that its arguments are without more general application, whether to other transnational experiments or to state contexts more familiar.

We shall begin, in the following section, with a critical look at some of the ways the common has been conceived in the European debate, drawing as these positions do on older theoretical traditions. In its less accomplished forms, the product of such thinking has been an unreflexive revisiting of past notions of national identity, this time played out as 'European identity', and often with a tone of disappointment concerning its ostensible absence.[5] This pattern has been widespread in both political discourse and empirical scholarship (Stråth 2002). Much such work has also shown a reluctance to consider the implications of its vision for the practices of democracy and citizenship. A considerable amount of writing proceeds in a purely sociological idiom, enquiring somewhat innocently into the existence of a European identity without examining more closely what exactly it is which may be politically necessary or desirable. One of the goals of this book is to develop a richer conception of the social underpinnings of political community, and to do so without losing sight of normative-theoretical concerns (Delanty and Rumford 2005).

Each of the perspectives we shall consider below is by no means so banal, and deserves the detailed examination it will be given. There are numerous criteria by which one may distinguish the different approaches: here they are analysed according to how thick they suppose the common element amongst citizens must be. By this is meant the level of regularity across the citizen body which is demanded: a thick, maximalist approach supposes a high degree of regularity such that, following whatever principle is invoked, citizens resemble one another rather strongly, whether in the attributes they display or the ends they pursue. A thin, minimalist approach allows for greater diversity, albeit potentially at some expense to the community's cohesiveness.

---

[5]One of the drawbacks of the idea of 'collective identity' is to conflate the matter of boundaries and of social cohesiveness, since it presumes homogeneity across a given social space and treats that homogeneity as the source of the cohesiveness of the collectivity thus formed.

Conceptions which tend too strongly either to maximalism or minimalism may have unwelcome implications for the democratic character of the political community. From a broadly pluralist perspective, an important element in any healthy democracy is political contestation. Where no single viewpoint can claim absolute validity, handling matters of common concern involves the identification and the making of choices, many of which will be contestable. The democratic process is what allows the range of competing political perspectives to be voiced and discussed, and its success depends upon there being vital and inclusive public debate, combined with widespread recognition that, due to the contestability of viewpoints, the outcome may be reasonable disagreement. The political system should invite citizens to be oriented to this debate, and to the opportunities provided by democratic institutions to shape decision-making on matters of common concern, so that widely held viewpoints are not systematically excluded.

Yet it may be argued that many of the existing approaches in the European debate, more or less minimalist or maximalist in their demands, are adverse in their implications for contestation and involvement, and rather of a depoliticising tendency. Having laid out arguments to this effect, the need for an alternative conception is advocated. It is suggested that this should have two features in particular: one being an emphasis on adversarialism, which implies subgroups of citizens tied to one another by specific common purposes without this presupposing a high degree of regularity and consensus across the whole citizen body; the second being an emphasis on substantive problems, which may foster an engaged citizenry by allowing a close link to be maintained to the everyday concerns of ordinary citizens. These guiding principles point to the elaboration of what one may call a 'political bond', towards which the chapter proceeds and to which the book as a whole is addressed.

Conceptualising the bonds of collectivity

A staple idea of social and political thought, and one that can be regarded as minimalist in the sense described, is that material *interests* can serve as the collective bond.[6] Such a perspective represents the default position in the older literature on the EU. In the 1940s/50s, the populations of European nation-states were seen as overtly hostile to one another, and it was widely assumed that any moves towards inte-

---

[6]This and the following section draw and expand on (White 2010a).

gration would have to quieten their passions by appealing to their interests. In the early post-war years these interests were understood by many as security interests, implying a *security bond* based on the need to establish peace in Europe. More commonly, once early federalist visions had faded, an economic perspective was advanced. With arguments redolent of the older notion of 'doux commerce', it was suggested that integration and polity formation could be advanced by enabling the pursuit of interests through commercial exchange.[7] The deepening of market interaction and functional integration was viewed as establishing a *commercial bond* between elites, leading to wider economic benefits for the member-state populations as a whole, who in turn would come to see their prosperity as entwined with that of their neighbours. The earliest act of integration was explicitly characterised by Jean Monnet in these terms: 'in itself this [the founding of the ECSC] was a technical step, but its new procedures, under common institutions, created a silent revolution in men's minds. It proved decisive in persuading businessmen, civil servants, politicians and trade unionists that ... the economic and political advantages of unity over division were immense' (Monnet 1963: 205). While this perspective was most common in the pre-Maastricht era, it survives amongst those who treat the common market and economic and monetary union as the principal features of the European polity. As Fritz Scharpf puts it, the type of legitimacy on which the EU rests is '*interest based rather than identity based*', and 'what is required is no more than the perception of a range of *common interests* that is sufficiently broad and stable to

---

[7]These ideas, traceable to the political thought of Bacon, Spinoza, Hume and Montesquieu, find their most complete theoretical elaboration in the political economy of Adam Smith (Hirschman 1996): 'Commerce and manufactures gradually introduced order and good government,' writes Smith, 'and with them, the liberty and security of individuals, among the inhabitants of the country, who had before lived almost in a continual state of war with their neighbours and of servile dependency upon their superiors' (Adam Smith 1990: Book 3 Chap. 4, 385). It was this type of society, consisting of aggregates of self-interested individuals bound together by the interests of commercial exchange, which would later be referred to by Tönnies as *Gesellschaft* (Tönnies 2001: 57) and via the work of Hayek it continues to inform modern libertarian theories of democracy. Hayek himself was an advocate of certain forms of European integration precisely on the grounds that by moving towards a polity held together by commercial interests one could expect the weakening of thicker bonds of nationhood at the state level, which he held responsible for undesirable acts of state intervention in the market and projects of economic redistribution (Hayek 1939/1948).

justify institutional arrangements for collective action' (Scharpf 1999: 11, 12).

In descriptive-empirical terms, there are reasons to doubt whether a bond based on interests, security or commercial, is sufficient to underpin a political community. To conceive the collective bond in these terms is to suggest that interests favour integration unambiguously. Yet interests are rarely unambiguous: they can generally be appraised in multiple ways, and are susceptible to redescription. An appeal to long-term interests such as security and growth is always vulnerable to counter-claims that conjure short-term or non-material interests, since what may be said to be in someone's interests depends crucially on how alternatives are defined (Connolly 1974). Interests are *comparative*, and therefore depend on ideational elaboration, which means any interest-based account of social order centred on pre-interpretational factors alone will be incomplete. Even under the settled conditions of Westphalian-state politics, interests are indefinite; they are all the more so in conditions where the boundaries of political community are in question.

If the empirical argument is inconclusive, for this reason one can take a critical approach to the normative implications of such a position. As critics of aggregationist models of politics have emphasised, a perspective which takes interests as self-evident is likely to accord a minimal role to political debate and contestation as a means for elaborating those interests and seeking an interpretation of the common good (Sunstein 1991). If political ends are given, citizens have little need to engage one another in an effort to define them: they need only delegate a small number of representatives to act on their behalf and execute the policies necessary to realising them.[8] While such a perspective may continue to acknowledge

---

[8]Confirmation may be had by looking at the kind of EU defended by those who regard it as grounded in material interests. For Scharpf, EU policy-making will need to avoid controversial issues and keep to a narrow range of 'policy areas of relatively low political salience in which its legitimacy is not really in doubt' since the outcomes produced are in the interests of all and/or harmful to none (Scharpf 1999: 203). Similar arguments are to be found in (Moravcsik 2002; Majone 1996; Majone 1999; Majone 2001). As has been observed, the notion that one can regard certain policy-areas as fundamentally uncontentious, and thus suitable to decision-making *without* political contestation by an EU technocracy, is problematic (Føllesdal and Hix 2006). Note also that the difficulty of separating out such issues renders implausible the notion that a minimalist bond of material interests at a supranational level might be combined at the national level with thicker bonds of collectivity supportive of democracy, for the former would most likely exert a colonising tendency on the latter.

'the people' as the final source of authority, there is little room for 'the people' as active agents engaged in self-rule (Elster 1986). Indeed, attempts to exercise democratic control over the management of these interests are liable to be portrayed as constraints on efficiency. It follows as little surprise that a commercial perspective tends to be suspicious of activity which cannot be understood in terms of the pursuit of individual advantage, and tends to admire citizens most when they act in private competition. Libertarians may welcome such a perspective – Hayek advocated market integration in Europe for exactly such reasons (Hayek 1939/ 1948) – but to the extent that they do so they weaken their commitment to the basic democratic idea of collective self-rule.

Naturally, such observations are not to imply that political theory should do away with the concept of interest: there may be ways to formulate it in less determinist terms such that it can be a starting-point for sustained political debate (Connolly 1974). If one acknowledges the fundamental ambiguity of interests, one makes space for citizens to be active in the articulation of different perspectives, and to seek common cause in the attempt to advance these. But it is exactly this type of reading one excludes by supposing one can separate out a set of concerns prior to political debate and regard these as the basis of the collective bond. To treat interests in this way as constitutive of the demos is a depoliticising move, likely to weaken public debate and to exacerbate wider trends in contemporary democracy towards the marginalisation of the principle of democratic control.

Reacting against this minimalist conceptualisation of the common, in which citizens tend weakly to mutual engagement, a quite different perspective instead plays up the importance of cultural attachments extending widely across the citizen body. In this maximalist conception of the common, it is held that political units require the support of a *cultural bond*. Historically, there have been two major ways to conceive such a bond: as involving ethical ties that constitute 'the people' as an organic unity extended through time and whose value is intrinsic, or as involving contingent ties which serve only the instrumental purpose of evoking attitudes of commonality, solidarity and trust within the population.[9] Both versions invoke markers such as territory,

---

[9]This distinction to do with the normative worth of national ties is distinct from the sociological one commonly made in nationalism studies to do with how and when these ties emerged, and on which there has been a long-standing debate between 'primordialists' and 'constructivists' (Anthony Smith 1998).

language, blood ties, historical events and feelings of belonging, though granting them a rather different status. The first perspective, promoted notably by the Romantic nationalist movements of the nineteenth century, has been rare in contemporary debates, though it finds expression in discussion of Christianity's significance for the EU and in the more enthusiastic references to Europe's 'common civilisation' and 'common heritage' (Delanty 2002).[10] The latter perspective, which deserves closer attention, presents itself as open and pragmatic, making no strong normative assumptions about the proper nature of common ties. Rather than essentialising a certain set of inherited attributes, it sees the community as bound by whatever combination of attributes its citizens may share and, importantly, believe or can be convinced that they share (Miller 2000). The community is in this sense 'imagined' rather than real, and since no outward markers are given *a priori* significance this approach generally marks a turn towards people's beliefs and feelings.[11]

Without prizing any one conception of cultural commonality, such a perspective seems to posit a level of homogeneity either unrealistic for today's Europe or, were one to take it seriously, repressive of those who do not easily conform to it. There is a danger that those who do not feel a particular cultural affinity with their fellow citizens come to be treated as suspect, and their legitimate presence in the community questioned. The potential for persecution and exclusion seems clear (Parekh 1995). Even in the ideal case where perceptions of cultural commonality accord perfectly with the extension of citizenship, cultural differences with those outside the community or those temporarily resident may come to be exaggerated in the attempt to make citizens aware of their distinctive 'identity'. The result may be a potentially dangerous hardening of physical boundaries and, as these acquire a sense of permanence and naturalness, of moral boundaries also.

Moreover, such a perspective can have negative implications for political contestation. Identity of culture risks being taken to entail identity of political ends, with the assumption that where there is cultural consensus there will be widespread agreement on the substantive

---

[10]See the work of Larry Siedentop, who comes close to declaring latent commonality amongst Europeans when he writes of the 'moral inheritance' they share and need to 'become more conscious of' (Siedentop 2000, Chap. 10, p.214), and Milan Kundera's famous essay (Kundera 1984).

[11]J. S. Mill provides a famous statement of this perspective in his discussion 'Of Nationality' (Mill 1975, p.380). For overviews of the literature on nationalism see (Canovan 1996; Anthony Smith 1998).

policies the political community should adopt. One sees this tendency when for instance it is suggested that the divergence of opinion amongst Europeans on how best to respond to global crises, and the failure to agree a common foreign policy, result from the absence of a cultural bond between the populations of Europe (Anthony Smith 1992: 56, 71). Political adversarialism, rather than the mark of the healthy democracy, becomes that which should fade once cultural disharmony is removed, and the conception of citizenship is a demanding but quite passive one, whereby good citizens display the regularity of opinion to which their cultural regularities should dispose them.

A standard counter-argument holds that the presence of a cultural bond is actually what allows political contestation to be pursued to the full, since underlying commonality ensures conflict never quite reaches the point of destructiveness. Plausible as this may seem in theory, one wonders whether such contestation is not likely to rely for its animation exactly on those other forms of collective identification (e.g. based on categories of class, or ethnic categories other than those that supposedly define the community) which are always prone to be suppressed when the talk is of cultural ties. Adversarial debate depends on citizens seeing other groups as people quite different to them: this is, speaking in stereotypes, how the poor may see the rich, or the country-folk the town-folk, and arguably it is exactly the sense of otherness which inspires people to mobilise to capture the political agenda.

Recognising the problems that result from a monolithic conception of identity, advocates of a cultural bond often emphasise the possibility of multiple identifications and the importance of situation (Miller 2000). There is much talk in the literature of 'multi-level', 'nested' and 'cross-cutting' identities, and even a 'marble cake' model has been proposed (Risse 2010). As we shall see in Chapter 2, a large body of empirical literature attempts to operationalise these distinctions and to measure the 'sense of belonging' or 'identity' which EU citizens display. While these moves may seem to relieve the culturalist perspective of its determinism, the result is a perspective so flexible, agential, and instrumental that one wonders what is meant then by 'identity' (normally understood as coherence and sameness) and in what sense shared beliefs and memories are shared. Are they shared always, or only when agents choose to share them? If the emphasis is on choice, must it be these things that they choose to share? The more cultural identification is pluralised and relativised, the less it can be seen as determining the viability of democratic institutions. Furthermore, the emphasis on perceptions and beliefs, born of the need to avoid reifying particular markers, raises epistemological difficulties concerning how to identify these cognitive phenomena. The danger is then that, faced with uncertainty about the beliefs that bind, one lapses back into essentialism and the predetermination of ends by treating certain cultural features as constitutive of the community, thus pre-empting debate over the nature of the common.

The ideal of a *cultural* bond is the clearest example of a maximalist conception of the common, just as the ideal of a *commercial* or *security* bond offers the prime case of a minimalist conception. Both ideals treat the viability of the polity as determined by a pre-political 'substrate' (Wagner and Friese 2002), with the emphasis resting on what citizens may be thought to *have* in common rather than on that they might commit themselves to *placing* in common. A third set of perspectives departs from these by imagining bonds of shared *values and principles*, where these are adopted on the basis of reasoned deliberation. This opens the space for a more dynamic and reflexive conception of the common, yet the tendency towards a too weakly or too strongly binding set of commitments persists. Such perspectives may be said to oscillate between minimalist and maximalist conceptions of the common.

In the one perspective, which gravitates to the first of these two poles, such values and principles are understood as *universal* in scope – despite their adoption for a particular polity – because they derive from a morality justifiable to all. Historically, the French Declaration on the Rights of Man and the US Constitution can be understood as attempts to define principles of universal appeal sufficient to bind citizens together in an attitude of patriotism towards their political institutions; attempts to constitutionalise human rights and the rule of law might be candidate examples in the contemporary European context. Such a collective bond may be considered minimalist in at least two ways. First, given the conditions of heterogeneity they are intended to overcome, the temptation is to frame these would-be universal values and principles very abstractly indeed, perhaps as little more than a commitment to proceduralism, to ensure their universal appeal. The concern then is that they become of marginal significance in day-to-day affairs, lacking immediacy to citizens and offering little spur to political involvement. Because intended to be compatible with a wide array of political programmes, such values can offer little guidance to specific forms of action, and are therefore likely to be a weak resource with which to mobilise citizens to collective ends. Only in the severest crises, when those values are fundamentally at risk, might citizens be reminded of their common bond.

Second, as sympathetic critics have noted, even if one accepts such values and principles could be formulated sufficiently abstractly such that reasonable objection would be unthinkable, yet not so abstractly as to deprive them of meaning and affective appeal, the political implications might not necessarily be attractive. Taking the argument on its own terms, there is the risk that an appetite amongst citizens for the universal could result in a cosmopolitan distaste for *all* political institutions – except perhaps the global – rather than a strong commitment to one set. Ethical universalism seems an insufficient source of motivation for political engagement in a bounded polity, since it seems to preclude a claim to the importance of any one specific site of political action (Markell 2000; Choudhry 2001). Judged as to how far they embody the universal, the institutions and practices of a neighbouring polity might be deemed more adequate and therefore more enticing as a focus of engagement, as might the activities of deterritorialised actors such as human rights NGOs. Conversely, the need to address the ethical failings of the polity in which citizenship is held by contesting its political agenda would presumably be held no stronger than to address the like failings of *all* the world's polities. Insofar then as universal values and principles were successful in inspiring allegiance, a weakening of engagement with the political life of the particular polity, either by emigration or a refocusing of attentions, would seem the attendant danger.

This is what leads some to conclude that a bond of shared values and principles would need to be conceived in more *particularist* terms. While arguably one can read the early Habermas as advocating the strong-universalist perspective just described, it is clear that in his more recent work the principles binding the community are understood to be mediated by particularist interpretation (Habermas 2001; Habermas 1992; Habermas 2006). Such a move will be especially welcome to anyone who doubts whether even the most abstractly framed values are really as universal as claimed. In this alternative perspective, moral reflection on the experiences of European history may play a special role, as a shared set of post-nationalist values emerges through engagement with the past and acknowledgement of the destructive tendencies of the Westphalian nation-state system. Lest reflection seem too abstract a process, often there is the suggestion that shared values be given tangible form with the creation of a European constitution.

By focusing on the discursive renegotiation of the common, this approach avoids the temptation to settle the debate prematurely in favour of a certain understanding of the universal and points to ongoing public debate. Yet in certain important ways it results in a maximalist conception of the common once more unconducive to contestatory politics and active citizenship. With its emphasis on the attainment of a rational consensus, the model is vulnerable to one of the criticisms made of deliberative democracy more generally: that it is depoliticising because it has an elitist bias, since it limits the involvement of citizens who are only weakly able to frame their interventions according to prevailing conceptions of rational debate (Sanders 1997). A disjuncture may then emerge such that certain values achieve consensus at the elite level – aversion to the death penalty, for instance – without these reflecting the achievement of a broader consensus across the citizen body, leaving many citizens (perhaps the majority) only with the options either to adapt or withdraw their consent. Insofar as these values are enshrined in a constitution and protected by judicial means, their interpretation becomes a matter for judges rather than the democratic process, potentially deepening the disjuncture. Even were one to accept the conceptual possibility of a genuine consensus that extended to all Europeans without being a top-down imposition, one would be strained to imagine the public sphere adequately free of power-political influences and the functional problems of language diversity such that this ideal consensus could take shape in an inclusive public debate (Grimm 1995).

Moreover, while it is an open question whether shared values sufficiently uncontroversial to be widely accepted would generate an affective response amongst citizens (certainly several advocates of such a bond at the European level seem unwilling to abandon a more mythical understanding of the collective at the national level (Weiler 1999)), those that might achieve such a response could well be politically unattractive. Appealing to emotions of shame and anger, one proposal for a more affective constitutional patriotism (Cronin 2003: 14), would involve couching much of contemporary politics in the language of morality. This holds problems: if political actors conclude that moralistic arguments appealing to values embodied in a constitution are 'trumps', it encourages them to frame political debates as clashes between right and wrong. This invites the adoption of an unquestioning disposition and a conviction of moral superiority, whereby opposing views are portrayed as 'mad' or 'bad', in turn leading to a hardening of intolerance and the demonisation of opponents. Much as one may sometimes sympathise with the moral judgements involved, such a move arguably weakens the political process by increasing the danger of anti-democratic responses from those whose views are thereby cast as illegitimate.

The conclusion one may take from examining proposals to focus on shared *values and principles* complements those arrived at previously. No conceptualisation of the collective bond is of such descriptive plausibility that it must be accepted at face value: the political implications of each are an appropriate element in their assessment. By demanding a high degree of regularity and consensus across the citizen body, rather like a *cultural* bond, a thick *values* bond is likely to downgrade the importance of political adversarialism in the life of the political community. Alternatively a formulation in minimalist terms, where that which is shared is universal, is depoliticising in a different way, since it may weaken attachments to the polity and since – like a *security* or a *commercial* bond, though by dissimilar reasoning – it may empty public life of the pursuit of all but the most general, and perhaps weakly identifiable, shared ends. None of these perspectives seems to provide a satisfactory perspective from which to conceive political community on a scale approaching that of the EU. A new kind of collective bond needs to be conceptualised, one that can serve as a normative ideal whilst retaining a basic level of empirical plausibility. The next section lays out some ideas for what one may call a 'political bond'. It will be sketched as an outline, to be developed further over the course of the book.

A political bond

A conception of politics which allows for persistent and acknowledged disagreement requires a collective bond inviting some notion of common endeavour whilst allowing for the possibility of a plurality of political goods and some degree of conflict in their pursuit. Some sense of common purpose with other citizens is indispensable, but one need not assume this should be extended to all citizens at all times. Perhaps there is inspiration to be drawn here from *agonistic* models of democracy, where the potential for persistent disagreement tends to be foregrounded (Mouffe 1993). In this body of approaches, it is precisely because there may be disagreement on how to interpret the most basic values of democracy itself, liberty and equality, that people may be inspired to participate in the political process so as to secure certain objectives and visions. Those defeated in the political contest at a given moment may be motivated to continue their engagement in the political life of the polity without conceding the superiority (rational or moral) of the position to which they have lost out. Political struggle in this view carries with it the potential for social integration. To be sure, it may be that the *possibility* of consensus, based not so much on the supposed demands of rationality but on a respectful disposition to 'hear the other side' and reach compromise where it can be reached, is something to hold on to for the sake of progressive politics. But a conceptualisation of the collective bond should treat consensus as a possible achievement rather than a presupposition.

A second and related challenge for formulating a more political conception of the common is to maintain a close link to the substantive problems of everyday life, enabling ordinary citizens to 'make sense of' the political community in terms closely related to their daily concerns. One would look to issues of direct significance to act as shared reference-points for the citizens of the polity, at once attracting their sustained attention and acting as a focal-point for adversarial exchanges. While it may be possible to recast constitutional patriotism in more conflictual terms so as to accommodate deeper political disagreement,[12] ultimately any conceptualisation of the common centred on constitutional values may lack the immediacy required to give citizens a sense of the daily significance of the political community and of the potential importance of developing relationships of solidarity with groups outside the local environment. To focus on substantive (i.e. resonant, non-abstract) problems is not of course to remove values from the equation: they remain embedded in the way problems are articulated and remedies advocated, and they will often be appealed to explicitly. But when describing the nature of commitment to the life in common, there may be advantages to a vocabulary more prosaic.

Some authors, attuned to the possibilities for a problem-oriented approach, have spoken of the EU as a 'community of shared projects' in which citizens are bound to one another by their shared or overlapping political objectives. The suggestion is that goals such as environmental protection, the eradication of world poverty and the pursuit of market integration can act as a basis for collective endeavour (Nicolaidis 2001: 473; Nicolaidis and Lacroix 2003). This intuition seems correct, but a number of points should be remembered. First, there may be very few (if any) tasks to which all in the political community are willing to subscribe, and even where consensus seems apparent this may mask the need to confront those within the community who obstruct their fulfilment. One needs to be particularly sensitive therefore to how the concern with a given set of substantive problems may be shared by some but not all, perhaps due to divergent interpretations of basic ideas of freedom, justice and equality, and to how one might conceptualise the fact that the pursuit of their remedy may proceed in adversarial opposition to others within the political community. Second, and related, these political objectives need to be open to ongoing reassessment: just as one should not suppose, for instance, that 'security interests' are sufficiently unambiguous to be

---

[12]Cf. the 'constitutional culture' described in (Müller 2007: 54ff.).

made the basis for a collective bond, so one should avoid the suggestion that the pursuit of military security could be singled out as the predominant justification for a European polity (Morgan 2005). Such goals need to be open to dissent and reappraisal.

One of the potential advantages of reconceiving the collective bond in project-oriented terms is that it allows one to avoid an image of political community centred either on the distinctive 'identity' of a quasi-unitary subject (as in the maximalist accounts) or on the spontaneous harmony of weakly-tied individuals (as in the minimalist accounts). It points instead to a rather different social logic, grounded in the idea of *comparison*. Acts of comparison may combine a recognition of underlying difference along any number of dimensions with the examination of similarity or equivalence with regard to one particular property. X and Y, whose distinctness is assumed, are compared with regard to Z, with the possibility that it is only with regard to Z that X and Y are at all alike. Thus when a person or a set of persons engage in comparison between themselves and other persons – this being the type of comparison relevant to our discussion of political community – they may assess the extent to which they share an equivalence of situation regarding a particular substantive problem or predicament (job insecurity, for example) while at the same time acknowledging any amount of diversity or disagreement along alternative dimensions of comparison. That which the persons share, insofar as some degree of commonality is noted,[13] is issue-specific and contextual, a reference-point invoked at a given moment. This contrasts with the logic of identity, which supposes that subjects enjoy (or are perceived to enjoy) sameness of attributes – that in some deeper, existential sense X = Y, in a way that is context-independent and is not restricted to a particular dimension Z.

The logic of comparison thus points to the recognition of some measure of readily identifiable commonality across subjects, in contrast to minimalist perspectives, combined with the acceptance of enduring otherness beyond the particular metric applied. Note also that it avoids any tendency towards postulating hard boundaries of inclusion and exclusion. For one may suppose that *some* dimension of meaningful

---

[13]Note that, whenever a comparison is made, simultaneously some degree of commonality between the target objects is implied, since even where difference along the relevant dimension is asserted, this is premised on the applicability of the same metric to these objects. This is one way to think of the 'relevant contrasts' we shall observe later in this work, which are rather closer to comparisons than might initially be thought.

comparison (and probably several) is always to be found between any two sets of persons. Where one possibility is ruled out by material factors (where, for instance, job insecurity is not a meaningful point of comparison because some persons are of pensionable age) it should still be possible to identify alternative dimensions of comparison (for instance to do with exposure to environmental problems). In this image of collective ties founded on equivalence through comparison, no permutations of inclusion and exclusion are ruled out *a priori* (in contrast to the maximalist perspectives discussed above), with the implication that boundaries to the world beyond the polity can never be naturalised or regarded as unbridgeable.[14]

Acts of social comparison can be regarded not just as a viable source of social integration but as one which offers significant possibilities for progressive forms of politics. One of the important preconditions for such forms is that citizens recognise at least some of the problems they consider themselves to be facing as not purely idiosyncratic and personal, but as located in a broader field of experiences. As political philosophers have reminded, some types of justice-claim are essentially comparative in nature, since they refer to the *relative* deprivation of groups of citizens rather than to the absolute condition of the individual (Feinberg 1974). Acts of comparison are therefore the very precondition of such claims being recognised at all, as it is through comparison with others that persons become aware of the nature and context of their problems, and the extent to which they should be seen as unacceptable. Furthermore, not only does comparison supply the frame of reference needed for problem-recognition, but it raises awareness of the possibilities which may exist for their remedy. Insofar as many sources of grievance cannot be addressed merely through individual responses but require some form of collective action to change underlying conditions, perhaps in opposition to those resisting such changes, acts of social comparison provide the basis for mobilising supporters to this end. Certainly not all forms of social comparison have these desirable effects – we shall return later to the ways in which some may be negative, and to the need therefore to give specificity to the *kinds* of comparison to be sought – but already at this stage it should be noted that there are grounds for considering a collective bond thus formed as potentially a politically appealing one.

---

[14]For this reason, though our focus is on the idea of a European polity, the possibility of a wider or a narrower political arrangement is maintained.

With these considerations in mind, one can sketch, in the form of a normative ideal, an alternative conceptualisation of the collective bond, one that will be taken forward for further exploration in the following chapters. This perspective is centred on the idea that human ties may emerge out of the sense of 'shared predicament', i.e. the sense of being faced with similar problems. What constitutes 'us' in this perspective is not some attribute that 'we' share or believe ourselves to share, but the sense that we find ourselves in situations which are alike. From this ultimately may emerge the sense that 'our' fates are entwined and that our problems need addressing collectively. 'We' may come to see ourselves locked into situations together, and therefore grant allegiance to those political institutions which seem to promise an amelioration of those situations. These ideas can be set out more exactly by dividing this alternative conceptualisation of the collective bond into three parts as follows:

1. The political common

This first element points to the significance of substantive political issues. A *political common* may be defined (postponing for a moment its specifically European elements) as *the assumed existence by members of the collective of important common problems in need of address*. At its core would be the myriad substantive problems which provoke a sense of injustice and the perceived need for remedy amongst sections of the citizen body. One thinks here of all the sorts of problem which ordinary citizens may be inclined to articulate as matters of concern – economic problems, problems to do with anti-social and criminal behaviour, problems to do with inter-cultural relations, environmental problems, and so on. Such problems would be 'common' insofar as they are treated by those who articulate them as shared with others, as liable to affect 'people like us' rather than just 'me', where the 'we' may differ according to the problem in question. There need be no consensus that every such problem affects everyone alike in the political community: on the contrary, a we-they dynamic would be involved, such that it is assumed that there are opponents to 'people like us' living within the political community whose position on these problems is quite different, or who may indeed be generative of them. Rather than binding all citizens to one another in an image of unity, the problems of the political common would pit some against others in a web of allegiances and conflicts. Note also that there need not be full agreement on precisely the nature and number of such conflicts, for this itself is a political matter. Where some see an authentic political struggle, others see mere squabbling – such is the nature of political disagreement and the processes of politicisation and depoliticisation. To be sure, dissensus on the composition of the political common could not be entirely unconstrained – any notion of political debate requires participants not simply to be talking past each other but to be hearing countervailing perspectives. A symbolic space which includes a core set of widely meaningful elements, including certain representations of the socio-political world and certain registers of evaluation, is indispensable[15] But none of this implies there must be uniformity across space and time in how political problems and conflicts are constructed and appraised.[16]

By speaking of 'assumed existence' the intention is to avoid taking a position on the ontological status of such problems. In contrast to interest-based approaches, one need not insist that such problems are 'real', or rooted ultimately in materialist concerns, for it is their appraisal and interpretation which is important. By suggesting that these problems would be considered 'important' and 'in need of address' it is implied that they would be the subject of a certain amount of affective involvement. They would be reference-points considered significant. It might be that those who articulated and appraised them would not necessarily themselves use the word 'political' to describe such problems, but they would have to treat them as both shared and significant. By referring to 'members of the collective', one implies an unspecified number of individuals affiliated to the polity. The origins of their membership is a question which can be bracketed for the reasons given above. Their number would be unspecified, since not all problems would need to be of importance

---

[15]This point may suggest that a political bond is derivative of a cultural bond, but several points should be noted: first, this is very different from the bounded symbolic space which authors in political philosophy have implied when advocating cultural underpinnings to political community (cf. the literature discussed). Culture in this conventional, 'container' sense has largely been abandoned by anthropologists and cultural sociologists in favour of a conceptualisation positing an unbounded field or constellation of unevenly distributed interpretative resources (Lamont and Thévenot 2000; see also Chapter 2). Second, the common symbolic space referred to here is explicitly political in focus: it does not draw its substance from the kind of cultural symbols – flags, hymns, stories of nationhood, etc. – which can be associated with a cultural bond.

[16]This is a point which tends to be underplayed in the scholarship concerning the possibility of a European public sphere, where great emphasis tends to be placed on the overarching unity of debate, hence studies of whether political issues are framed alike across the media of the EU member-states (Gerhards 2002).

to all persons in all places: there is scope for variety here, though one would want 'most of the people' to make 'at least some assumptions' of this kind – to be able to articulate grievances in need of address, in other words.

One can suppose that a rich political common composed of many diverse kinds of problem would be conducive to preserving the integrity of the community. Insofar as common problems are perceived, it is per- haps likely that some would be seen as 'going together' because they have similar origins or similar effects, as opposed to others which relate to quite different aspects of life, with the consequence that a political common would be composed of a plurality of *problem domains*, each with a different thematic focus. This could be normatively attractive. If opponents are constructed in relation to problems, and there is a plu- rality of problem domains, then there will be a plurality of we-they for- mulations rather than a single axis of confrontation. Different kinds of problem will provoke different ways of formulating opponents, and any one formulation will relate only to a subset of the problems of the common, thus constraining the likelihood that the community frag- ments into a series of discrete adversarial groups who exist in segrega- tion or choose to separate from each other. The feasibility of pointing to a particular section of the citizenry and saying 'we have nothing in common with them' would be reduced by the multiplicity of resources for collective positioning. Thus in substitution for the idea of an all- embracing 'we' such as 'the nation' or 'the community', one would envisage numerous lines of intersection between multiple, interdepen- dent constituencies (Connolly 1995: xix–xx).[17]

---

[17]Some readers may detect an echo of the pluralist thought of Robert Dahl, who gives a sharp analysis of how a political community may be held together by the multiplicity of its divisions (Dahl 1966: 371ff.). Societies, he suggests, dis- play high levels of 'coincidence' when individuals who agree (or disagree) on one issue tend to agree (or disagree) on another, leading to a bipolar distri- bution of opinion which may prompt centrifugal dynamics. Alternatively, when coincidence is low, a varied array of oppositions will emerge, and provided one does not become dominant – as it will only if people care about some issues much more than all others, *and* if they agree on which these salient issues are – one will instead see an interlocking set of we-they relations take shape, collec- tively knitting the community together. While Dahl's discussion is heuristically of great interest, its ontology is more materialist than that we shall sketch in the next chapter, where the focus is on discursively-embedded forms of subjecthood, not social roles determined exogenously by societal structure.

2.   Political subjects, counterparts and opponents

In order to foster a collective bond appropriate to a polity such as the EU, the acts of collective positioning thus inspired would need to fulfil two conditions. Firstly, as the basis for a transnational demos, one would want those presumed affected by the problems in question to be conceived not as a narrowly defined territorial group such as 'people in our country'. While it might be valid for a subset of problems to be treated in this way (and indeed there may be some problems for which a localist perspective is preferable), it would be undesirable if this were extended to all, since not only would treating the problems as purely domestic to individual member-states provide little basis for a collective bond wider than this, it would also negate the possibilities which political community beyond the Westphalian state holds for developing wider frames of reference and a political debate informed and enriched by a wider range of experiences. Instead one would want to see the assumption that, in addition to those included directly in the 'we' by which the problems are narrated – call them the *political subjects* – there exist others elsewhere in the EU who face similar problems and whose experiences are in this respect analogous – call them *counterparts*. As this implies, problems would not need to be described as affecting specifically 'Europeans' as a whole, since this would imply a strong level of consensus across the board and the nullification of major lines of internal division. But there would need to be some sense of transnational 'shared predicament', of there being at least some groups in other EU countries comparable to 'us' in terms of the problems they face. By the same token, other EU countries one would want to see treated not just as unitary actors but as environments worthy of comparison because they feature others who face similar problems. One would want to see reference not so much to undifferentiated wholes ('the French' or 'the Spanish') but to the comparable experiences of those living within these countries (*in* France, *in* Spain).

The bond between *subjects* and *counterparts* would be based on the sense of shared predicament, the recognition that, notwithstanding all their multiple differences, in certain respects their situation is alike. It would – at least initially – amount to something less than an awareness of direct interdependence, or active solidarity in the sense of a concerted effort to equalise burdens and benefits across persons. While this type of strongly-bound partisan 'we' might be a desired endpoint, the relation of subjects to counterparts would stand as an earlier stage, one of self-orientation and learning as developed through social comparison. Counterparts would, for the subjects, be a largely imagined category – real-life encounters would be rare, given their distribution across space – but their presumed existence would help to cultivate receptivity to, and would in turn be consolidated by, new information concerning the experiences of others outside the local environment. As a disclosing, educative process liable to enrich the kinds of political subjecthood subsequently achieved, it would have some worth of its own and need not be understood as merely transitional. The bond between subjects and counterparts would also entail rather more than a general sense of common humanity: to the extent that others share in problems similar to 'ours', 'we' take interest in their experiences because through the practice of comparison there may be something to be learned about the situations in which we find ourselves, inspiration to be drawn from 'them' concerning the extent to which the problems faced may be ameliorated, and because occasionally it may be desirable to seek joint political action in remedy of them.

This positioning of the subjects and their counterparts would have to be coupled with tolerance towards those who are assumed to be opponents, i.e. those who threaten their well-being. While, if one holds that conflict is constitutive of the political, a 'we-they' dynamic of some kind is always present, still it would have to be agonistic rather than antagonistic: opponents would have to be treated, in Mouffe's language, as adversaries to be convinced or politically defeated, rather than enemies to be destroyed or banished from the community (Mouffe 2005: 20). They would need to be seen as legitimate sharers of 'our space', even if much disliked. While the subjects/counterparts and their opponents would have little in common other than their conflicts and their membership in the community[18] – in contrast to maximalist approaches to the common there is no overarching 'identity' that links them, nor a diffuse sense of solidarity or a common set of values beyond the basic democratic values of liberty and equality – their adversarialism would have to stop short of the break-up of the community. The struggle against opponents would have to be treated as ongoing. Ultimately this would not be something for which one could give grounds – opponents would be tolerated

---

[18]Note we are referring here to what binds together the *categories*: the 'we' of the subjects finds its meaning in the conflict with 'they' the opponents. Really-existing individuals should be understood as enmeshed in multiple subject positions, and therefore tied to one another not just by a single conflict but by multiple lines of both adversarialism and allegiance.

not because they bear a particular attribute which links them to 'us', but simply because, to speak with Wittgenstein, 'this is what we do' (Wittgenstein 1976: §217). Nurturing this attitude would be a role for civic education, combined with the development of institutions which render plausible the idea that authority may change hands at regular intervals. Again, that acts of collective positioning would be made according to *problems*, and that there might be multiple sets of problems at stake, would perhaps make the task of fostering this tolerance easier, since a plurality of domains would mean that those seen as opponents with regard to one set of problems may be seen as counterparts in connection to another.

3.   The credibility of political projects

A political bond would be completed by the assumption that seeking to address these problems through the political institutions of the polity constitutes a worthwhile endeavour. It is this conviction which would serve to connect citizens to the institutions ruling in their name. It implies several things about how the problems of the common would need to be seen. They would first have to be treated as problems which can and should be tackled, rather than as just 'facts of life', and tackled in organised collective terms rather than on an *ad hoc* individual basis. If they were seen such that there was no sense of their possible remedy, the problems associated with the political common would be as likely to inspire a retreat into the private realm as a concern for collective action. Likewise, if these problems were assumed to be resolvable on a personal basis, whether by individual intervention or adaptation, there would be no reason to make political claims intended to influence decision-making. Only if they were seen as requiring *collective* address would these problems have integrative force. The level of popular participation in decision-making would not necessarily have to be high, but it would need to be readily assumed that political approaches are worthwhile. The sense of shared predicament would have to be linked in other words to a sense of the worth of *political projects*.

To constitute allegiances supportive of a European polity there would have to be the assumption that the nation-state cannot alone provide the means to address all these problems adequately, but that some (though by no means all) require Europe-wide approaches to be successfully tackled. Such measures would have to 'make sense' in principle, even if the Brussels institutions in their current form, and the policy-making they have given rise to, were assumed to be deficient. As will be argued further in Chapter 5, such a perception would probably be rooted in taken-for-granted under-standings of the nature of such problems, including assumptions about their transnational origins and effects, combined perhaps with the sense that they are not so global in scope as to resist address at a European level. The sense that certain problems need to be tackled at the global-regional level if they are to be tackled at all would be an important factor in entrenching popular acceptance of the related institutional structures. In this way European-level political institutions would become natural reference-points in the agonistic encounter with adversaries, with each 'we' seeking influence over these institutions' agenda so as to advance their political objectives.

Admittedly, this extension of political contestation to the European level would take place within the context of existing popular attach-ments to the political institutions of member-states. Yet there seems no reason in principle why it should entail the abandonment of those attachments. As long as there remain certain domains of problem for which political action at a continental level is deemed unnecessary, more local approaches would retain appeal. Furthermore, engagement with European institutions might be pursued precisely so as to enhance the ability to influence state-level decision-making, rendering the political contest complementary across multiple venues. Of course, the problem of divided allegiances *might* arise if citizens saw their attachment to national institutions and practices not in political but cultural terms: if, for instance, they regarded them not so much as familiar arenas in which to advance a political project, but as the unique means by which 'our' cultural com-munity represents and governs itself. A strong *cultural bond* at the member-state (or sub-state) level would undoubtedly raise challenges for this vision. But the prospect of persistent nationalism is challenging for *any* concept-ualisation of bonds across national boundaries. To the extent that its per-sistence is a realistic prospect, the way to moderate it is not by an appeal to material interests, wider cultural attributes, or shared values and principles, but through the elaboration of a political language for transnational collective positioning of the kind described.

With each of these three elements present one could speak of a col-lective bond, and given that it is addressed to the framing of public concerns one may refer to it as a *political* bond. It points on the one hand to the 'horizontal' allegiances of citizens to other citizens, based on practices of social comparison and the mutual concern which a sense of shared predicament before common problems may generate. It points on the other hand to the 'vertical' allegiances of citizens to the institutions of political authority, grounded in the purposes to which such institutions might be directed. Such citizens, rather than atomised, would have a web of links extending out towards others: yet towards those with whom 'we' do not share problems there is no particular bond other than a common focus of attention (on those things widely held to be problematic) and mutual acceptance as members of the same political space. There is no generalised 'sense of belonging together' (Mason 2000), and no presumption of a harmony of goals: indeed, the absence of consensus and the consequent desire to control aspects of the political agenda are what provide the impetus to come together. Nor does this conceptualisation presume coherence across issue-areas: indeed, a certain irregularity may usefully soften the symbolic boundaries constructed towards the world outside the polity. It does not assume a high degree of political participation – there is no presumed consensus on the value of active citizenship – yet it may foster the conditions in which participation is deemed attractive. On membership questions it would be as ambiguous as all formulations of the collective bond: it would not provide clear criteria for inclusion or exclusion, since who shares in the same problems is something on which plenty of debate may be had. There is no myth here of 'the people' as a single collective extended through time. The conceptualisation fits well, on the other hand, with the two other senses of 'the people' which have been highlighted, that of the final source of authority, and the more empirical sense of a set of individuals engaged in influencing the course of decision-making.

It has been one of the themes of this chapter that the question of how to conceptualise transnational allegiances, rather than being mainly empirical, is of a political character, since whatever position one adopts implies consequences for the kind of democracy which is possible. How one responds to these basic questions says much about which contemporary political trends one approves of and wishes to see replicated at a transnational level. This is why we have approached the question of the common in Europe with an eye to how it may connect with wider developments to do with the health of contestatory politics, the principle of democratic control and the role of citizens in public life. The argument has been that many of the existing approaches to this question conceive either of a quite minimal degree of commonality amongst citizens or that they rather overplay the degree of regularity which is necessary, and that both of these moves may have depoliticising consequences. By minimising the sense of common purpose amongst citizens one is liable to diminish the expectation and possibility of exercising democratic control over matters of common concern; conversely, by overstating the degree of common purpose one may narrow the sphere of reasonable disagreement and circumvent some of the very debates which it is the peculiar virtue of democracy to make possible. What one wants from an explicitly political conceptualisation of the collective bond is a perspective which allows greater scope for political adversarialism and which points towards revitalising the principle of collective self-rule. A political bond as it has been outlined so far, centred on the three elements of the *political common*, *collective positioning* and *political projects*, seems to provide this, but it is just the bare sketch of an ideal, a starting-point for further exploration.

Each of these three elements will be the subject of a chapter, where they will be developed further with an empirical eye. Ideals, it should be said, involve both an act of modelling and of idealisation: they are at once an attempt to depict the world, as it currently exists or may become, and at the same time to do so in a way that accentuates certain features considered desirable. Ideals are not susceptible to empirical (dis)confirmation, since they are intended to organise one's understanding and suggest diagnoses rather than directly correspond to a real-world situation, and it may be that their purpose is served even if they never take on the status of an accurate model of existing reality. At the same time, to treat them as purely theoretical constructs, and to evaluate them only on the grounds of internal consistency, is to deprive them of much of the critical and suggestive force they may have, and to overlook an important means by which they can be elaborated further. Empirical research represents a useful way to pursue and discipline a line of thought, and 'theory without some kind of exemplification is no theory at all' (Barnes 1995: 61), just as empirical research needs to be concept-driven.

There are undoubtedly tensions between political theorising and sociological research. Simplifying a little, one may say that the role of the sociologist has traditionally been to look for the rules which govern the behaviour of a collective and its elements, seeking uniformity and order so as to explain and predict. A political philosopher on the other hand, concerned with the possibility of human freedom and the renewal of political life, has often been sceptical of such rules, or has wanted to insist that any such rules are limited in scope and leave aspects of life undetermined. There is no straight contradiction between these perspectives – each can acknowledge a boundary beyond which the other is sovereign, even if they disagree on its location – but it is evident that a project which seeks to combine them must tread carefully. The work that follows proceeds by setting the theoretical ideas sketched in this chapter in a dialectical relationship with a small-scale empirical study. The concept of a *political bond* is applied to a body of empirical material, on the one hand to assess how smoothly the concept may be employed and how it might be refined, and on the other to explore the material in a theoretically informed way. The next chapter sets out the strategy and the methods used.

2
Studying the Allegiances of Europeans

The political attachments we shall explore hinge on how citizens understand the world, identify its problems, and conceive the possibilities for reacting to these. They are anchored in subjective appraisal. Clearly the image of *homo economicus* conjured by rational-choice approaches is unsuited to their study (Downs 1957). Such models work best as exercises in deductive reasoning, and the difficulties which arise in their empirical application have been well documented and need not be repeated.[1] Moreover, they point to an interest-based conception of political community, something we have had reason to criticise. Nor can we be guided by *homo sociologicus*, the protagonist of much classical social theorising who plays out his role in a social totality held together by forces of production, the division of labour, or behaviour-determining values and norms. Holism of this kind, despite the appearance of radical divergence from the individualism of economic approaches, tends to share the basic assumption that the ideational is epiphenomenal, that order is achieved independently of people's interpretation (Reckwitz 2002).[2] Further, in its image of society as the outcome of normative consensus, it supposes the kind of maximalist conception of the common one may wish to avoid. This work therefore concentrates on those approaches to citizenship and mass politics broadly classifiable as *interpretative*.

---

[1] See for instance 1995's special issue of *Critical Review* 9 (1/2).
[2] Some who seek to explore empirically a culture- or values-based bond fall into this category – not those examining *perceptions* of commonality (these will be considered below) but those attempting to trace the distribution of objectively observable attributes. Such studies explore whether, for instance, individuals in post-communist Europe share the same values as their western counterparts. See (Fuchs and Klingemann 2000; Gerhards and Holscher 2005; Ester et al. 1993).

Such approaches come in a variety of forms (White 2009a). Some treat interpretation as a matter of individual cognition and adopt what may be called a 'mentalist' approach, as in the tradition of political psychology. Others focus on transpersonal phenomena, notably patterns of language usage and symbolic practice, drawing *inter alia* on the insights of language philosophy, interpretative sociology and anthropology. These latter approaches are interpretative in the more profound sense that not only is the focus on how people see and experience the world, but it is assumed that accessing these meanings is itself an interpretative exercise, one which requires the researcher to draw on their own resources of understanding rather than seek to step back from these.[3] The following pages elaborate the rationale for interpretative research in this deeper sense, as well as a shift in focus concerning the kinds of citizen perception which should interest scholars of European society and politics beyond the nation-state. In the latter part of the chapter, attention focuses on the study to be developed in the chapters that follow.

Political philosophy by other means

How people interpret the political world is the concern of many strands of literature in political science and sociology, most of which take established state structures as their research frame. Generally the focus is on how people form opinions connected to the political processes of the state where they hold citizenship, and the population for which findings are intended to be representative is likewise defined by citizenship. Much US opinion-poll research follows this pattern, concerned primarily as it is with the workings of American democracy. In Europe, analogous national traditions of research have been augmented in recent decades by a large literature studying how people interpret the social and political world *beyond* the state of which they are members, particularly their appraisal of developments connected to European integration. A significant part of this research draws on data provided by the EU's polling body, Eurobarometer. While this data remains heavily dependent on research conducted at the national level, aimed at representing the populations of member-states and sub-divisions within these, it nonetheless endeavours to produce findings generalisable to a wider European space.

---

[3]For discussion of interpretative perspectives in general, see (Sewell 1992; Hollis 1994; Taylor 1971).

One can divide this literature into two large families, looking at two different aspects of European integration. The first is addressed to citizens' *socio-cultural identification with Europe and Europeans*; the second is addressed to attitudes towards the *EU institutions*. Studies of the first kind have examined whether for instance respondents declare themselves willing to trust other Europeans (Niedermayer 1995; Scheuer and Schmitt 2007), the extent to which they feel a sense of cultural likeness with other Europeans, the extent to which they report a 'feeling of belonging' to Europe, or the extent to which they claim a 'European identity', either in preference or in addition to such an identity at the national and other levels (Carey 2002; Bruter 2005; Herrmann and Brewer 2004).[4] Scholars have looked at the degree to which a sense of belonging to the category of 'Europeans' varies across socio-economic groups, and is strongest amongst high-status and well-travelled groups such as businesspersons and white-collar workers (Fligstein 2008). In the second family of literature, studies have examined the extent to which citizens approve of their country's membership of the EU, in correlation with what such attitudes vary (Gabel and Palmer 1995; C. Anderson 1998; McLaren 2002), how much they know and understand about the workings of the EU, and whether they trust its institutions (Thomassen 2007; Thomassen 2009). These two literatures are sometimes brought together, examining for instance whether apparently persistent feelings of *national* identity are the major hindrance to the development of positive attitudes towards the EU's political system or European integration in general (Hooghe and Marks 2005a; McLaren 2006).

These two families of literature comprise the main research done on popular forms of identification in Europe under conditions of integration. From the perspective of our enquiry they have two major shortcomings, one to do with research focus and one to do with methods. If one considers first the focus of research into citizens' socio-cultural identification with Europe and Europeans, one notes immediately how it closely corresponds to the search for a *cultural bond* described in the previous chapter. It seeks as the necessary underpinning to political structures the existence of social ties much as they were understood in the nation-state context. The emphasis is on patterns of identification coextensive with territorial units – Europe, the nation-state, the region or the world – and it is presupposed that these are the most salient

---

[4]Cf. (Kohli 2000; Duchesne 2008) for overviews.

formulations for the self and other Europeans. What tends to be lacking is a sense of how cross-national bonds may develop in denominations other than the territorial, extending for instance to some social groupings in a territorial space but not all, based perhaps on a logic of comparison, and extending differently on different issues.[5] Also generally missing is sensitivity to the adversarial relations which may properly accompany political community – how, for instance, citizens may have good reason to oppose and *dis*-trust certain fellow citizens on certain issues, and how indiscriminately benevolent dispositions may be normatively undesirable. One also sees a tendency for the attachments sought to be conceived as unreflexive brute feelings, with little attention to their desirability and the political purposes for the sake of which they might develop. Seeing them in this way as pre-political attachments, their normative appeal is put beyond question. Such a move can be defended only if one makes the empiricist claim that these feelings of attachment simply are what they are, and permit only a single interpretation. Yet such an argument is too ambitious, given the overwhelming reliance on one data source. These points apply no less to the more sophisticated accounts which distinguish between different kinds of 'European identity', e.g. civic or ethnic (Bruter 2005; Risse 2010), or between 'inclusive' and 'exclusive' forms of national identity (Hooghe and Marks 2005b).

The second family of works, looking at attitudes towards the EU institutions, might seem preferable insofar as it avoids some of these maximalist tendencies. Indeed, the questions posed are important. Yet the attitudes these approaches anticipate are generally cast as existing separate from the context of substantive purposes – they concern perceptions of trustworthiness or corruption in the abstract, rather than the capacity to deal with particular issues of concern. Allegiances to institutions are thereby separated from the reasons for which they might be held. The distinction between attitudes to institutional procedures in general on the one hand, and the desirability of particular acts of policy-making on the other, is too often ignored, or where it is acknowledged it is generally without probing of the criteria by which citizens judge policies, and the schemes of meaning within which opinions form.

One of the shortcomings of existing scholarship is therefore its research focus: it tends to inquire into the kinds of collective bond which, as

---

[5]Eurobarometer regularly asks respondents to evaluate their personal situation, their country's, and that of Europe in general, but does not enquire about non-territorial forms of collective subjecthood.

the previous chapter argued, are not necessarily of the type one should want to seek. How one defines research questions is a matter of normative significance – it is political philosophy by other means – yet the approaches generally taken are, from the perspective advanced in Chapter 1, problematic.

The second limitation is methodological, having to do with the research methods used and the assumptions underpinning them. The widespread reliance on Eurobarometer data has the consequence that concepts as complex as European identity, solidarity and trust are reduced to a very limited range of indicators so that they may be equated with the responses given in opinion polls. Such a move involves several forms of reductionism. First, the referent of these terms is treated as something cognitive, a feature of individual minds taken in isolation rather than something anchored in situations and social contexts, with all the problems that mentalist approaches to the social may lead to (White 2009a). Second, a strong assumption is made about the centrality and stability of this cognitive thing (usually expressed as 'beliefs' or 'attitudes') in the minds of those who participate in the research.[6] It is a kind of EU-centrism which supposes that respondents should have a set of beliefs or attitudes on the subject to hand.[7] Third, this cognitive thing comes to be regarded as sufficiently accessed by a small number of polling questions – despite the fact the analyst cannot know what criteria respondents bring to bear on these questions, and despite the fact respondents may not themselves be in a position to make explicit and summarise on demand the bonds of attachment

---

[6]It can be argued that Eurobarometer polls are intended to have exactly this performative effect, problematising e.g. the notion that citizens' automatic identification should be with the nation-state and promoting the idea that 'feeling European' is as natural as 'feeling British' (Cf. Shore 2000: 51–2).

[7]See e.g. (OPTEM 2006). While this large-scale qualitative study contains some interesting findings, it seems likely to have overstated the extent to which citizens look to the EU as a response to their concerns (pp.8–9) simply by virtue of the structure of its Discussion Guide (Appendix III). Already from the second question (p.73), respondents are invited to focus their attentions on the EU by being told that 'one of the factors likely to play a role in the future is the European Union and how it will develop.' Thus the everyday concerns which they articulate in response to the first question are automatically given a connection to matters European, and this can hardly but encourage the 'europeanisation' of subsequent responses. See also the speed with which Standard Eurobarometer surveys (e.g. Eurobarometer 62, 2005: 23ff.) move from asking about issues of general concern (Q33) to asking about the role played in them by the EU (Q34).

they feel.[8] The problem is compounded in many cases by the use of cluster-concepts like 'identity' and 'public opinion' to suggest the specious unity of a range of quite disparate ideas. Needless to say, these problems arise not because researchers are negligent, but because the application of quantitative methods relies on making large reductions to the complexity of the social world, first so that large amounts of data can be collected, and second so that such data can be converted into numerical form without loss of information. Such methods are clearly ill suited to studying the meanings which Europe and the EU come to assume in people's lives more generally. While such methods can usefully elicit short answers to direct questioning, they are little able to explore the kinds and the depth of significance attached in contexts beyond the question format.

Such observations suggest the need not only to redefine the research focus but to seek new methods of inquiry. There is a need in particular to look not just at what people say when prompted specifically to consider matters European but at the reference-points they invoke of their own accord, the extent to which these include transnational elements, and only as a later step to consider how these correspond to the question of political community in the European context. Some of the more promising research methods are to be found in the small number of existing works drawing on sociological approaches. A valuable study by Ulrike Meinhof uses interviews involving visual prompts to investigate the reference-points routinely invoked by border communities in East/West Germany and Germany/Poland, producing the important finding that European reference-points are invoked quite rarely (Meinhof 2004). Sophie Duchesne and her collaborators have used focus groups to study how citizens construct and contest narratives to do with the EU, as part of a wider examination of conflict and consensus formation in everyday discussion (Duchesne et al. 2010; see also Chapter 6). Interviews have been used to enrich Eurobarometer data and newspaper analysis in the work of Juan Díez Medrano (Díez Medrano 2003), while Adrian Favell has examined how elite EU citizens conceptualise

---

[8]See e.g. the questions Eurobarometer has regularly posed concerning people's attitudes to EU-related issues: 'Generally speaking, do you think that [your country's] membership of the European Community is a good thing, a bad thing, or neither good nor bad?' 'In general, are you [very much/to some extent] for or against efforts being made to unify Western Europe?' 'In the near future do you see yourself as [nationality] only, [nationality] and European, European and [nationality] or European only?' (Gabel and Palmer 1995; C. Anderson 1998; L. McLaren 2002; Carey 2002).

and take advantage of the opportunities of EU citizenship, plus face constraints on their ability to do so (Favell 2007). These works are indicative of the concerted efforts of certain scholars to bring a wider range of disciplinary resources to the study of EU citizenship (Checkel and Katzenstein 2009; Robyn 2005). Though not all seek to connect their findings to the explicitly political questions at the core of the present study, nor to engage in the development of concepts, all are a useful indication of how research may proceed beyond the familiar paths.

Towards an interpretative sociology of the political bond

The bonds of collectivity cannot be sought purely in the opinions voiced in quantitative surveys, for these do little to illuminate the underlying structures of meaning in which opinion-formation is embedded. The natural move for those seeking to avoid the premises and methods of a mentalist approach is to turn instead to the study of symbolic (i.e. meaning-guided) practice, with language as the pre-eminent example. Taking this as the target of enquiry promises a richer insight into citizens' self-understanding and appraisal of the world around them. It enables examination of the concepts people invoke themselves rather than those put to them by the questioner, and allows a better grasp of the associations those concepts bring with them.

There are multiple perspectives on how one should see practices of language usage and their political significance; one which has attracted considerable interest is that associated with Habermasian *deliberative democracy* (Habermas 1984). This perspective focuses on language as a medium of intersubjective argumentation. In a definition which has been taken up in the EU literature, one author casts the deliberative model as the 'rule of reasons' (Forst 2001).[9] Language is given a very particular significance: it is the means by which free public reason can be exercised, allowing distorted or undesirable political views to be overcome through reasoned debate (Habermas 1984: 99). For those interested in empirical questions, attention is likely to be focused on how far those engaged in interaction take advantage of the opportunities for deliberation and consensus-formation, and the extent to which there exist the necessary conditions for such opportunities to arise (hence the interest in the European context in the possible existence and character of a European 'public sphere' (Gerhards 2002; Eder and Kantner 2000; Risse 2010)).

---

[9]The model has been treated as both a normative ideal of democracy and as an explanatory model for existing processes – (cf. Eriksen 2005).

Yet while reasoned argumentation is undoubtedly one of the prime aspects of language usage, arguably there is just as much to be studied at the tacit level, i.e. those aspects of usage which go largely unquestioned and are *not* submitted to reasoned reflection. Thus an important counter-perspective on language sees it not so much as a passive medium but as something which shapes, enables and constrains those who take it up (Schatzki 1996; Polanyi 1966). This points to a focus less on opinions, beliefs and attitudes – as in mentalist perspectives – or reasoning and argument – as in deliberative-intersubjectivist perspectives – but on the common-sense assumptions and routinised discursive practices which underlie these, in which the terms of debate are set and the possibilities for subjecthood and political understanding laid out.

Approaches from cultural sociology and interpretative social theory have much to offer both in conceptualising such a perspective and rendering it suitable to empirical research. An emphasis on the ideational *resources* for interpreting the world available to speakers as part of the social environment they inhabit is an important point of departure.[10] By seeing the individual as drawing upon resources or 'repertoires' which predate her and constrain the possibilities open to her, yet which she redeploys in new ways and whose reproduction she actively shapes, the voluntarism implied when each individual is conceptualised as constructing the ideational world alone can be avoided without reverting to a social determinist perspective which reduces the individual to the passive bearer of structure (Sewell 1992: 7ff.). In contrast to the holism of traditional sociological approaches, there is an emphasis on the possibility of human beings actively to renegotiate their cultural milieu rather than merely be constituted by it. Consistent with this, the language of 'identity', with its implication of cross-spatial and cross-temporal sameness, is abandoned or sharply problematised (Brubaker and Cooper 2000), and greater attention is given to how forms of subjecthood and interpersonal bonds are constructed and 'achieved' through symbolic practice. The study of *symbolic boundaries* is one way research in cultural sociology has proceeded empirically (Lamont and Molnár 2002); modes of justification and orders of worth have been another important field of enquiry (Boltanski

---

[10]As classic statements, see (Swidler 1986; Swidler 2001). The terminology of 'resources' and 'repertoires' is admittedly perhaps just a suggestive metaphor, since these are elements one must infer and which cannot be accessed directly; there is also an evident instrumentalist flavour to the metaphor. Still, on balance it is a useful one. On certain nuances of application, and some limitations, see (Silber 2003).

and Thévenot 1999; Boltanski and Thévenot 2006), together with questions to do with their uneven distribution across different social and territorial environments (Lamont and Thévenot 2000).[11]

With the major exception of the work of Luc Boltanski and Laurent Thévenot, these approaches have been little applied to the concerns of political theory and philosophy. Students of politics in general have tended to adhere to older sociological and anthropological traditions which treat cultural systems as bounded spaces heavily determinative of the actions of individuals living within them (Wedeen 2002). This is unfortunate insofar as these more recent approaches may be the more suitable for combination with a political-philosophical preference for conceptualising the ideational world in ways that permit discrimination between its more and less desirable elements. Even if one does not wish to endorse the deliberative ideal of human subjects consistently engaged in reflexive reasoning and the questioning of presuppositions, and instead assumes that most people for most of the time are heavily dependent on existing ideational packages, still one will want to leave space for the exercise of moral and political evaluation by citizens at their best, and to avoid conceptualising community in terms of brute feelings or the dictates of law-like norms. It is when a certain set of dispositions is naturalised, and consecrated as constitutive of a certain grouping's 'identity', that political and social theorising are liable to enter into tension.

The study which follows treats political allegiance as a phenomenon mainly of tacit understanding, of the taken-for-granted elements which generally precede conscious deliberation and reflection, though they are never quite immune to individual revision or renunciation. In line with the arguments of Chapter 1, rather than treating political community as a matter of stated feelings of identity, belonging or trust, or explicit ascriptions of value, it is explored in the common-sense assumptions and reference-points people invoke when discussing matters of political relevance. *Discursive practices*, i.e. patterns of coordinated talk, are taken as the site for study, and it is through the enactment of these that the collective

---

[11]In Britain and parts of continental Europe, similar questions to these are studied under the rubric of discourse analysis, with studies looking at the 'interpretative repertoires' speakers in discourse situations invoke as they engage in discursive practices such as the construction of identity, acts of legitimisation and delegitimisation, and the building and mobilising of coalitions. For an overview, see Torfing in (Howarth and Torfing 2005). In discursive and rhetorical psychology, see (Potter and Wetherell 1987; Billig 1991). Looking at the organisation of talk at the micro-level, see conversation analysts such as (Antaki 1994).

bond is maintained and reproduced.[12] *Contra* mentalist approaches, and the quantitative methods with which they have been associated, it is not individual beliefs which are taken as the unit of analysis, but the patterns of assumption identifiable in discursive interaction. These are understood as textual rather than psychological phenomena, i.e. transpersonal things manifest in what is said or pointedly not said in a given discursive situation. For our purposes, the assumptions and reference-points of interest are those to do with the kinds of political problem deemed important, how problems are linked to one another, how they can be explained, and the extent to which it is plausible to address them in some organised, collective fashion. Identifying assumptions of this kind requires interpretation: they are never self-evident, and it is always possible to add more to those one has identified. Analysis is therefore no more a purely objective exercise than any other form of empirical research – though it may be better grounded than that which relies on hypothesising about invisible states of consciousness. As one shifts away from a focus on the individual mind to sites of social activity, the study of group environments becomes superior to the use of survey questionnaires.

Assumptions, it is suggested, are not made at random. At any given discursive moment, some are appropriate and others less so; more generally some tend to go together and others not, and some tend to appear accompanied by certain concepts and ideas in clusters. Certain assumptions – e.g. that all heads of state will die tomorrow – are likely to provoke surprise and censure in the text, if made at all. It is possible therefore to speak of at least a basic level of order, and thus the necessity that participants to the discursive practice exercise competence in the way they speak. It is this which allows the researcher the possibility of drawing generalisable conclusions, since these features point to the existence of patterns which extend beyond the collection of individuals who happen to be present. It is also this which allows the researcher to simplify what would otherwise be unmanageably complex.

Aside from on the making of assumptions, the focus will also be on discursive practices of *positioning*. Rather than speaking of 'identity', individual or collective, as something which is brought to bear on a discussion by its participants, we shall examine how texts exhibit subject positions which are taken up, ascribed or resisted by the speakers. Drawing on the work of Rom Harré, subject positions are conceived as

---

[12]This matches with a number of talk-centred perspectives on citizenship in which discussion is treated as a form of political practice (Perrin 2006; Duchesne and Haegel 2007).

locations in discourse to which individuals attach themselves using pronoun grammar, thereby embracing the conceptual repertoire which comes with that position (Davies and Harré 1990). Positioning refers to the discursive practice whereby individuals assign subject positions to themselves and others. It is a relational activity (others are positioned as one positions oneself), and it can extend beyond the intentions and awareness of the actors involved (indeed, actors are part-constituted by positioning).[13] Chapter 4 will look closely at how 'we's' and 'they's' are constructed in discussion, what kind of relationship is posited between them, and how certain subject positions carry implications of agency and others of passivity. It will look also at acts of cross-spatial comparison, which involve positioning others as experiencing similar situations to those faced by 'us'. Just as certain assumptions tend to go together, so too do certain subject positions. Thus it becomes possible to pick up from Chapter 1 the idea of 'domains' of patterned discourse, and to regard individual self-understanding as an ensemble of multiple forms of sub-jecthood (Mouffe 1993: 20, 97). All these terms of analysis are explicated further in the course of the study.

Outline of an empirical study

The research with which we shall explore the allegiances of a *political bond* involves assembling groups of lay people – i.e. those with no profes-sional interest in politics – and getting them talking about problems in public life. The focus is on informal talk, unlike the close attention to media discourse one tends to find in public-sphere analyses, or the articu-lations of well-organised social movements one finds in the literature on contentious politics (Imig and Tarrow 2000). While the media undoubt-edly have a key role in supplying the repertoires with which everyday talk unfolds, media messages are very often supplemented by other resources drawn from daily life, with outcomes which are unpredictable. Moreover, things given prominence in the media are by no means automatically given the same prominence elsewhere: reading, listening and watching is selective, and topics and messages can be ignored as well as borrowed (Gamson 1992). Similarly, scholars who focus on claims-making by

---

[13]As a psychologist, Harré's focus is generally on interpersonal positioning in the small-group setting, but the concepts have been applied also to the intergroup level, whereby groups of individuals position themselves as a 'we' at the same time as constructing a 'them'. See Sui-Lan Tan and F. M. Moghaddam, 'Positioning in Intergroup Relations', in (Harré and van Langenhove 1999).

organised societal actors risk overlooking the broader and less conspicuous social configuration from which these emerge. A political bond needs to be sought in the wider citizenry and not just in its most structured and vocal elements.

The extent to which ordinary people 'talk politics' in their daily lives is of course a matter of some debate, even taking a broad understanding of what constitutes political talk. Some studies based on participant observation, mainly in the US, have emphasised the tendency of non-elites actively to avoid such discussion, considering taboo the expression of strong and opposing views, and unwilling, as individuals, to put themselves in a position where they might have to justify opinions (Eliasoph 1998). Other studies, by contrast, have suggested it is by no means uncommon, at least amongst those of close acquaintance (Cramer Walsh 2004). Context is certainly important: familiar surroundings and faces are likely to be conducive (Conover et al. 2002). As will become clear, the discussions which form the basis of this study were not isolated events: they contain cross-references to conversations had between participants on prior occasions, and were thus enmeshed in a broader history of discussion. Our focus is principally qualitative, however, on the *kinds* of discursive practice which can be observed rather than on the frequency with which they arise in different contexts. We look at how a certain set of people talk when given the opportunity to do so, and treat the provision of opportunities as a separate though important issue.[14]

The discussions conducted were loosely structured: while certain topics were placed on the agenda by the researcher using thematic index-cards, participants were generally given freedom to choose what to talk about and when. (Full details on methods are in the following chapter and the Appendix). The goal was to minimise the significance of the researcher's *a priori* assumptions about what was 'relevant' and 'important' to the discussion whilst maintaining a minimum level of comparability between interviews. As indicated, too many studies of lay perspectives on European politics start with the assumption that the EU is important to people and go on to ask interviewees what they think about it. Hence one sees studies which present a rich amount of data concerning how people

---

[14]Participant observation would have been one way to access information of this kind, but it would not have been suitable to the goal of exploring patterns of discourse in multiple locations and linguistic environments. If one wishes to draw data from numerous settings, participant observation is generally unviable because of the level of familiarity needed with those one is studying. This process is likely to be all the longer if one is identifiably a 'foreigner' in some such settings.

respond when invited to express views on matters European.[15] Instructive as these can be, such an approach replicates one of the problems of opinion polling, the tendency to exaggerate respondents' level of concern with the topic in question by forcing them to address it directly. It also prevents the study of how, and to what extent, this topic is woven spontaneously into discussion. Such a question is often pressing when studying the mass politics of the EU, since not only does anecdotal knowledge suggest a certain level of public disengagement with the subject, but because it may be that matters of political community are best explored as tacit phenomena rather than as the stuff of formulated opinions. While the study that follows draws links to this literature where appropriate, as well as to quantitative data, it is expressly designed to avoid foregrounding the EU from the outset.

This principle was observed by approaching the topic of interest tangentially, getting participants to talk about political issues more generally and then examining what they chose to bring into the discussions spontaneously. This meant giving them considerable freedom to set the discussion agenda, and probing directly on matters related to the EU only towards the end of the discussions.[16] The use of *group* discussions rather than one-to-one interviews has a number of benefits: the power-advantage of the interviewer over interviewees is reduced, and the interviewer is less in a position to dominate the discussion either by direct intervention or silent authority. Indeed, after the first 20 minutes or so, the researcher can adopt a fairly low profile (though of course, his presence is surely always felt, as perhaps is the presence-to-come of an academic audience). Furthermore, group discussions allow one to look at such interactional features as responses, reactions, consensus and jokes, and to get a better feel for the 'common sense'. The role of the individual's whimsy in setting the course of discussion is also reduced in the group environment, since interviewees are accountable to each other for what they choose to talk about: that which is collectively deemed inconsequential is likely to be drowned out in discussion (Morgan 1997; Bloor et al. 2001; Kitzinger and Barbour 1999).

Taxi-drivers were chosen as the interview subjects. As subjects for empirical research, taxi-drivers have been used before. Diego Gambetta

---

[15]See e.g. (Bruter 2005), where the focus-group moderator initiates the discussion with questions which are strongly Europe-related.

[16]This technique of delaying direct probes on the topic of research interest until late in the interview, so as to explore the extent to which it is invoked naturally, has been referred to as 'funnelling' (Morgan 1997: 41).

and Heather Hamill interviewed taxi-drivers in Belfast and New York to explore the cues that are used to make quick decisions about which strangers are likely to be trustworthy (Gambetta and Hamill 2005).[17] In their sociological study, taxi-drivers were interesting because their daily vulnerability to being cheated, intimidated or attacked meant they were likely to be particularly skilled players of the 'trust game'; they were interesting, in other words, because they were in a position of heightened sensitivity to rather ordinary problems. Likewise, in this study of lay politics, taxi-drivers were chosen with the idea that their conversation may exhibit in concentrated form some of the assumptions widespread amongst lay people. On the one hand their job puts them in a position of particular sensitivity to a wide variety of political developments: they are amongst the first to be affected by changes in consumer behaviour, changing patterns of labour mobility, or changing patterns of crime and policing. On the other hand they are exposed to a wide set of currents in society (newspapers and the radio in particular, and the experiences of others as narrated to them), militating against the possibility that theirs is a world unto itself. Also, the self-understanding of many taxi-drivers is arguably as people of practical wisdom and common sense. Unlike, for example, academics, students or perhaps artists, they show little inclination to emphasise personal creativity by formulating opinions which strongly diverge from those around them; rather, it seems, they take some pride in saying pretty much what 'everyone' is saying. Of course, one should be wary about whether they do this accurately, whether they in any sense represent the 'voice of the people' as some of them claim to, and there is no doubt that some of the concerns they voice are idiosyncratic, such as annoyance at the parking violations of civilian drivers who park on their ranks. But it is generally their stated intention to speak as other people speak, and so their talk makes an interesting site for the analysis of discursive resources which are available more widely.[18] Furthermore, they have no reason to be unusually favourable or hostile to the EU, something which might have had a bearing on the kind of issues to be explored.

---

[17]Studying the experiences of South Asians in the North of England, see (Kalra 2000). A useful overview of the taxi-driving industry is contained in Chapter 9. Taxi-drivers have also been used in the field of neurology to study brain activity during the process of memory recall: their significance here lies in their need to activate large amounts of stored memory to navigate a city (Maguire et al. 2006).

[18]Note also that taxi-drivers are well used to conversing with strangers on matters of everyday concern – it is a role readily available to them and which does not need to be developed anew in the interview situation.

While they are of interest here mainly for the patterns to be found in their conversation, taxi-drivers also may have some significance as actors in themselves. They can be treated as belonging, across the countries and cities studied, to a class position which is politically important. The large majority of taxi-drivers are without higher education (a few individuals in this sample had attended university for a couple of semesters, but left before completion).[19] While average earnings are inherently difficult to calculate for taxi-drivers, anecdotal evidence suggests that for each of the countries studied, the majority of drivers may be considered to earn below the average income and to occupy that socio-economic space which extends, on a typical stratification scale, from the working class to the lower-middle class or petit bourgeoisie.[20] There are of course many theories of class and political mobilisation (Eder 1995), and given this study does not treat the ideational as socio-economically determined, these questions are not explored here in detail; nonetheless, it can

---

[19]An interesting study in itself would be the stereotypes to be found in different countries concerning who one is likely to find behind the wheel of a taxi. A considerable number of German social scientists gave warnings before this research was begun that the researcher was likely to encounter taxi-driving social-science students, anxiously studying him as he studied them. Sadly, it seems there were none (though maybe future scholarship will prove otherwise!).

[20]Calculation of average earnings is difficult: first, much depends on the hours the individual chooses to work, and whether those hours are in the day time or night time, during the working week or at weekends. Drivers who work weekend nights may earn considerably more than those doing a weekday day-shift. Second, many drivers are wary of revealing their income to anyone who might turn out to be a tax-inspector. Data on average earnings, as for instance compiled by the British Office for National Statistics 2006 report, should therefore be treated with scepticism. The internet chatrooms taxi-drivers themselves use to compare earnings offer a better approximation – see e.g. www.taxi-driver.co.uk or www.taxiforen.de/forum. These suggest, at the time of interview, earnings after running costs (licensing, maintenance, fuel, possibly car rental etc.), and before tax, of around €25,000 in Britain, €20,000 in Germany (lower in the east), and €6000 in the Czech Republic, each of which is lower than Gross National Income per capita as listed in the World Bank's World Development Indicators (WDI) 2006 database. Drivers working night hours in capital cities (absent in this study) may nonetheless earn higher amounts. Perhaps less important (in terms purely of earnings) is the distinction between drivers who are self-employed (and own their taxi) and those who are employed by a firm, of which there was a mixture in each of the cities interviewed in (though in Britain there was a larger proportion of self-employed drivers than in Germany and the Czech Republic, and some variation between cities). There is no clear economic hierarchy between the two, since while those who are self-employed keep a larger share of their profits and may work for longer hours, those who work for a firm tend to have a more reliable turnover of jobs and may not have to purchase their taxi.

perhaps plausibly be said that it is such people whom political movements have to engage so as to be politically meaningful, and that by studying their discursive practices one can study the resources which are there to be mobilised and the common-sense assumptions which inhibit their mobilisation. It is sometimes suggested, both in the EU context and in democracies more generally, that those in the upper-middle and upper classes of society tend to be more supportive of the polity and the institutions under which they live than those lower down the socio-economic scale (Crompton 1998). To the extent that this is so, it is the working classes and the lower-middle classes that one needs to study if one is to assess a polity's viability. Finally, there are some practical reasons for choosing taxi-drivers. They are accessible, since with the right incentive their time can be secured, and since they can generally be found clustered in one or two places. They generally display camaraderie with each other and are rarely intimidated into silence. They are also people who are used to selling their time, suggesting a two-hour interview does not represent a major interruption or distortion of their schedule. One can speculate that in this sense the interview is not *as* unnatural a phenomenon as it might be for certain other social groups operating to different daily routines.

A total of ten interviews were conducted: three in Britain (Reading, Swansea and Norwich), four in Germany (Lübeck, Kassel, Erfurt and Würzburg) and three in the Czech Republic (Liberec, Plzeň and Ostrava). Looking at cities in more than one country alerts one to features of discourse which might be invisible if one looked at just a single country and language, and allows one to look for common patterns. While the total number of interviewees is small in statistical terms (37, all male) it is well suited to the close textual reading necessary for this kind of project. The countries were selected with presumed diversity in mind: Germany being a large, established member-state of the EU and having land borders with several countries; Britain being another large state but with a shorter and more troubled membership of the EU behind it, and an island status; the Czech Republic being a much smaller country, one which has recently undergone significant political change since the fall of communism and which at the time of interview had just recently acceded to the EU. The cities (approximately 100,000 to 300,000 inhabitants in size[21]) were

---

[21]Ostrava, at around 300,000 inhabitants, was the largest. Reading, Lübeck and Erfurt have populations in the range 200–250,000; Swansea, Norwich, Kassel and Plzeň have c. 150–200,000 inhabitants; Würzburg and Liberec, depending how one measures them, are sized 100,000 to 150,000.

generally chosen with geographical spread in mind, although Erfurt was selected more specifically so as to include a former East German city: this meant having, as well as variation by country, something of an east-west axis, intended to act as a brake on thinking instinctively in national terms. With several of these locations near national borders, one may also investigate the (non-)prevalence of nation-based categories in the discourse of those plausibly most likely to draw on them. Capital and second cities were avoided on the assumption that taxi-drivers there were more likely to be recent arrivals from outside the country or to be part-time workers (e.g. students). Groups of four drivers, sometimes three, were enlisted at taxi-ranks using a financial incentive. Having parked their taxis and turned off their meters, drivers accompanied the author to pubs or cafés for approximately two hours of discussion. Participants were usually familiar with one another – in many cases, already talking to each other when approached – and were familiar with the surroundings in which they were interviewed. Whilst a small handful of participants were internal migrants or first-generation immigrants, all had been living in the city of interview for at least a decade.

It is worth reflecting briefly on the logic of the cases thus constituted for research, in particular the extent to which we shall be looking for cross-spatial variation in the results. There is a common tendency amongst comparativists to assume that it is *social groups* which are the relevant units of comparison, and thus to focus attention on defining which social groups to study. British, German and Czech taxi-drivers, understood in this way as groups, might seem to be the currency of this study. However, whether one defines such groups by criteria of nationality, regional location, socio-economic position, or any number of factors and combinations of factors, one risks both reifying a collective as well as making unwarranted assumptions about these being the most relevant criteria to an understanding of variations in the pattern of results. A number of problems may follow.

First, it may be that the criteria one uses to constitute the cases are far less appropriate to the matter in hand than one assumes. Whereas with quantitative research one may be in a position to make a statistical claim about the level of variation subsequently found between cases, and thus to acknowledge the unimportance of these criteria where necessary, with qualitative research the need for interpretation is all the greater, and by rounding up the usual suspects of nationality, ethnicity, class and gender when constituting the cases one can easily at the moment of research design set oneself up to exaggerate their importance. In European studies this is a problem the researcher is likely to be especially aware of, since often one of the points of interest is exactly the extent to which the old categories of collectivity associated with political modernity are still of relevance in the context of transnational integration – whether for instance nationality still has the same hold on people's imaginations and allegiances as supposedly it did in the past, or whether new social configurations centred e.g. on the European or the local are gaining ground. However, where cases are constituted according to the criterion of nationality, or indeed any other category of collectivity, there will then be a strong temptation to ascribe any noteworthy differences subsequently found to this factor.[22]

Second, not only may one draw false conclusions that fail to conjure the relevant groups, but it may be that the very idea of there being groupings of this kind founded on some principle of likeness independent of patterns in the object studied (here patterns of talk), but in correlation with these, is misplaced. Students of culture have long been plagued by the difficulties of supposing that ways of talking, thinking and acting correspond to the boundaries of recognisable groups. Even where an essentialist perspective is explicitly rejected, 'groupism' (Brubaker 2004) can easily become embedded in the research design, encouraging the researcher to develop a special talent for spotting homogeneity within putative groups (and within their constituent individuals) but a blindness to the importance of individual interpretation, creativity, inconsistency and transgression. This is problematic at a social-theoretical level because one of the important implications of the notion of the duality of structure is that, given social structures exist and are reproduced through interpretation, individual creativity matters hugely in their change and transformation (Giddens 1984). It is problematic also at a political-theoretical level, since again it embeds scepticism about the potential for individual reflexivity. There is the danger that acts which were choice-laden, and potentially susceptible to reassessment, come to be seen as pre-ordained by facts about the individual's biography.

Given these problems, the study which follows makes few attempts to link patterns of discourse and practice with particular biographical

---

[22]One of the underlying difficulties is that there are usually far more axes of commonality and difference than one can control for when constituting the cases.

facts. Instead of comparing social groups, however defined, the emphasis is on comparing snapshots of discourse and practice as taken from different spatio-temporal locations. Each focus group is understood as an observational site where one can examine, in a particularly concentrated and vivid form, the nature and diversity of repertoires which actors have available to them. The 'parent population' from which one is drawing is then understood not as a social group but as a discursive field or a nexus of practices, the precise extension of which is left open, allowing the avoidance of strong assumptions about how these cleave to particular individuals. Naturally, the danger is that one arrives at a kind of a-sociological quietism on these matters, such that one has nothing to say on the significance of the social milieu in which people are embedded, something perhaps no less problematic than any tendency to social determinism. Thus in the study that follows, where important variations between countries or between western and post-communist areas seem evident, these will be highlighted in the analysis. Importantly, so as to go some way to circumventing the groupist trap, such findings will be treated as indicating the significance of different territorial *experiences*, rather than a comparison between nationalities. Likewise, we shall speak of the uneven territorial *distribution* or *availability* of cultural repertoires, without speaking of their adhesion to particular social groups, and without supposing that any one such repertoire is adopted uniformly in any given spatio-temporal location.[23]

Full details of the recruitment process and the factors which may have affected it can be found in the Appendix, but a brief introduction of the participants and the cities of interview can be made here.[24] The first interview was carried out in October 2004 in Reading, a city approximately 40 miles west of London and a commercial centre for the Thames Valley region. Over its history it has had strong industries in the production of cloth, beer and biscuits, and has benefited from its location on the main route from London westwards towards Oxford, Bristol and Wales.

---

[23]A similar rationale is adopted in the work of Lamont and Thévenot, who state their concern as with 'documenting how [...] schemas [of evaluation] are unevenly present across national cultural repertoires,' on the assumption that 'different national communities are not equally likely to draw on the same cultural tools to construct and assess the world that surrounds them' (Lamont and Thévenot 2000: 6–9).

[24]The names have been changed.

The four participants were drawn from the taxi-rank at the main train station, soon after lunch, and taken to a pub across the road. They were: Malik, second-generation Pakistani background, early 30s; Derek, white, mid-50s; Saeed, first-generation Pakistani background, mid-50s, resident in Britain since the 1960s; and Hanif, second-generation Pakistani background, early 30s. The second interview was conducted a month and a half later in Swansea, a coastal city approximately 40 miles west of Cardiff, near the old mining and copper industries of south Wales and once a maritime port of some significance. Unlike further north, English rather than Welsh is generally the first language. The participants were recruited – with some difficulty – at the taxi-rank next to the Quadrant shopping centre and taken to a nearby pub as it was opening at 11am. They were: Luke (white, early 30s); Dean (white, early 30s); Alan (white, early 40s); and Marvin (white, late 40s). The third interview was conducted a few days later in Norwich, an old Anglo-Saxon town in East Anglia with historical connections to continental Europe based on trade (mainly wool) and migration (including the arrival of large numbers of Walloons and Huguenots in the sixteenth and seventeenth centuries), and a history until recently of producing clothes, shoes and chocolates. The participants were Malcolm (white, mid-40s), Bill (white, early 50s), Les (white, mid-50s) and Gary (white, mid-40s), all of whom took little convincing to take part.

The German interviews took place in March and April 2005. The first was in Lübeck, one of the old Hanseatic towns near the Baltic coast, famous for marzipan and Thomas Mann. Recruitment began early in the morning at the main train station and was met with considerable enthusiasm, some drivers expressing regret that they were unavailable. Those who participated were: Jochen (white, mid-50s); Werner (white, mid-50s); Hamid (first-generation Iranian, early 40s); and Niklas (white, mid-30s). The second interview was held a few days later in Kassel in central Germany – a city bombed heavily in World War II, today known mainly for hosting every five years the Documenta exhibition of modern and contemporary art. The participants were drawn, easily, first thing in the morning from the large taxi-rank at the city's modern out-of-town station, Kassel Wilhelm-shöhe, and interviewed in an upstairs café overlooking the station. Included in the discussion were: Dieter (white, mid-50s); Sebastian (white, mid-30s); Peter (white, mid-50s); and Hans (white, mid-50s). The third German interview, in early April 2005, took place in Erfurt, an old, well-preserved city in the former East, long famous for its connections to Martin Luther, who attended university there and lived on several years as a monk. Taxis were rarer here, despite the rain, but after an hour of searching three willing volunteers were found and accompanied to a café opposite the station. They were: Harald (white, mid-50s); Uli (white, mid-40s); and Matthias (white, late-30s). Ten minutes into the discussion a fourth participant was added: Axel (white, mid-30s).[25] Recruitment for the last of the four German interviews – in Würzburg, a wine-producing city in northern Bavaria, heavily bombed in World War II – was very difficult. Possible reasons are discussed in the Appendix. The taxi-rank at the main station, a large one with a swift turnover, looked promising. For several hours though only the enthusiastic endorsement of one driver had been secured – Ralf (white, early 50s). He left occasionally to take jobs, returning each time to see how things were progressing, to restate his interest and to try and cajole some colleagues. Long after the researcher's lack of success had become a joke, a running joke, and beyond a joke, Ralf was able to win the participation of Oskar (white, mid-30s). Oskar subsequently enlisted by mobile phone a third driver, Ulrich (white, mid-30s).

The Czech interviews were conducted in August 2005. The first took place in Liberec, a city in northern Bohemia which enjoyed wealth in the nineteenth century on the back of its textile industry. It was at the centre of the Sudetenland dispute in the 1930s (when its population was mainly ethnic German), and large numbers of ethnic Germans were expelled at the end of World War II in accordance with the Beneš decrees. The participants were gathered easily at the main rank in the town centre and taken to a large, upstairs restaurant just as it was quietening after the lunch-hour. The participants were Vladimír, (white, early-40s), Zdeněk (white, early-50s), Radoslav (white, mid-30s) and Tomáš (white, late-20s). The second Czech interview was in Plzeň, a relatively prosperous business and industrial centre about half-way between Prague and the German border, famous for its *Pilsner Urquell* beer. Experiencing considerable difficulty in recruiting, the author alternated between the two main ranks in the city, one on the main square and one at the bus station. Neither had much of a turnover. Eventually one keen driver appeared, Pavel (white, early-30s). He came and went for a while until the participation of Michal was secured (white, late-20s). Michal rang up a driver who was off-duty at the time, Robert: (white, mid-20s). By that time it was early evening; the discussion was had in the only place quiet enough to make a recording, a grand, Habsburg-style café in the centre of town, in which the drivers and the researcher were the only customers. The third and final interview was conducted in Ostrava, a former mining and steel-making city in the east

---

[25]For details on Axel's late arrival, see the Methodological Appendix.

of the country, close to Poland and Slovakia, which has recently seen most of its industry closed down. It was probably the poorest of the cities interviewed in, and – despite also being the largest – it had barely a taxi-rank anywhere. In the city centre, the square where a few taxis would normally park was being dug up, so they were displaced. Fortunately there was still a taxi hut there, and inside were three very willing drivers: Miloš (white, mid-30s), Zbyněk (white, mid-40s) and Jan (white, late-50s). There was no fourth driver easily available. It was mid-morning; their local pub (*pivnice*) turned out to be closed, so a decision was made for the hotel brasserie across the road.

3
Articulations of the Political Common

Chapter 1 outlined the idea of a political bond. In such a perspective it is substantive political problems which are made the focal point for the collective bond, in substitution for alternatives such as interests, cultural markers, or values. It would be the sense of shared predicament arising from facing problems in common with others that would form the basis for collective ties. One of the first questions this raises, and one with some significance for contemporary democracy more generally, is whether the capacity and inclination to articulate matters of common concern can be found in contemporary populations. Is there the willingness to voice problems that relate to 'us' rather than just 'me', a sufficient level of engagement in affairs extending outside the private realm, or are ordinary citizens too incompetent or too 'depoliticised' for this to be taken seriously as a starting point? Can one, to resume Chapter 1's vocabulary, speak of there being a 'political common' – that is, the assumed existence by members of the collective of important common problems in need of address? And if so, how best does one characterise its composition?

It is this first element of a political bond which is explored and developed in this chapter. A theoretical perspective from which to understand the commonality of problems is elaborated, based on the ideas of the preceding chapter, and the empirical material is studied for how far common problems are constructed in discussion. The chapter identifies a series of problems articulated and developed in each of the country groups – Britain, Germany and the Czech Republic – and, to put this in context, notes also various problems articulated rarely or not at all. Then, picking up the idea of problem *domains*, it looks at how certain problems tended to be clustered in discussion. The analysis suggests three domains of particular importance – *Economics*,

Society and the Law, and *Relations between Peoples* – and points to a fourth set of problems, to do with *Quality of Life*, which, though they were articulated with some frequency, tended to be marginalised in these discussions. With these observations one has the contours of a political common, both as a theoretical concept and as an interpretation of one body of discursive practice. This forms the basis for an exploration in subsequent chapters of the kinds of group positioning one finds with regard to these problems, the extent to which these problems are assumed amenable to organised address, and more generally what these patterns imply for a European polity.

Problématiques, problematisations and common problems

Let us begin with the format of the interviews. Once each group of taxi-drivers had taken seats around a table, introduced themselves and ordered their drinks, the discussion was opened by directing attention to a series of topic cards spread out on the table. There were 17 of these, each consisting of two images and a verbal caption, and each designed to refer to a topic with some connection to public life.[1] The English-language captions were as follows: Peace & War, Treatment of Outsiders, Overseas Aid, Medical Care, Education & Training, The Legal System, Policing, Health & Safety Standards, The Environment, Science & Research, Transport, Money & Prices, Purchase of Property, Markets & Production, Taxation, Corruption, and Work. These were the author's own creations, designed to mix breadth of coverage with openness to interpretation. The list covered the major topics which it was felt participants might be inclined to develop, and excluded a number which in other spatio-temporal contexts one might wish to include (abortion rights in the contemporary US, for instance). No such list can be comprehensive of the full range of issues in public life, and it was fully expected that the cards might be of unequal interest to the participants; the intention was to provide a starting point from which discussion could begin. Some blank cards were provided so that participants could add to the 17 cards any extra ones they felt were missing, but this generally proved unnecessary.

The participants were invited to look at the cards for a few minutes, and then as a group to arrange them in piles according to 'what goes

---

[1] See the Appendix for black-and-white reproductions of the cards. The exercise is inspired by (Coxon 1999).

naturally with what', giving justification for their choices as they did so. This tended to result in ten minutes or so of discussion. As a second step, the participants were asked to provide a title for each card-pile, summing up why those cards belonged together. Again, roughly ten minutes of debate followed. The third step, which initiated the bulk of the discussion, involved participants selecting certain problem-areas to talk about in more detail. They were encouraged to focus on those they considered most urgent, although each topic was touched on at least briefly, in some cases at the end of the discussion at the researcher's prompting.[2]

In the Wittgensteinian tradition, rule-based behaviour is understood not in terms of the application of theoretical rules to given situations but rather as competence in practice, the capacity of 'knowing how to carry on' (Barnes 2001; Schatzki 1996: 49ff.). This competence is understood as a social phenomenon, as a basic convergence in practices and the capacity for successful coordination and adjustment among peers, rather than individual distinction on an absolute scale.[3] Conversational competence, by extension, can be seen as the ability of individuals mutually to coordinate their talk based on a certain convergence in discursive practices: to make interventions which others can respond to, and to carry on from what others say, so as to achieve some level of ordered and sustained interaction. This is an important idea for the purposes of this chapter. By convening participants in an interview environment, supplying them with prompt-cards, and asking them to justify the choices they make with these, one is creating a situation in which participants must 'carry on'. The cards themselves could by no means determine the discussion, any more than a

---

[2]Opinion surveys often ask respondents what they consider to be the 'most important problem facing the nation'. There is a danger that this approach overlooks those aspects of life which respondents consider important, but not problematic (cf. Wlezien 2005). In introducing these interviews a combination of wide formulations was sought such as 'problems in public life', 'important issues' and 'things that need addressing', to avoid prematurely narrowing the range of discussion. However, as will be made clear below, the focus in the analysis is on those things described not just as important but as a source of concern, these being the most frequently articulated.

[3]N.B. The word 'competence' may be prone to misinterpretation: it refers here not to an elitist judgement by the researcher ('have the participants got their facts right?') but to the capacity of participants to coordinate successfully with one another, using the cards where necessary as props. This point is picked up at the end of the chapter.

collection of cards themed on equine diseases could structure the discussion of an unremarkable group of political theorists. At least some of the topics would most likely provoke little engagement, while others might lead to sustained conversation. Only if the participants were able to reach beyond the situation to pre-existing knowledge could an ordered discussion emerge. Tacit understanding of this kind is crucial. Likewise, in open discussion, participants would require a certain amount of know-that and know-how in order to respond to each other's points and develop them. Without this competence, one would probably reach silence, or a fundamental shift in topic. It is one of the considerable advantages of conducting *group* interviews that one is able to study the ability of individuals mutually to coordinate their talk in this way.

Before looking in more depth at some findings, let us clarify our terminology. The words and images on the cards can be understood as *symbols* which may or may not be received meaningfully by an observer. To competent observers who know how to read them, they refer – by convention – to a series of practices, material objects or situations which henceforth may be called *problématiques*.[4] For example, 'Taxation' refers to a set of practices which involve, roughly speaking, the state extracting money non-arbitrarily from its citizens. When a *problématique* is talked about, and is talked about in negative terms (e.g. 'How dare the state take that hard-earned money!', or 'Why don't those people pay higher taxes?'), one can say that it is being *problematised*.[5] Of course, not all problématiques will be problematised. But those which are one can then refer to, in the everyday language sense, simply as *problems*. Whereas problématiques are abstract and undisclosed, problems are formulations of a more specific sort; they come with a certain spin. Nonetheless, they can be more specific or less: both 'war' in general and the 'war in Iraq' might be treated as problems, and it would be a question of judgement whether one sees them in the relation of category to item. Problems, one may say, can be articulated in a plural but not unlimited number of ways. To suggest there is just one way would be to adopt an ideal-language perspective,

---

[4]This term is preferred to the everyday word 'topic' used above, since 'topic' is strongly discourse-centred, whereas problématique may be taken to imply an experiential and situational basis as well.

[5]Of some relevance here, there is a small literature in social and political science on 'problem definition' – see (Cobb and Rochefort 1994).

whereby the stuff of problématiques (practices, material objects and situations) can be problematised either correctly or incorrectly. On the other hand, to say there is an *unlimited* number of ways in which problems can be articulated would be to disregard the conventions of language usage and the historicity of discursive repertoires.

Our terminology, though slightly 'p-heavy', serves to remind of the relational and constructed character of problems: the 'real world' does not consist of a collection of pre-existing problems which individuals subsequently discover and ponder, but rather of raw, ambiguous things which can be read in different ways and for the interpretation of which individuals rely on transpersonal resources. Problems are the things which emerge from an act of engagement with the world. When, in the analysis that follows, something is referred to as a problem (e.g. the 'problem of immigration'), the implication is that it is *treated* as a problem, not that we – as the authorial voice – consider it necessarily to be a problem. One is not obliged – at least when engaged principally in analysis – to reach a position oneself on how accurate or appropriate each act of problematisation is.

Fortunately, these distinctions need not be continually invoked in the course of the analysis. What one encounters when studying discourse are not problématiques but problems (understood as problematisations). Once individuals grasp at a problématique, sensing there is something important there, and once they put it in words and treat it as something problematic, already one may say that they are talking about a problem. Therefore for much of the empirical analysis in this and the following chapters, it will be possible to speak simply of 'problems': participants were invited to talk about problems and their articulations can be referred to as such. But even if one does not have to invoke it frequently, it seems that one could not do without the concept of problématique, since the study involves the act of drawing comparisons between different discussions, and different sections of a single discussion, something which requires that the analyst be able to say, at least occasionally, 'they're talking about the same thing.' When two groups complain about 'asylum-seekers', for example, both are problematising the problématique one might call 'immigration'. That they are both doing this is, of course, an act of interpretation rather than objective observation, and depends on the researcher himself being a competent participant in the same language-games as those used by his interviewees. The necessary familiarity has, one hopes, been built up over the course of the interviews, multiple readings of the transcripts, and life more generally.

A political common would be formed of 'common problems'. Here it can be made clearer what is meant by 'common'. Again, the choice of *group* discussions is crucial. The essence of conversation, one can argue, is sense-making. Participants in conversation try to make sense, to 'carry on' in a meaningful way, and they must expect their partners in discussion to do the same, so that some kind of conversational development can take place. There is a *cooperational* basis to conversation, such that participants orient themselves to the interventions of other participants (Grice 1975: 45–7). Conversation is, in this sense, a question of agreement in discursive practice and of mutual coordination and adjustment. By convening group interviews, one creates a conversational environment in which all interventions are subject to peer judgement. Participants are encouraged to say things which they assume others in the group will be able to react to and develop, since ensuing silence is widely assumed to be the mark of a weak intervention. Successful interventions in the group interview, one may say therefore, are characterised by their public relevance. Participants generally do not seek to make interventions which are highly idiosyncratic and which other participants would not know how to react to: even autobiographical narratives must, in the group context, be offered in such a way as to highlight their common significance. And should a participant diverge from this pattern and say something which appears strange to the others, this oddness is likely to be evident. The intervention may explicitly be rejected as peculiar, or more likely it will be ignored, resulting in another participant taking the conversation in a more meaningful direction or, in the worst case, resulting in silence and the need to 'restart' the conversation.

This is what allows one to say that those problems which are successfully introduced into a group discussion are the kind of 'common problems' which can be associated with a political common. They could not be purely private problems, problems affecting just 'me', since those problems will be screened out as the conversation develops; rather, they are likely to be the kind of problems which affect 'people like us', where the 'us' is some kind of we-formulation which may differ according to the problem at hand. The use of 'we' pronouns is important, but crucial is not so much their occasional appearance – this may be due simply to an individual speaker wanting, for whatever tactical reason, to position himself as part of a larger group – but their acceptance and development by certain or all other participants to the discussion. It is this successful generation in discussion of reference points to which others can orient themselves which expresses the

common. Likewise, when certain problems are repeatedly linked together in discussion, and when participants accept and develop the linkages made by others, one can treat this as indicative of a more basic
convergence concerning what topics go with what.

Clearly what is needed at this point then are some criteria by which
to assess whether interventions in discussion are successful and thus
whether the problems described can be considered common. Indicators
of 'success' used to select passages for analysis include the following.
Evidently, where problems are talked about and developed in a considerable amount of depth by more than one participant, this indicates
their common salience, particularly if all participants are active; likewise if the same problems are pursued in depth across multiple interviews. Significant is when interventions are closely tied to one another,
in particular when one sees the joint construction of an argument by
more than one participant. The presence of cross-references in discussion is also important: when participants want to 'go back' to an earlier
passage of discussion, or when they simply make a link to something
which was said earlier, this implies the significance of that intervention
and that the problem in question is interwoven with others. Descriptions drawing on more than one source of information (for instance,
both the media and personal experience) may indicate the importance
of the problem in question. Shared affective responses, such as more
than one participant expressing outrage or frustration, or a particular
enthusiasm to discuss a certain problem, can be indicative.[6] Together
with this, expressions of *opinion*, particularly when this occurs early in
the interview when participants have been non-committal so far, can
be an indicator – as long as this statement of opinion is then followed
up (even if just to rebut) by at least one of the other participants. In
the discussion in Norwich, for example, the card-arranging exercise at
the beginning was interrupted for some time by an irrepressible flow of
interventions from Malcolm, Bill and Les about the inadequacy of the
police and judicial system in dealing with local crime. In effect, the
prompt-card was so successful that even this loosest of interview
formats was disrupted.

Many problématiques were problematised in all or most of the interviews, and these are the ones focused on below. Principal among them,

---

[6]On the last two, see (Gamson 1992). These criteria subsume the two axes
of centrality commonly spoken of in political psychology – 'cognitive' and
'motivational' – though no such distinction need be made here.

to list them briefly in our own words, were: unemployment, crime, immigration, relations between majorities and minorities, extremes of wealth, military conflict, prices, wages, culture clashes, education, anti-social behaviour, the quality of policing/justice, corruption, taxes, debt, and regulations. It is the articulation of problems related to these that will be treated as the core features of a political common.[7] It is not proposed that they be treated as distinctly 'European' or 'EU-oriented' problems. In how far, and in what way, a European dimension is evoked in their discussion is something that will be considered in the following chapters. Nor is it argued that these problems are distinctly 'European' in the sense that interviews with taxi-drivers in other parts of the world would not generate a similar array of concerns: our focus of attention is always on the possibilities held out by the discursive practices in question, not the extent to which they are exclusive to a particular set of people; or, to recall the earlier distinction, on their potential bonding effects rather than on membership criteria for inclusion and exclusion.

Importantly, several of the problématiques referred to on the prompt-cards were very little talked about, something which confirms that the presence of the cards could not determine the course of the discussion. Topics were chosen with selectiveness. For example, almost nothing was said in the open discussions that could be linked closely to 'Science and Research', and, in contrast to a card such as 'Money and Prices', it was never referred to, pointed at, or tapped during the discussions. 'Health and Safety Standards' was talked about rarely (there was some discussion amongst the Plžen group about who had a fire extinguisher in their taxi, but little more). 'Medical Care' was rarely problematised: none of the participants told of experiences with hospitals or doctors, although the economic aspects of healthcare (e.g. who contributes to

---

[7]The problems articulated in these interviews generally correspond to those identified as salient in survey research. Cf. in particular (OPTEM 2006: 7–8), where the concerns found to be particularly prevalent amongst the populations of the 25 EU member-states in 2006 include: employment and working conditions, economic aspects of globalisation, decline of the welfare state, prices (including house prices), widening wealth inequalities, immigration, terrorism, petty crime and antisocial behaviour, and occasional mentions of environmental threats. See also the Standard Eurobarometer data on issue salience, where these concerns also consistently emerge (usually with economic ones, unemployment and rising prices especially, to the fore). Such data say little of course about how concerns may be interconnected, which is the question we turn to below.

its funding, who gets it for free) were regularly discussed.[8] Occasionally in the discussions one participant would deliberately try to bring one of these 'neglected' cards into the conversation – possibly in a spirit of politeness towards the researcher – but such a move would barely be followed up by other participants. For example, in the Reading group, Derek made an intervention which he linked to the cards 'Science and Technology' (thus adapting the card's title, 'Science and Research') and 'The Environment'. He began talking about how an old mill in Oxfordshire (Sonning Mill) was about to upgrade its power source so it could run on hydroelectric power generated by the flow of the Thames, saving electricity for its owners and doing something good for the environment. The other participants, who just seconds before had been engaging actively with him on the problem of unemployment, made no effort to respond here. Derek started to ramble, and the anecdote became increasingly personal: 'I used to deliver corn there when it was a mill, I used to deliver corn there ... yeah, two and a quarter in the rape sacks of corn ... I used to go in there with an old Bedford lorry ... years ago ...'. Malik made a joke about Derek's age, everyone laughed, and then there was silence. It fell to the researcher to restart the discussion by referring back to the passage of conversation on unemployment which had preceded Derek's 'tangential' intervention; conversation flowed again.

Of course, one must be careful not to take such reasoning too far in a counter-factual direction: the fact that such problématiques were little developed in the interviews does not rule out the possibility that in further discussions they might be problematised more. The point is a comparative one: certain cards, and anecdotes framed in certain ways, tended to be developed much *less* than others. One should add that participants in this group and generally were by no means averse to

---

[8]The low salience in these ten interviews of healthcare as a medical rather than economic issue may seem surprising, since polling data often suggest the opposite (see e.g. (Hobolt and Klemmemsen 2005), and a poll by GfK NOP in August 2006, which cites healthcare as the greatest priority to UK citizens: www.gfknop. co.uk/content/news/news/Challenges_of_Europe_UKrelease.doc). This could be to do with our all-male sample – conceivably men express less concern on this issue than women. Alternatively, it could be that healthcare is seen as an important issue (a 'priority'), but that its provision as currently stands is treated as unproblematic. Another interpretation would be that, because opinion polls can say nothing about opinion formation, they fail to distinguish between those issues such as healthcare on which respondents are merely registering a basic concern and those which are of day-to-day significance.

anecdotes drawing on personal experience: these were a regular feature, and could successfully generate plenty of discussion. Derek, for example, told another autobiographical narrative a little later in the discussion, but this time it seemed to meet far better the criterion of common relevance. Malik was discussing burglars:

> M: … The problem that I think is ridiculous, right, say like you've got a trespasser on your property, you know, burglar or something, that comes into your house … and he's probably got the intent that, if he's caught, if he's got a gun he'll shoot you. But in the process of it all, if you were to shoot that person, if you were to harm him, or GBH, ABH him, any of those, in any way, you could actually be sued. I mean, I find that ridiculous. The fact that you can't protect your … [D: That's always been, funnily enough …] Well, it hasn't *always* been …
>
> Hanif: You've got an example [points to Derek], you've got an example for this [chuckles] …
>
> Derek: Yeah, just exactly what he said. [M: Oh OK, I didn't know …] Caught a man in my house … The dog was going absolutely raving mad, we'd gone to bed … we have this fox that walks along the wall, this fox … he knows when it's there and he goes mad … I'm laying in bed and the dog's going absolutely bananas … 'whatever's up?', I've got to get up and stop him barking, I've got up, come through into the kitchen, there's a big French window there and there's a bloke out there. The dog's going mad at the window and there's this fella stood there. I couldn't undo the door, my missus always locks it … couldn't … in the mad panic … 'Christ, if this bloke's got a knife' …

This is an anecdote which Derek was able to continue at length with the full engagement of the other participants – note that Hanif was already familiar with the story and was encouraging him to narrate it. Hanif would subsequently steal the punchlines. Key points in the narrative became clear: it turns out the police, when they arrived, were too casual about the incident, were more interested in having cups of coffee, and took seven hours to collect Derek's statement ('That's ridiculous though,' says Malik). A detailed discussion followed concerning the problems of law enforcement and how they should be handled. In this case and many others, a personal anecdote was picked up and developed at length, indicating that the problem in question was not an idiosyncratic one but rather the kind of common problem liable to affect 'people like us' more generally.

Problem domains

The card-arranging exercise, in which participants were asked to place cards in piles, brought out various assumptions about certain problems naturally belonging together. The resulting card arrangements in themselves were instructive, and three or four similar groupings of cards recurred, along with others which varied from one interview to the next. Perhaps most instructive was the accompanying discussion, in which participants justified to one another their suggestions and debated how best to summarise each card group with an overarching category. The flow of the subsequent discussion also suggested certain problems and ways of speaking might naturally cluster – particularly in those moments when participants made links to earlier parts of the discussion, when they agreed that a certain set of problems had already been covered, or when they felt it was time to 'move on' to a new topic. Observations of this kind suggest that, rather than treating the problems discussed as separate from each other, each with a distinctive repertoire of assumptions and typical acts of positioning, it is possible to speak of them as clustered in *problem domains*.

Domains can be thought of as groupings of problems (understood as problematisations of problématiques), the concepts used to link them, and the patterned ways of speaking available to speakers as resources with which to discuss them. They are the substance of a political common. We shall approach them as features of discursive practice rather than of the speakers' psychology, although it is true that various participants used vocabulary suggestive of domain-based cognitive frameworks (e.g. 'problem-area', 'field', 'group', 'packet'). By 'patterned ways of speaking' one should understand not strict repetition and regularity, in the sense that certain problems are *always* talked about in a certain way, with particular assumptions and we-formulations attached. This would be a crude and determinist perspective. Individual speakers are always capable of innovation in the way they articulate a problem, and it is always possible to draw unexpected links between one problem and another with a suitable amount of creativity. Rather, these patterned ways of speaking should be seen as brought together following the principle of 'family resemblance', just as Wittgenstein suggests is the case for those things we describe with the word 'game', which we treat as linked in some way but for which a single set of common properties does not exist (Wittgenstein 1976). As Schatzki observes, 'the unity of a discourse does not lie in the repetition of the same objects and concepts, but instead in the possession of delimited diversities of them' (Schatzki 2002: 13).[9]

Of course, an alternative conceptual move would be to treat 'ways of talking' as separate altogether from particular substantive issues. Domains could be thought of, in principle, as just sets of problems in themselves, discussed in unpatterned ways. Likewise, they could be thought of as patterned ways of speaking applied to any number of different problems: one could for example take as organising principles 'class', 'morality' and 'race', or one might speak, like Boltanski and Thévenot, of different 'orders of worth', and make no particular link between these and specific situations of concern. This approach is rejected here for several reasons. Firstly, given that problems are treated as constructed phenomena, as *problematisations* rather than unambiguous material facts, it would be quite meaningless to conceive them as separate from the discursive formations by which they are constructed. Only problématiques could be treated in this pre-discursive way, but then the question of what links are made between them, and hence of domain-clusterings, would not arise. Secondly, treating domains only as patterned ways of speaking without any association to substantive problems would not be suited to the overall purposes of this project, which include conceptualising the collective bond in an explicitly problem-oriented fashion, and exploring the polity implications of the types of decision-making authority invoked in connection with these problems. Focusing only on the orders of worth which speakers invoke, without foregrounding the problems in connection to which these are expressed, would be an approach more of sociological than political-theoretical interest. Thirdly, there are strong empirical grounds, and not just in this data, for suspecting a link between the two. In an interesting study of citizenship in the US based on focus-group interviews, Andrew Perrin looks at the different 'logics' which citizens apply in discussion of political topics. Important ones highlighted include notions of interest, of morality and justice, and of feasibility (Perrin 2006: 60ff.). While Perrin notes that there is no intrinsic connection between

---

[9]Cf. Sewell's discussion of 'schemas', understood as 'generalisable or transposable procedures applied in the enactment of social life' which 'can be applied to a wide and not fully predictable range of cases outside the context in which they are initially learned' (Sewell 1992: 17).

these and particular political topics – economic issues for example need not necessarily be discussed according to the logic of interests, and discussion groups with differing socio-demographic make-up may vary somewhat in the frequency with which they apply different logics – his main conclusion is nevertheless that 'by far the strongest influence on how citizens talk in the focus groups was *what they were talking about* – the scenario they were discussing' (Perrin 2006: 31, 102). Problems and ways of speaking are found to be quite closely linked. A domain-based approach which links the two is empirically as well as theoretically attractive.

This perspective does not discount the possibility that some problématiques may be problematised in more than one way, such that they can be talked about as a problem of one domain or another. The concept of 'affordance' is useful here. Harré notes that 'the same material thing may have a great many different possible ways in which it can be used. Each is an affordance. ... Thus a floor affords walking, dancing, placing furniture; a window affords a view of the lake, an escape from a threat, a view for a peeping Tom; a knife affords cutting, threatening, opening a window catch, and lots more' (Harré 2002: 27). Likewise, problématiques may be thought of as having varying degrees of affordance, such that some may be articulated as problems in multiple ways. A problématique such as 'violence' seems amenable to problematisation in more than one of the domains outlined below. However, given that the focus here is on talk, and that talk features problems rather than problématiques, these considerations are ornamental to our work.

On the basis of an analysis of the interview material, three problem domains in particular can be identified. These can be considered central aspects of a political common and are treated as tenable categories for all of the countries studied, though with some important variations. These domains will be considered in turn.

1. Economics

'That one is easy,' says Tomáš in the Liberec group as he points to the pile of cards which the group has formed out of 'Money and Prices', 'Taxation', 'Markets and Production', 'Work', 'Health and Safety Standards' and 'Purchase of Property'. 'That one is easy, it's a question of everything to do with finances. It's the cost of living, it's consumers, it's prices ... it's everything to do with finances.' His comment finds a receptive audience in the other participants around the table, who make their presence felt not by disputing his point but by modifying it.

A brief debate ensues as to whether the best title is 'financial problems', 'financial situation' or 'financial system', but agreement forms quickly that 'they're basically the same'. 'Financial Situation' is adopted and the discussion moves on. This experience can be considered typical of the groups interviewed, and the first domain we propose can be called the *Economics* domain.[10]

The initial card exercise offers strong grounds for this reading.[11] Often the first cards to be put together (the 'first pair' (Coxon 1999)) subsequently became the basis for a pile labelled 'economics', 'finances' or something of this sort. A brief look at how the interview in Lübeck developed should clarify this point. Having had the protocol for the discussion explained, the participants were invited to think about how best to order the prompt-cards:

> Author: Perhaps you could spend a couple of minutes thinking about how these cards might go together. If you had to make little groups out of them, how would you do so? There's no right or wrong way, whatever seems natural.
>
> Jochen: How many groups should it be?
>
> Author: Up to you, up to you. [90 seconds of contemplation]
>
> J: So, what would I say ... start with the economy, with Taxes ... they belong together, right, Markets and Production are directly linked with Taxes because taxes can strengthen or weaken the economy. [Werner: yeah] And ... Science and Research ... also has something to do with the economy, because innovation strengthens the power of the economy.
>
> W: Yeah, I'd also put those together. And Work too ... [J: Work too ...] Work too ... [J: Work too ...]

The vocabulary on the cards is not being clumped together aimlessly: Jochen creates a small narrative to explain the relationship between them, and his narrative is validated by Werner's interventions, in turn accepted by Jochen. When asked to summarise the collection of cards with a title, the group considered 'Markets and the Economy', 'Working Life' and 'Financial Security', but considered each too narrow:

---

[10]For a visual summary of the card exercise, see the table in the Methodological Appendix.

[11]This page and the next draw on (White 2009b).

'Occupation and the Economy' was the title eventually chosen, to express the link between daily life and more distant processes. Of further interest is what happened a few minutes later: the card 'Money and Prices' had for some reason ended up in a different pile, but questions started to be raised as to why. Jochen said that he felt at the beginning it should have been placed with 'Occupation and the Economy'; Niklas, Hamid and Werner agreed, and it was moved over. The episode suggests the momentum generated by the placing of cards is not so strong that it cannot be overturned by arguments appealing to common expectations of what goes with what.

When asked to go into further depth on the problems considered most significant, Jürgen invoked once more 'the economy' and, with the active support of Werner and Niklas, used it to link together a whole series of concepts which had not been written on any of the cards:

> I think the biggest problem here in Germany at the moment is the economy. [W: yeah] The economy and work of course. Unemployment and ... zero economic growth, or hardly any economic growth, and the unemployment which goes with that. Domestic purchasing power, the lack of domestic purchasing power. Also under this heading with money and prices I'd say the introduction of the euro is very relevant, because the euro – due to the exchange rate – has brought disadvantages in purchasing power, considerable ... [N: price rises] ... Yeah, it's led to price rises, and so also the purchasing power, the domestic demand, has gone down, because people have less money at their disposal.

Some notion of 'the economy' or 'economics' clearly comes across here as an organising concept, along with the more specific problems associated with it. A later cross-reference (this time by Werner) suggests the naturalness with which the participants orientate themselves in discussion using the concept of 'the economy'. The conversation had been looking at the problem of inadequate contributions to the system of health insurance: 'The easiest solution for this problem would be full employment. If there weren't five million unemployed people there, if they were paying into the pension and health insurance, then we wouldn't have all these problems ... [N: yeah]. We're back to this first subject again – the economy. It all links together.' A passage from the Plzeň group is similar, in that a cross-reference is made which can only be meaningful to more than one participant (as it evidently is) if there is a shared understanding that certain problems are linked by the concept 'hospodářství' (the economy). Robert says: 'Markets and Production, we've talked about that, that's generally … [Pavel: I think … yeah, the economy, certainly …] We talked about work, we talked about investment, what's that, that's the economy. We can still talk about the economy of the Czech state as a whole, how it manages its resources.'

One sees here a distinction being made, as it was in other groups too, between the more daily or personal aspects of economics and the larger-scale or more remote aspects, though these were generally closely enmeshed in discussion. Beyond the words 'economics' or 'economy', a variety of terms was used to make such links. The Reading group had no doubts that the pile they had formed using the cards 'Markets and Production', 'Work', 'Purchase of Property', 'Money and Prices' and 'Taxation' was 'all to do with money', and this was taken as the title. Likewise for the Würzburg and Plzeň groups, it was 'all to do with money' or 'all to do with finances': the Würzburg group explored 'commerce' and 'economic policy' as possibilities before settling on 'Economy and Finances', while Plzeň quickly opted for 'Finances'. In Kassel, 'Political Economy' (*Volkswirtschaft*) was chosen over 'Economy' on the grounds that 'it affects the whole people, not just the economy alone but more deeply.' In an interesting twist, the Erfurt group explicitly rejected one participant's suggestion of the label 'economy' for the three cards 'Markets and Production', 'Taxation' and 'Purchase of Property', opting instead to call it 'Capitalism'. Although they did not create a card pile with this title, Ostrava also invoked the term readily.

One concludes that an important domain of problems making up the political common has, despite the nuances, something more or less to do with economics. Certain problems were articulated more in some discussions than others: the banking system was an important issue only in the Czech discussions, and corruption (which, as several groups pointed out, straddles various areas of public life and which for analytical purposes will be discussed both as part of this domain and the following one) was given particular prominence by the Czech and the Erfurt groups. However, a considerable number of economic problems were articulated frequently *across* the groups, without noticeable variation according to nationality. These included wages, taxation, unemployment, social security and insurance, prices, debt, relations between rich and poor, privatisation, the decline of local industry, and the adequacy of the education system in equipping people for employment. These can be treated as the core problems we shall be dealing with when studying the *Economics* domain. Not only were they articulated frequently and followed up by several participants, but they tended to be discussed in language that was impassioned. One had little difficulty in identifying a sense of injustice when these problems were discussed (Gamson 1992: 7). See for instance Malcolm and Bill from the Norwich group, discussing rich rock stars who cling to their money:

> M: You look at Bono, who's stood in front of Blair and Bush, he fucked off on his private jet ... [B: He's got a castle in Dublin.] Bono, fucking get a life. Strip yourself bare, strip yourself bare and leave yourself with a million. Give the rest away, you toss-pot. [B: Yeah, that's right ...] [...] Elton John, at least he gives away his wealth. He did, you know, he gave away his wealth. That bastard McCartney earns £520,000 ... [B: He earns £60 a second ...] How much money does one person need?

Comments such as 'that's not right' and 'it shouldn't be like that' were common, as when Dieter in Kassel spoke of the problem of personal debt: 'mobile phones for example, it's a real problem for young people, there's children of 13, 14 or 15, they're already in debt because of the payments, it's a trauma, something like that really shouldn't be happening. There should be regulations so that something like that doesn't happen.' As will be seen in Chapter 5, the sense that a situation was unfair or intolerable by no means meant that clear remedies to it were identified, or even expected. The 'should' was not always accompanied by a 'could'. But the inclination to problematise, and to treat these problems as affecting 'people like us', was widely evident. A sense of involvement, rather than 'cynical chic' (Eliasoph 1990), was the dominant tone.

2. Society and the Law

None of the groups spontaneously offered the phrase 'Society and the Law' to describe an arrangement of cards or as a point of reference in open discussion. Both 'society' and 'law' were freely invoked in all discussions, and the clustering of problems and discursive resources suggests a strong overlap in the semantic range of each, but to label this domain 'Society and the Law' is an interpretative act. Moreover, a plurality of perspectives is being covered under this heading. Similar words carry different connotations in different countries, and aside from the core problems and motifs whose clustering is evident in all the discussions there are some important variations. Treating 'society' and 'the law' as constituting a single domain should serve to illuminate some of these differences.

The problems at the heart of this domain are those of neighbourhood behaviour, crime (including corruption), policing, the justice system, and education – the latter here understood as a social good which benefits the community as a whole rather than the economic prospects of individuals. All of these can be thought of as having something to do with rules, morality, or the institutions by which rules and morality are enforced. For the discussions in Britain the concept of 'law and order' captures these neatly, as this passage from the Reading group indicates:

Malik: And then we've got here [looking at the card pile that the group has formed out of 'The Legal System', 'Education and Training', 'Policing', and 'Corruption'] ... I suppose that's more along ... Law and Order isn't it, law. Cos the policing, everything, is law [...] it's either you're against it or for it ... Corruption's against it, Policing is for it, Education and Training obviously ... and the Legal System. Law?

Author: How do you feel? What's the general consensus?

Saeed: They come together ...

Derek: In a way, yeah ... I mean that's law [points at bulk of pile] but that's corruption [points at 'Corruption' card; chuckles] ...

M: Corruption yeah but it's *against* the law isn't it, so it comes under the same sort-of umbrella of law.

D: Well ... in a way, I suppose, you could say, yeah ...

Author: Education you're keeping as part of the law as well?

D: Well, inasmuch as that's where you're first educated about all things. You're told off by your mum from the day you do something wrong, aren't you, so I'd connect it.

M: And also, if you do something wrong out there the police pull you over and what do they say, 'ignorance is no excuse' or whatever. You're supposed to know it. So you have to be educated and you have to be trained in certain aspects ... everyday things ...

Author: Sure, sure. OK, so are we deciding on 'Law' for that group?

D: 'Law and Order', 'Law and Order' I'd say, 'Law and Order' ...
M: Yep, no problem with that ...

If the police and the legal system are taken to be the institutions of enforcement (the ones who 'pull you over'), corruption is taken to be a breach of the law, and education as the means by which law-abiding people are raised. Consensus is evident: Malik and Derek exchange points smoothly, and at the end Derek reaffirms Malik's original heading 'Law and Order'. The discussions in Swansea and Norwich are in keeping. Swansea generated the heading 'Justice/Law' to describe the corresponding card pile; the Norwich group made the same link between education and the law, emphasising the problem of discipline, and bringing in the concepts of 'public disorder' and 'antisocial behaviour' (including drug and alcohol abuse) to characterise the challenges facing the police. The notion of 'society' that comes through in these British discussions is a fairly restricted one: the extent to which fellow members of the population are, in the legal sense, rule-followers rather than rule-breakers. Crime is a very central problem in the British discussions, and the healthy society is the crime-free society.[12]

This is a little different from what one finds in the German discussions. While these groups do generate headings like 'Legal Security' (Lübeck), 'Legal Order' and 'Legal System' (Kassel), and 'Rule of Law' (Erfurt), problems of crime and inadequate policing occupy a smaller proportion of the discussions. At the end of the Lübeck discussion, the group was asked specifically whether they had day-to-day difficulties with the police, a question which would have been provocative in the British context. Niklas concedes merely that 'there are occasionally a few small problems ...'. Jochen and Werner talk briefly about speed-cameras before concluding that it is difficult to think of any other particular problems, and Hamid concurs. Nor was this a particularly mild group – Kassel and Würzburg are similar in this respect. Rather than discussing crime and crime prevention, amongst the German groups there tended to be more talk about other aspects of conduct in society. Adhering to the rules is about showing concern for others and for public spaces, and the healthy society is the one in which a sense of community feeling has been retained, a society which has not

---

[12]British preoccupation with crime is also discernible in surveys: see e.g. Euro-barometer 69 (3), 2008, p.26.

descended into selfishness and egoism. In this 'social sphere' or 'social realm', as the Würzburg group terms it, the emblematic villains, as will be seen in the next chapter, are not just the criminal law-breakers but the people who spit out their chewing-gum on the pavement, and the passive onlookers who fail to speak out against this kind of offensive behaviour. 'Somehow everything's splitting apart,' fears Peter in Kassel, 'everyone speaks just for themselves now.'

In the Czech and the Erfurt discussions there is particular emphasis on corruption and social hierarchy, and the police and the justice system are given prominence as institutions which embody these. Corruption is considered so omnipresent that it is a reliable basis for jokes and sarcasm: Robert in Plzeň declares to general laughs: 'but please, that's not a problem in the Czech Republic!' while Miloš in Ostrava exclaims on seeing the relevant cards 'Corruption! My God, that's a wonderful topic! ... Legal System – basically that doesn't exist here!' Along with this unquestioned assumption, in the Czech discussions one finds much tighter clustering with the law-*making* process, something consistent with there having been a weaker distinction between the legislative and the judiciary under communism. Harald in Erfurt talks of politicians being 'people who are elected and are supposed to build up the legal system', and a passage in the Liberec discussion moves swiftly from 'bad laws' to 'the legislators, the parliament, which functions really badly.' A discussion of corruption in the police and the judicial system can thus merge with a discussion of corruption amongst elected politicians. While there is repeated mention in the Czech groups of society (*společnost*) and the law (*právo*), the hierarchy motif of the former is never far from the rich versus poor motif of the economics domain, and the latter always carries overtones of state authority in a quite broad sense.

Amongst all the groups, these problems to do with the following of rules tend to be described as being experienced in a very local environment. Much emphasis is given to the city, and in particular 'the streets'. Derek in Reading describes those 'who don't fit in' and who 'don't want to most of the time. That's why they're like that. ... You see them sitting on the streets, they're outsiders, they're drug addicts, they get into a system and they can't get out of it and they need it ... and they thieve and they do all the things ... then you see them laying all round the town don't you. They're outsiders, cos you wouldn't want them living next to you cos you'd be frightened to tread on their needles or whatever, you know. [...] You don't want to be horrible, you say "oh I'll give him a pound", but you wouldn't really want to touch his hand would you?' During the discussion in Ostrava, Miloš sees something happening outside the window. He uses it to extend a point he is making about the thoughtless behaviour of those further up the social hierarchy: 'Here's a beautiful example of that. The Mercedes here. Along comes Mr. Businessman, lets out the children and parks so that no-one can park in the next space next to him. That's ... you can see this guy wants to show off, "I've got a different kind of car, a Mercedes, and I'm going to put myself here." It's a display. And now the kid sees it, the kid ... I don't know how old he is, but in ten years he'll be doing the same. Because "that's how Daddy did it, so I can do the same." That's Education and Training.' Offensive behaviour is evident in the smallest things and the environment is intimately proximate. This is a theme which will become familiar in the following chapters.

3. Relations between peoples

With a great deal of indignation, Luke from the Swansea group recounts the following experience: 'I took a soldier home in the week, he'd just come back from Iraq, seven months over there, and it's five boys in his platoon, or battalion or whatever you call them, Welsh Fusiliers they were, and they're based in Aldershot. And they'd been back about three or four days and they'd lost a couple of their close friends, and they jumped in a taxi with a Paki, and the Paki started shouting "you lot ..." – he knew they were in the army, he was taking them back to the base – "you lot there ..." you know, giving it all that ... And they pulled the Paki out, and they warned him two or three times "we've got close friends over there who've been killed, we don't even want to be over there ourselves", and he kept on and on, "you lot ... you're all over there killing innocent people" and all the rest of it. Well, they pulled the Paki out didn't they and leathered him. They did him, and now they're in prison. So it goes back to them again doesn't it.'

Apart from being rather shocking, this anecdote is interesting in several ways. Two social groups seem to be implied here: that of the soldiers (and their close friends), whose Welsh/British identity is fore-grounded and for whom Luke seems inclined to express sympathy, and the Pakistani taxi-driver who associates himself with the civilians who have been killed in Iraq. Luke's sense of injustice seems to be premised on the unwillingness of the Pakistani driver to distinguish between the soldiers and the orders they are carrying out, and on the fact that the soldiers end up in prison, simply, as it were, for defending themselves. Treated as perfectly natural is the willingness of a Pakistani person to associate with the plight of Iraqis; indeed, it is his ethnic background

– the only thing we are told of him – which is crucial to how the speaker makes sense of the whole anecdote. The suggestion is that 'they' constitute a single grouping. Thus an episode in a taxi is framed as part of a wider confrontation between groups. This kind of discursive construction of 'peoples' and the relations between them is based on a distinctive set of interpretative repertoires, and these make up our third domain.

Certain problems in the *Economics* and *Society and the Law* domains prompt references to minority groups, as we shall see: the supposed economic cost of refugees, for example, or the supposed willingness of immigrants to steal. But there are a whole series of problems and patterned ways of talking about them not reducible to the logics of these two domains, and where one finds different acts of demarcation with regard to shared predicament, and different understandings of the potential for agency. The core problems in this domain are threat and intimidation as represented collectively by other peoples; conflict, whether in the form of wars between nations or configurations of nations, or non-military conflict in the course of daily encounters; and the need to accommodate different cultural practices, and the perceived erosion of practices considered distinctive of 'our' way of life. A wide range of problems are thus brought together and treated as expressions of a single or related set of phenomena. Each is discussed at least to some degree in the three countries, albeit with nuances. In the Czech discussions this domain is less central than in the British or German ones: the assumption seems readily made that the Czech Republic has little significance on the international stage, and these participants draw on a more limited range of personal encounters with ethnic minorities. It is significant that both the Liberec and Ostrava groups explicitly decide to leave discussion of these problems until last, preferring to focus first on the themes of the previous two domains. Their discussion of Roma/gypsies tends to be framed according to the *Economics* and *Society and the Law* domains, although not exclusively, as will be seen. The British and particularly the German groups, on the other hand, tend to discuss the problems of this domain rather early on, and make frequent digressions and interruptions so as to return to them. A further issue of salience in the British discussions is terrorism (and this before the London bombings of July 2005); the German groups meanwhile devote considerable time to reflecting on their country's history and its legacy for today. Despite these variations, one finds a core set of basically similar problems being articulated across the country groups.

Historically, the problems associated with this domain would probably be regarded as distant ones rather than a part of daily life. Conflict between peoples would perhaps have seemed a remote idea, the kind of thing undertaken by soldiers in far-away fields and resolved by diplomats in smoke-filled rooms. To some extent this impression lingers – various participants speak of these problems as 'not really affecting us here' – but there is a counter-perspective, usually mentioned by someone else in the discussion, which emphasises the very proximity of these issues. When Derek from the Reading group proposes the heading 'Affairs outside our environment' for the card pile consisting of 'Peace and War', 'Treatment of Outsiders' and 'Overseas Aid', on the grounds that 'we're not at war particularly here in our environment if we're looking at us sat here in the town. So ... that's sort-of overseas affairs, I mean, I can't do nothing about,' Malik responds that 'Treatment of Outsiders is not overseas affairs – it's even in Reading itself.' Titling this domain 'Relations between Peoples' is intended to capture the link made in these discussions between what the political scientist might call 'foreign policy' or 'international relations' on the one hand and domestic 'race relations' on the other. The link is evident in Luke's anecdote above, and can be seen as the Erfurt group discuss a heading with which to categorise the pile they have made consisting of the cards 'Peace and War', 'Overseas Aid' and 'Treatment of Outsiders':

Uli:	I'd say ... I'd say ... 'Foreign Policy', or something like that ...
Harald:	Yeah, it's ... here I'd put ... you see, it's not just foreign policy. For me it'd be 'Humanity'. I'd have 'Humanity' as the title.
Matthias:	... With the person being in the foreground ...
H:	... 'Overseas Aid' ... yeah, that belongs there too. They all belong together somehow. Yeah ... but if I put that here then ... 'The Person', or 'The Future', or something, it depends ... [U: 'Future Prospects' ...] Yeah, but you have that over here too ... [U: 'Human Togetherness' ...]
M:	Sure but humanity one could have here ...
H:	Yeah ... need to think through carefully ...
Author:	You said foreign policy before ...?
H:	Yeah, foreign policy belongs in there. But 'Treatment of Outsiders' I see as something not just abroad but here too ... [U: Here ...] That's a problem right here in

Germany too. Everywhere really, because in my view there's nationalism everywhere. Everyone has a certain national pride, and nationalism develops out of that. Quite simply. So that's why it's hard to order the cards. These things ... [pointing at cards] ... If there's none of that [Peace and War] then there's none of that [Treatment of Outsiders], and without that then none of that ...! [laughs]

U: If that was OK [Peace and War] then you wouldn't get immigrants ... [H: Exactly ...] If the poor countries weren't so poor then people wouldn't come to us, they'd rather stay at home. They're driven away by war and so they come to us. That's why foreign policy is crucial.

'Humanity' is a word which recurs here, and 'Human Foreign Policy' is a category heading they consider later in the discussion. Their (self-imposed) challenge is to express why foreign policy and immigrant populations in Germany are issues which 'go together'. When, for the sake of simplicity, they settle on 'Foreign Policy', it is stressed that this should be understood 'keeping in mind the human dimension'. 'Culture' is another key word which recurs, for instance when examining the rights of Muslims to build mosques in Germany. It connects what happens in the local environment to places more distant: 'When we're abroad,' says Uli, 'in an Islamic country, we're meant to conduct ourselves in a reasonable way. Women are supposed to cover their arms and not wear shorts. But we have to build mosques here and everything for the Muslims. That's not right. With us it's always expected that we behave in a reasonable way, but here everyone's allowed to behave however they want.' The Lübeck and Würzburg groups both choose 'Foreign Policy' as their heading for the two cards 'Peace and War' and 'Overseas Aid', but in discussion link to these the question of immigration (the card for which was put with the piles 'Internal Security' and 'Rule of Law' respectively); for the same two cards, the Kassel group considers 'Global Interaction' and 'World' ('it's a topic which really spans the globe', says Sebastian, with Hans' agreement) before settling on the title 'Inter-State Relations'. For the Norwich group the appropriate heading is 'the World', whilst in Reading the participants, after a lengthy discussion which will be looked at later, choose 'Conflict', Malik explaining 'because, you know, you're going to have conflict with outsiders; because of conflict at times you have to have Aid, and Peace and War is obviously again is conflict ...'. In Swansea, having arranged the cards such that there is a pile consisting of 'Peace and War', 'Treatment of Outsiders' and 'Overseas Aid', the group is so eager to start talking about asylum-seekers that the category-generating exercise is put to one side. In the Czech groups, as might be expected given the domain appears less central, participants do not arrange these particular cards together with the same consistency, and the category headings are hence rather disconnected: 'Security' for the Liberec group (referring to the cards 'Peace and War' and 'Treatment of Outsiders'), 'Global Problems' for the Ostrava group (referring to 'Peace and War', 'Overseas Aid' and 'the Environment'), and a rather amorphous category for the Plzeň group based on the concept of Education.

The link between 'foreign affairs' and domestic 'race relations' which comes through during these discussions of the cards, in particular amongst the British and Germans, is a feature of the discussions as a whole. Perhaps the most obvious example is the link made between Jews and the Israeli state, visible in a passage from Lübeck:

Jochen: ... But it troubles me sometimes when *Spiegel* [a news magazine] – it's *Der Spiegel* isn't it, where the guy at the top is a Jew? – when they always come out with this stuff, when they raise the finger and say to us Germans 'you evil ones have done something bad again' ... [Hamid: ... Yeah, he's the financer ...] 'We need to remind you of your past, otherwise you'd forget it again ...'

Werner: Yeah, and what are they doing with the Palestinians ...?

J: Yeah ... yeah, naturally you're not allowed to bring that into the equation ... [W: ... yeah ...] what they're doing there. The German press is naturally pro-Israeli ... [W: ... yeah ...]

In the Würzburg discussion, Ulrich makes a point about the British public's reaction to the Iraq war: 'There was certainly a lot of outcry about the war in Britain. Have the English still got soldiers over there ...? [Ralf: I think so, yeah] ... But ... this policy isn't much liked there either.' Oskar then makes the link to minority groups: 'It's led to domestic problems there too, because there are lots of Muslims living in Britain [R: ... yeah ...] and they're putting the British under fire because of Iraq. They still have it under control, and Blair is trying at the moment to extend his hand to them a bit.' In a discussion of the

Balkans conflict of the 1990s and the refugees who arrived in Germany, Axel points to the Serbian café across the road as an example of how Serbs have unjustly prospered while it was Albanians who were the legitimate refugees.[13] Wider conflicts are played out and are visible just by taking a walk around town. Luke in Swansea tells Alan to watch his words because there's 'a Paki' in the pub: 'in Swansea now, in a local pub, and you've got to watch what you're saying. [...] Shouldn't have to.' The local pub in one's own town is, it seems, the kind of place where these problems of intergroup relations should not have to be faced: the outrage is exactly that these problems are being encountered within the local environment. The same immediacy comes through in a passage from the Kassel group:

Dieter: [...] And there's not going to be war between countries any more, instead war takes place between people(s),[14] who sit directly next to each other but which have completely different cultures from each other, and I think ...

Hans: It seems to me that ... your own fears are coming out there ...

D: Yeah, they're certainly there, they're there ...

Peter: I mean ... you can see it, just go out in the street and have a look ...

H: That's ... that's exactly what I mean. The fears aren't just with you, the fears are also with exactly those people that you're suggesting are threatening. Why isn't it possible for the reason that we're all human beings to go over to them and enter into dialogue with these people? [...]

P: Germans, they don't stick together. Foreigners – just go along the *Holländerstraße*, if you hit a foreigner in the face there ... [D: yeah] ... within five minutes there are ten of them standing in front of you. If you hit a German in the face then ten minutes later there's still no-one there.

Dieter's reference to 'war between people(s)', which seems to be endorsed by Peter, is not accepted by Hans, either in this passage or in other sec-

---

[13]While this example might seem to blur the demarcation against Muslims which we shall see to be characteristic of this domain in its current form, there is no indication here that Axel or the rest of the group considers Albanians to be Muslims; even if this knowledge is available to them, it is given no weight.

[14]Original: no longer 'zwischen Ländern' but rather 'zwischen den Menschen'.

tions of the discussion. The basis on which he rejects it however is that conflict is not inevitable, not that such 'peoples' are a misleading construct. His notion of 'dialogue' clearly postulates two entities, to be encountered 'on the street' as well as further afield.

A final point of importance concerning the composition of this domain is the assumed relationship between a country's government and its people. It was visible above that Luke (and presumably also the soldier who told him the anecdote) makes a distinction between the views of the soldiers based in Iraq and of the government which sent them there, whereas he naturalises the identification of the Pakistani taxi-driver with Iraqis. A general pattern seems to be that for parts of the world considered geographically or culturally 'proximate' a distinction between states/governments and peoples is readily made, whereas for more 'distant' places they tend to be elided.[15] Thus in the Norwich group one sees Malcolm criticising US treatment of Ethiopia and explicitly drawing a distinction between government policy and the people by saying 'don't get me wrong, cos I like America, I think the average American is fine,' whereas one sees Bill making no distinction at all between the government and the people when referring to an African country, even one whose government is acknowledged to be repressive: 'the biggest rip-off at the moment, we're actually paying overseas aid at the moment to Zimbabwe, where you've got the worst dictator ... Certain parts of Africa deserve it for the treatment of AIDS and poverty, but I'm afraid Zimbabwe don't. Mugabe is a dictator ... he's got torture chambers – any opponent is oppressed. So I'd abolish that one for him.' That AIDS and poverty-relief should be withheld because the country's *leader* does not deserve it indicates a merging of people and government in perception of this more distant location. How the boundaries of the 'proximate' and the 'distant' are drawn is one of the first questions considered in the next chapter.

These three domains – *Economics, Society and the Law,* and *Relations between Peoples* – can be taken as important components of the political common, whose existence they in turn confirm. Participants across all the groups were able to talk in depth and to coordinate well with one another in discussion of these problems, drawing on patterned discursive formulations to do so, and – as will be seen further in the next

---

[15]The tendency to emphasise the homogeneity of out-groups and the heterogeneity of in-groups has been well documented in social psychology (Duckitt 2003).

chapter – tending to articulate them as problems liable to affect people like 'us'. Participants did not necessarily link them directly to themselves: as taxi-drivers, none was unemployed or liable to become so in the near future, certainly not by the factory closures repeatedly mentioned. But although it was not a problem liable to affect 'me', it was nonetheless one that could hit people like 'us'.

Roughly the same kinds of problem emerge across the set of interviews, and they are linked together using concepts which can be considered functionally equivalent. While important variations of nuance emerge in the following chapters, this should not disguise the underlying similarity. In Chapter 1 it was noted that absolute convergence across the sites of study, aside from being unlikely, was theoretically unnecessary, since all political communities display some degree of dissensus amongst citizens not just on how to see their own position *vis-à-vis* a defined set of problems, but also on the very matters to be problematised – a point sometimes overlooked by scholars exploring the existence of a European public sphere who emphasise the necessary unity of public debate. Without taking up such a demanding goal, the possibility of identifying three broadly alike domains of political concern indicates some degree of discursive order across the field of study.

The way these domains are described here is clearly not the only possible way. There would be some grounds in the interviews for conceptualising the analysis according to institutional domains rather than problem domains, with headings such as 'national government' (perhaps even just 'politics'), 'local government', 'European', 'global' and 'private'. A domain along the lines of 'State Provision' would have been a natural one with which to read the Czech and the Erfurt texts (i.e. those from the post-communist cities): both the Ostrava and Liberec groups brought together 'Transport' and 'Medical Care', using the headings 'State Sector' and 'State Services' respectively. Likewise there would be some support for adopting a principle of immediacy, with domains such as 'day-to-day', 'emergency', 'past' and 'future'. These were sometimes offered by participants, though less regularly than the thematic division which we shall take as the crucial one, and hardly at all were discussions structured along these lines. In the approach we shall follow, questions to do with political institutions are examined separately in Chapter 5 in terms of the plausibility of *political projects*, as distinct from the substantive problems such a project might address. Questions to do with immediacy are integrated into discussion of problem-salience.

The three key domains – *Economics, Society and the Law,* and *Relations between Peoples* – should not be thought of as closed systems or sharply bounded spheres. The most appropriate metaphor is that of the constellation. Picking up what was said earlier, some problématiques ('comets', one might say) can be problematised in terms of more than one domain. Take 'immigration' for example. This problématique – the permanent or semi-permanent movement of people across state borders – certainly does not have to be treated as a problem (it can be welcomed), but if it *is* problematised then this can be done in more than one way. For example, it can be talked about as something which costs 'people like us' our money or jobs, or as something which makes us more vulnerable to criminal behaviour, or which forces us to live next to those culturally different to us. Immigration in other words can be articulated as a problem in terms of the *Economics* domain (along the lines of 'they're a burden!'), in *Society and the Law* terms ('they're all criminals!') or in *Relations between Peoples* terms ('they're completely different to us!'). These different kinds of framing will sometimes be contested, a fact which reaffirms the dynamic relationship between speakers and the resources they draw upon. When participants articulate a problem, they are talking about a problématique in a particular way, and are drawing on particular discursive resources to do so. As suggested above, one can suppose that the relationship between problématiques and discursive resources is not free-floating – certain problématiques seem to be problematised in certain ways – but at the same time there is scope for some flexibility in the process of problematisation. At an analytical level, this means that occasionally there can be difficulty in deciding how a particular passage of transcript should be read and with which domain(s) it should be associated. This does not mean however that the domains merge into one, rendering the concept redundant. Many everyday concepts have precisely this radial structure, and an analogy can be drawn with the domains used to talk about the weather – the seasons. A sunny day – equivalent to a problématique – can be a feature of summer, autumn, winter or spring, resulting in occasional uncertainty as to how to talk about a particular phase: are these two days of sun the beginning of spring, or just a brief respite from the gloom of winter? In the face of such difficulties, we continue to talk of the seasons, without feeling that we make ourselves absurd. Domains are to be thought of in a similarly pragmatic spirit.

Interviewing groups other than taxi-drivers would no doubt have resulted in some different problems being brought to the fore and others being marginalised. The participants in this study were exclusively male: one may speculate that a study involving females might produce not just alternative we-formulations applied to the same set of problem domains, but a clustering of problems distinctive enough to suggest the conceptualisation of a domain based on gender-related problems. This is not a thought we are in a position to pursue. The supposition, based on the reasons for which taxi-drivers were chosen, is that their discourse is likely to feature many of the patterns that would arise in discussions composed of different social groups, and that the domains which have been conceptualised here would be tenable more widely, notwithstanding the variation one might find at the 'superficial' level of opinions.

Economics, Society and the Law, and *Relations between Peoples* are the domains which will be carried forward for further analysis. They are comprised of the problems which were talked about in greatest depth and with greatest frequency, and which were described by participants themselves as the most important. However, that they are not comprehensive of all the problems discussed in these interviews, and that they should therefore not be considered as definitive of the political common, can be made clear by looking briefly at a fourth, more marginalised, set of problems one might treat under the heading *Quality of Life.* We shall return to this set of problems in Chapter 6, when discussing how the political common might evolve over time.

4.   Quality of Life

During the initial card-arranging exercise, several groups created a card-pile which they titled Quality of Life comprised of cards such as 'The Environment', 'Health and Safety Standards', 'Medical Care', 'Science and Research' and 'Transport'. Participants in the Lübeck group linked together environmental problems with transport pollution by drawing on a story in the news at the time about the dangers posed to human health by 'fine-particulate pollution' (*Feinstaubbelastung*). The Würzburg group also linked pollution, transport and health when narrating how the introduction of a road toll for lorries on the Autobahn had led to heavier traffic in the city as drivers switched to smaller roads to avoid it. However, despite passages such as these, which indicate a clustering of issues, such problems were generally not discussed in depth by any of the groups. Amongst the British groups they were hardly mentioned at all. Amongst the German groups they were mentioned a little more. Amongst the Czechs groups they were mentioned a little more still, pollution in particular, perhaps because the experiences of adaptation to the demands of EU membership acted as a spur to problematisation. But generally they were marginalised in discussion.

One expression of this marginalisation is simply the avoidance of talking about them, as one sees most clearly with the British groups. When Malcolm in Norwich is looking for a heading to describe the two cards 'Environment' and 'Science and Research', he suggests 'Try Not To Think About It!' Bill agrees that the environment is a subject 'for the future, really'. In the case of the German and Czech groups, where there was slightly more talk about these issues, marginalisation takes the form of downplaying the significance of environmental problems compared to those encountered in other domains, notably *Economics*. Uli and Ralf in Würzburg, discussing measures mentioned on the radio to reduce fine-particulate pollution, immediately think about what their impact will be on the economy, of 'all the euros that'll have to go on that.' When Zbyněk in Ostrava talks about the visible improvement in pollution levels in the city, he concedes it is 'terribly important' but feels that the Green Party rather exaggerates the problems; Miloš follows this by arguing that the reason for these improvements is the decline of local industry, with all the unemployment this involves.

Whereas the significance of the problems associated with our three principal domains – Economics, Society and the Law, and Relations between Peoples – is never seriously doubted by any participants in discussion, the seriousness of these problems to do with what one might, if it were better developed, call the Quality of Life domain tends to be doubted by at least some participants whenever they are mentioned. One sees this particularly clearly in the German and Czech cases; in the British case, so little problematisation of this kind takes place in these interviews that the marginalisation is almost total.

Overview

This chapter set out with the goal of examining how far our speakers show the ability and willingness to orientate themselves collectively to political matters of shared concern – the kind of we- rather than I-oriented concerns one can associate with a 'political common' as outlined in Chapter 1. Could one find sufficient evidence of the recognition of and engagement with shared problems for the sense of shared predicament to be a plausible foundation for political ties?

The conclusion we have arrived at is affirmative. When invited to talk about problems in public life and when given a few prompts to react to, our participants were able to develop detailed discussions using various shared concerns as points of coordination. There was considerable consistency across the groups in the kinds of problem evoked, and evidence of widely shared discursive competence for at least three domains of problems. It has been argued that the fluidity seen in the articulation and discussion of these domains was in contrast to the rather more disjointed efforts to be found in connection with other problématiques, as visible in the ignoring or the awkward acknowledgement of certain prompt-cards and peer interventions. This diversity of outcomes makes it possible to distinguish with some confidence a series of problem-areas which may be thought of as 'common', and therefore to claim empirical plausibility for the idea of a 'political common'. To be sure, it is by no means a definitively determined entity, and there are many areas of public interest touched on briefly or not at all in these discussions – e.g. questions of ecology and gender relations – which different interviewees might well have chosen to engage. There are also the ambiguities of interpretation characteristic of all empirical study, in particular the study of discursive practice. It is, however, a political common with enough clearly defined features to proceed to explore these in greater depth.

The consistency with which common problems are put forward in these discussions seems to speak against assumptions of citizen apathy. 'Depoliticisation', it seems, cannot be understood simply as indifference towards matters of common concern.[16] Grievances remain easily articulated, and they are assumed to be shared with others rather than merely private. The notion that problems today tend to be experienced primarily as individual problems rather than ones capable of generating interpersonal bonds does not find backing in these discussions (Bauman 1999: 53). Even if one accepts that certain contemporary societal changes have encouraged a trend in this direction, and even if one acknowledges the specificity of the discussion situation, it remains the case that speakers show themselves willing to articulate problems affecting not just them themselves but others like them, and that these moves are in turn recognised, accepted and followed up by other speakers.

---

[16]In their study of the US, Hibbing and Theiss-Morse suggest that ordinary citizens care deeply about political *processes* but that their preferences on *policy* are quite weak (Hibbing and Theiss-Morse 2002). However, this second category of theirs ('policy preferences') fails to distinguish between views on the policies to be adopted and views directly on the substantive problems deemed in need of address. In our interviews the richness of the latter comes through clearly, while the former will be dealt with separately in Chapter 5.

Nor does one find reason to support a Schumpeterian account of the incapacity of non-elites to engage in substantive political issues (Schumpeter 1943: 62, 257). As should become further evident in the following chapters, one does not need to be of the inclination to romanticise 'everyday life' or 'real people' in order to find considerable political competence in these discussions – if one understands competence in the way we have suggested, as the capacity to elaborate discussion in coordination with peers using knowledge of the know-how as well as know-that kind. In political psychology, competence or 'sophistication' tends to be understood in ways easily quantified: in terms of cross-topic and cross-temporal consistency in polling responses (ideological constraint, and the presence of 'attitudes' rather than 'non-attitudes') or in terms of the capacity to demonstrate knowledge of the purely know-that kind by reproducing elite messages and publicly recognised facts.[17] Treating competence as an individual phenomenon, to be measured against the standards of elites, these approaches quickly lead to the abandonment of participatory conceptions of politics. Even scholars who emphasise the capacity of ordinary citizens to hold opinions tend to take as their puzzle how this is achieved in spite of their lack of relevant knowledge.[18] If there is a puzzle at all, one might see it rather as why certain individuals are willing to denigrate the competence they have by declaring themselves too busy to keep track of political issues.[19] In the face of a rich ability to articulate common problems, this seems the more surprising phenomenon.

The intention in speaking of a political bond was to investigate whether substantive problems may be substituted for alternatives such as interests, cultural markers or values as the focal point of the common. What has been observed in this chapter lends some backing to this perspective, in that the capacity to articulate and elaborate common problems in need of address seems evident in the empirical material. The next chapter explores how the concept may be taken further, examining the contours of collective allegiance which these problems inspire.

---

[17]Cf. (Zaller 1992; Delli Carpini and Keeter 1996) and some contributions to (Elkin and Soltan 1999).

[18]Cf. the literature on heuristics, e.g. (Sniderman et al. 1991).

[19]The definitive study on this is (Eliasoph 1998). In our interviews some such comments arose – Hamid in Lübeck declared 'we're so busy I think with our own lives that we don't have time to follow foreign and domestic news ... we've got hard work to do, 14 or 15 hours a day, and families to think about.' For further consideration of reactions to the word 'politics' itself, see the Appendix.

4
On Subjects, Opponents and Counterparts

If the articulation of common problems is to form the basis for political attachments, it clearly becomes of special importance what kinds of social grouping are evoked in discussion of such problems, and the relationships indicated between them. Problems bring people together and push them apart, and both dynamics need to be accommodated in a political conceptualisation of the collective bond. This question of *collective positioning* forms the focus of this chapter. Our interest is in the various social categories which arise in each domain, the patterns of sympathy and opposition they are tied to, and the perceived spatial scope of these conflicts. These are discursive patterns in the same sense as described in Chapter 3 and, in theoretical terms, Chapter 2: routinised ways of speaking which, though always susceptible to renunciation by individual speakers, nevertheless recur widely across the discussions, and whose adoption is generally taken for granted rather than marked by hesitation or reflexivity.

The discussions as always are treated not so much as a glimpse at individuals, though names will become familiar, but as a site of discursive practice. What gets said is interesting not because it indicates the 'identities' of participants, but because it is a pool in which one finds accumulated some of the discursive resources commonly drawn upon for collective positioning, and whose political implications one wants to study. Two broad questions are of interest in particular. The first is whether these acts of positioning are consistent with a political bond of any kind – that is, whether they exhibit the basic tolerance of 'the other' necessary for a democratic political community. The second concerns the scale of polity they would seem to support – in particular, whether they carry a transnational dimension, and in how far this is specifically 'European'. Following the logic of exploratory research, the aims are double: on the one hand to use the empirical material so as to further develop our concepts; on the other hand to use these same concepts to make a reading of the contemporary situation.

Sensitising concepts for the study of collective positioning

An extended extract from the interview conducted in the Czech town of Liberec provides a starting-point for laying out the conceptual apparatus. At the point where we join it, the discussion has been running for approximately 50 minutes, with regular interventions from each of Vladimír, Tomáš, Zdeněk and Radoslav. The focus has been on problems of unemployment, job insecurity and the inadequacies and possible abuse of the benefits system – issues that can be associated with the *Economics* domain. Problems to do with wages and working conditions are drawn into the discussion over the course of this passage. An intervention from Tomáš conjures up the figure of an unemployed person faced with the dilemma of whether he should accept a low-paid job:

T: … You've got to remember though, if someone gets CK4500 on benefits or CK6000 in wages, that's a difference of just 1500. Who's going to … what will-power is going to make you work for 6000 if the state gives you 4500?

Z: That's exactly it, a young person is going to prefer to be on support than to go out and work for 6000. As a young person he'll still get hold of a side-job. So he's better off like that than if he went out and did something, isn't he.

V: And on top of everything he'd have to get up at 6 in the morning. Like this, he doesn't have to get up at all. [Z: Hang on, at 6 he needs to be at work already …] So he gets up at 5 then …

T: But it's the same with everything. Working time, which in the Czech Republic is now 181 hours a month … [Z: Yeah, we've got plenty of hours …] We have the most in the whole of Europe. But the problem is, like all of us know, it's 181 hours which are obligatory and then on top of that you have overtime. People have to go and work at the weekends too …

Z: … Those supermarkets etc., they run non-stop, right, from Monday to Sunday, it's non-stop …

R: … People don't get much pay for it at all …

T: ... Of course, it's not enough pay to live on ... [R: ... It's not ...]

Z: ... They've got a bit of security, but not much ...

V: Well, in exchange for that security they've got masses of hours to do. [T: ... Of course ...]

Z: Nothing's for free. And all these entrepreneurs who've come in from outside, they know we're a cheap source of labour ... [T: ... Of course ...] so therefore they throng to the country. They make sure the wages don't go up fast so they don't have to dip into their pockets.

R: Exactly, and there are companies where when they're behind schedule they give you the chance to do overtime, so you do get more money but you're still not gong to get what you'd need to satisfy you. And there are some companies which ...

Z: You don't have to do overtime and they pay you fairly, but you have to have qualifications ...

R: My wife for example, works in BabyCup, and if they don't get the goods ready and send them out ...

Z: They'd get a salary, but not as high as if they got the goods out on time ...

R: ... Basic wages, but they don't pay them overtime. And I say: 'Why are you working there so long? I wouldn't do it, I'd go home at 3.30.' And they whisper, 'if you don't like it ...'

Z: There's another five or ten waiting at the gate ... [R: ... yeah, exactly ...] That's always the way it goes, cos that's how it is here.

R: The bosses don't value people. If they valued them, they'd give them 50% higher wages.

Z: Why should they value them if they know that outside there are another 15 or so waiting for each job? [R: ... Exactly, that's why ...] Why would they cry for you?

T: They should pay workers holiday-time like in the west ... [Z: Yeah, that too ...] [...]

Author: Can these problems be prevented somehow ...?

T: No ... first of all, these are companies from abroad which have come here to make a profit out of the cheap labour-force. And as soon as that cheap labour runs out, they'll pack up here and move on.

Z: Because that's not a factory that manufactures ... That's the problem, they just assemble here, they don't produce anything. If they produced something then you'd have some certainty they weren't going to run off ...

T: It's a clear example ... the mistake is the government's, because they give them tax holidays. There are firms here which ... Škoda, my suspicion is that it's been only this year that they've started paying taxes, I don't know ... it's ten years that Škoda-Volkswagen have been running, isn't it ten? ... [Z: Because they expanded, yeah.] So in order to get Volkswagen to come here for Škoda, they got a ten-year tax holiday from the state and Škoda doesn't pay a crown in tax, for ten years. That's a huge amount of money. So clearly they enticed them over, they paid, but if they do that for every company then the state really isn't going to make any money. And then they behave towards people ... [Z: Yeah, it's the same in the Mošnov industrial zone ...] It's the same. They get given so many subsidies ...

Z: They can pick and choose now in the industrial zone, they don't want to employ Czechs any more, Slovaks go there now, to Denso[1], it's all just Slovaks.

R: Yeah, Slovaks do it for a certain amount of money ...

Z: ... Under their conditions ...

T: ... Yeah, there isn't as much work where they are as there is here ...

Z: ... Because there they haven't got work and those conditions suit them, since that way they get more than if they were still over there. [R: ... yeah ...] [V: Thanks to the exchange rate of course ...]

T: The problem is, here there's 10% unemployment, and there's plenty of people who aren't even registered ... [Z: ... registered ...] And politicians don't admit to it ... [Z: ... That's just the tip of it, those 10% ...] That's just the tip of it. I'd calculate that here there's 12% or 13% unemployment, definitely. There are plenty of people who don't even go to register at the job centre. [Z: Yeah ... look how many homeless people there are, they're not registered anywhere.] Those are things which the state doesn't admit, they just show off numbers to the world. [Z: Of course.] For them

---

[1]A manufacturer of advanced technologies for the car industry.

> it's clear that every number which is visible, whether it's 20% or however much – which would be awful … they assume there's no hidden people there, they take it as a clear figure for unemployed, that it's definitely 10%, so they say 'yeah, people are doing fine,' but the reality is completely different.

We shall postpone until the next chapter two issues very much to the fore in this text: how the problems articulated are explained, and how far they are assumed susceptible to remedy. Instead, the focus is on the references one sees to those affected by them, and to those who stand as their opponents. As regards the first, several instances in this passage highlight the difficulties of those in low-paid and insecure jobs, forced to work long hours with badly paid overtime. Factory work is highlighted, with Radoslav's reference to his wife forging a direct link to the participants themselves. Tomáš's parenthetical 'like all of us know' positions the group as sharing in the problem of long hours and overtime, and the connection is affirmed by the usage of 'we' and 'you' pronouns – though several times it is individuals who are referred to ('a young person', individual 'he's' and 'she's', the five or ten individuals waiting at the gate). These people, it is suggested, live in the real world, where low wages and unemployment are major problems, rather than in the artificial realm of state statistics. They are without special advantages, and do not have the qualifications with which to find more attractive work. Though in this extract they are not summarised in a single term, one could easily adopt the phrase Tomáš uses elsewhere, 'ordinary people'. The 'we' also has a national dimension: Czech workers are distinguished from Slovak ones, though both represent a 'cheap source of labour', and both face the problem of being constrained to take undesirable jobs.

Those described in this way as being affected by the problems articulated can be termed the *political subjects*. They are the social groupings that speakers construct so as to define their relationship with the problems under discussion. While they do not constitute 'the identity' of the participants (since speakers invoke different subject-positions at different moments in discussion as they move from one set of problems to another), they are categories and implicit groupings towards which the participants orient themselves. The subjects are *political* in several senses. Firstly, they are defined in relation to the problems of the political common set out in the previous chapter. These are problems treated as shared rather than purely individual, and for which speakers demonstrate a transindividual competence when handling them in discussion. The subjects are thus political by association with the shared substantive concerns that could form the basis for political community. Secondly, the subjects are political in the sense that they are the kinds of imagined groupings that political actors (e.g. parties or social movements) might use to mobilise people to their cause, or which they might seek to redefine so as to make everyday discursive practice more compatible with their cause. Thirdly, in some cases such groupings will have been actively shaped by past efforts at political mobilisation, e.g. by actors seeking to define those in whose name they act. The subjects, as common discursive formulations, represent a political resource on the basis of which collective political initiatives may be organised – the success of which will depend also on the kinds of assumption examined in the next chapter – as well as to a greater or lesser extent an outcome of past political action.[2]

The construction of political subjects involves at the same time the construction of those who differ from them. It requires 'boundary-work' (Gieryn 1983; Lamont and Molnár 2002),[3] since we-description is at the same time a relational act of positioning, and requires the evocation of 'others' so as to clarify and give meaning to the 'we'. Demarcated in this passage as *opponents* of the subjects, one sees in particular the entrepreneurs and companies which 'come in from outside' and offer bad conditions to their workers. Supermarkets and manufacturers are mentioned, taking advantage of the attractive situation the state affords them in the form of subsidies and tax holidays. There are 'bosses [who] don't value people', as expressed by the low wages and lack of holiday-time they offer, and by how they compel their workers to do overtime. They are in control and they know it – they only have to 'whisper' a reminder of this. These companies are here to make a profit, to fill their pockets. As soon as the profits dry up 'they'll pack up here and move on'. Because such companies are only assembling goods, they are always liable to 'run off', leaving people unemployed.

---

[2]As will be seen, the categories of political subjecthood evoked in these discussions tend not to refer to disembodied opinions or ideological traditions, as in 'left', 'right', 'socialist' or 'liberal'. Insofar as they retain a retain a reference to *people* rather than ideas, they suggest the individual's association with them is something short of wholly voluntary, and to this degree while political they may be considered *imperfectly* so. Cf. below.

[3]On relationality and political subjecthood, see (Tilly 2002).

It is the actions of these opponents which exacerbate or cause problems for the subjects, and it is only through some kind of settlement with them, consensual or imposed, that the problems articulated may be addressed.

The possibility that others within the political community may be positioned as opponents is one of the essential characteristics of the perspective on allegiance outlined in Chapter 1. Such a perspective maintains the possibility of accommodating political disagreement and the absence of diffuse solidarity, so long as this disagreement does not lead to calls for the banishment of opponents from the community altogether. It is a perspective which draws on agonistic conceptions of politics, in which the life of the political community involves multiple acts of the construction of an 'us' and a 'them'. Unlike in Carl Schmitt's conception of the political, this is understood not in terms of a binary distinction between 'friends' and 'enemies'. Rather, a key distinction is made between two kinds of positioning of opponents: that which casts them as *enemies*, with whom a purely hostile, antagonistic relationship unfolds, and that which casts them as *adversaries*, with whom an agonistic relationship is maintained and with whom the life in common is possible (Mouffe 2005: 20).

This distinction is a useful sensitising idea, though we shall appropriate it in a certain way. In Mouffe's work, the distinction is elaborated with movement politics in mind, and is intended to conceptualise how the holders of opposing political ideologies must regard one another so as to be consistent with agonistic democracy, and the kinds of ideological position which can be ruled out as anti-democratic. Although her concept of exclusion can be ambiguous (Abizadeh 2005), and although her terminology refers explicitly to categories of *people* (friends, enemies and adversaries), her perspective focuses mainly on the inclusion and exclusion of *ideas*, and of people only insofar as they associate themselves with these (Mouffe 1993: 4). This is a little different from the kinds of positioning one finds in everyday discourse, where it is very often descriptions of people and their actions, not explicitly their ideas, which are to the fore. In the extract above, it is groups such as 'bosses' or 'entrepreneurs' which are positioned as opponents, not political ideas more generally. Indeed, it may be that this explicit linkage to categories of people makes possible, or at least augments, the very sense of injustice with which these problems are articulated. To 'put a face' on a problem is to make it tangible, to give it urgency, whereas to treat it as an abstraction (such as 'poverty' or 'hardship') may be to neutralise and normalise it (Gamson 1992: 7). We shall thus give a rather literal sense to the categories of friends (political subjects), enemies and adversaries which accepts them as categories of people. While this implies using the terms with a slight difference of emphasis, it does not do violence to the political philosophy in which they operate. After all, the ideas-people distinction is a fuzzy one. In particular, whenever social categories are invoked, an array of category knowledge is brought with them (e.g. concerning 'what bosses do', what they 'represent', under what conditions they thrive, etc.), and it is in these clusters of assumptions, and the broader domains in which they are embedded, that ideas return to the fore.[4]

In empirical terms, determining whether in a given text those positioned as opponents are being treated as *adversaries* or as *enemies* is always a matter of interpretation. Some guiding criteria might be as follows. Where the behaviour of the opponents is assumed contingent on particular circumstances and therefore potentially susceptible to change or 'correction', the sense they should be engaged with is likely to be stronger, and so one may infer their status as adversaries. Where alternatively the behaviour of opponents is essentialised, such that it is assumed their conduct is a function of their fundamental nature (perhaps with connotations that this nature is not rational), this is likely to be accompanied by the sense that there is little point in trying to engage with them, and therefore their status as enemies may be inferred. In sociological terms, it is a question of the *permeability* of group boundaries, with the boundaries surrounding adversaries more porous than those surrounding enemies (Lamont and Molnár 2002). Relatedly, the level of threat associated with the two kinds of opponent may be distinguished: those that compromise the well-being of the subjects, and about whom a sense of irritation is conveyed, can be thought of as adversaries, in contrast to those from whom the threat is of a more fundamental, existential kind, who are described more with a sense of fear than irritation. In this passage from the Liberec group, the opponents (the companies and their bosses) are portrayed as causing hardship rather than a threat to existence. There is also the sense that they are merely doing what any rational subject would do in their position, that is, taking advantage of a favourable situation. Notice Zdeněk's comment in response to Radoslav (to which Radoslav

---

[4]Conversation analysts – e.g. (Antaki 1998) – have shown particular sensitivity to how speakers' selection of social categories draws accompanying ideational features into the discussion.

in turn agrees): 'why would they value them [the workers] if they know that outside there are another 15 or so waiting for each job?' There may be little that can be done to tackle the opponents, but that is because of the assumed nature of the circumstances (wage competition, an accommodating state, etc.) rather than because of the assumed nature of the opponents themselves. The category of 'adversary' therefore seems a more appropriate one here. As will be seen below, this is characteristic of the *Economics* domain more generally.

Mouffe's account of the political conjures up a rather sparse terrain peopled by friends, adversaries and enemies. Though their existence is not explicitly ruled out, there are no fourth groupings of political importance in her account. The emphasis is on alliance and opposition. The notion of a political bond, on the other hand, does raise the prospect of at least one other politically significant kind of grouping. This would be what one might call the 'counterpart'. Counterparts, strangers living outside the home environment, would be linked to the subjects in that they are assumed to be confronted with similar problem(s). They share in the same predicament, though they live 'there' rather than 'here' – with these locations being a matter for definition in the text.[5] The bond between subjects and counterparts is not necessarily one of active solidarity, nor are they necessarily engaged together in collective political action – the counterpart is something less than a 'friend' or fellow subject, though may become one – but nor is the relationship between them assumed to be of a 'zero-sum' kind whereby the one can benefit only at the expense of the other – the counterpart is something more than an enemy or adversary, though again may become one if circumstances change. The significance of counterparts would lie in how their assumed existence serves to make sense of the political community. The evocation of counterparts broadens the reach of the political common, such that the problems of which it is comprised are seen to be facing not just an immediate 'we' quite narrowly defined, but a larger, more dispersed ensemble of 'people like us'.[6] Where counterparts are assumed to exist, a wider political bond becomes possible.

---

[5]Definition of the 'home environment' is something one wants to avoid pre-empting, but broadly it should be understood as the space of experience evoked by speakers for themselves and those considered directly interdependent with them. It should not necessarily be equated with political units such as the state.
[6]'People facing predicaments like ours' would be the more correct formulation, though it is cumbersome.

Such a bond in the European context would require that at least some of those living outside the home environment, in other EU countries for instance, be assumed to be facing problems of a basically similar kind.[7] While counterparts might also be evoked *within* the same country – in different regions for example, or in different occupations – of particular interest for our purposes is the spatial *scope*, i.e. the greatest extension, of the comparisons made. Evocations of shared predicament would not have to include 'all Europeans' of course – for this would be to do away with the agonistic dimension altogether – but they would have to extend to at least some groups associated with other European countries. If counterparts were assumed to exist only close to the home environment (in 'our country', for instance) but not elsewhere, then people in other parts of Europe would most likely be seen either as wholly irrelevant – no bond of any kind would exist with them – or as enemies to be excluded from the community, or as permanent adversaries against whom the struggle is constant. While the existence of adversaries is by no means contradictory of a political bond, if they were always demarcated in national categories then a political community coextensive with the EU would be unlikely to have common-sense plausibility.

The notion of the 'counterpart' is a conceptual one which does not translate easily into readily discernible features of the text. Lacking the immediacy of subjects, enemies and adversaries, counterparts are not often explicitly constructed in discussion (though they do appear, as will be seen). While the concept serves a useful sensitising function, a more empirical phenomenon for study is the nature of comparisons and references to places. An important precondition for the assumption of counterparts is that territorial units in the EU be treated not just as unitary *actors* but also as *environments*, as locations where events unfold. Whenever, in the discussion of substantive problems, other countries are mentioned as actors (France or 'the French', for example), without internal differentiation, then the speaker is emphasising territorial boundaries which cut across the EU and treating these as the relevant facts in play. While such a perspective of course does not necessarily lead to the fragmentation of political community – indeed, it is

---

[7]The assertion would be of equivalence rather than sameness – if it is asserted that the *same* problem is faced, this would imply a strong degree of interdependence, and one might prefer to speak of shared political subjecthood rather than a subject-counterpart relation.

likely to have a place in any federal or decentralised polity – it would need to be counterbalanced by other acts of positioning which do not foreground these territorial divisions, else any sense of the common would be lost. Moreover, not only does one look for other EU countries to be treated – at least in part – as environments, but as *similar* environments, in which problems arise and are encountered in a fashion analogous to those experienced by the subjects in the home environment. Such environments are *comparable*, in the everyday sense in which this means not just that a comparison is possible but that subsequently similarity can be affirmed. Reference to the conditions found in other countries only for the purpose of *contrast*, i.e. to emphasise dissimilarity, would again be to undercut any sense of the common. Only where there is this assumption of similar environments does the conceptual notion of the counterpart become possible, and thus the political bond as a basis for political community.

As was suggested in Chapter 1, social comparison involves the interplay between a dimension of comparison (Z^8), an evocation of subjecthood (X^9) and the evocation of a comparator deemed more or less similar (Y^{10}). Scholars in sociology and social psychology have had much to say on the processes at work here, developing a number of related concepts such as the 'reference group' (Merton 1957; Shibutani 1955).[11] An important point emerging from this literature is that acts of comparison are purposive, and can be quite varied in their purposes. *Evaluation* is one: speakers engaging in a comparison between a 'we' and a 'they' are liable to be making an assessment of both, whether it be of their competence, their good fortune, or their moral standing. As social identity theory (and older notions of *ressentiment*) highlight, similarities or differences may be stressed so as to position the speaker and a particular reference group in a favourable light, so as to attract sympathy, or indeed so as to assert the relativity of all forms of evaluation (e.g. by evoking multiple registers of evaluation which produce conflicting assessments of status) (Tajfel 1981; Tajfel and Turner 1986). Here com-

---

[8]Here: affectedness by a given problem.

[9]A 'we', or an 'I' presented as a representative of many (e.g. 'I as a working man', rather than 'I as Michael').

[10]Rather than an individual or set of individuals familiar to the subject, this is likely to be an imagined social category, carrying a limited range of associations.

[11]More recently, see (Suls et al. 2002; Guimond 2006). Studies of transnational comparison within Europe have been sparse, but see (Brown and Haeger 1999; Delhey and Kohler 2006).

parison shades into some of the boundary-drawing practices described above. More distinctive is comparison for the purpose of *orientation*. By evoking the existence or absence of others who are similar to the subject along a certain dimension, the speaker contributes an act of contextualisation, one which probes to what degree the subject's situation is distinctive or is replicated more widely. As indicated earlier, this may also be the first step in constructing or expressing feelings of sympathy with others. Even where counterparts are not evoked explicitly, comparisons for orientation create the conditions for their emergence.

By highlighting the importance of comparisons, one can make a link back to the empirical material. One can look at the places with which they are drawn because experiences 'there' are held to be largely similar to those 'here' within the home environment with regard to a particular problem or set of problems. In the Liberec passage above, the home environment seems to be the Czech Republic, as indicated by the figure for hours worked and the suggestion that companies are 'thronging' to the country. Emphasis is particularly on developments in the neighbourhood of Liberec itself, with a number of references to local industry. One sees some comparison with conditions in Slovakia, and a numerical comparison with 'Europe' on the question of hours worked, but neither is much developed. Here are two further extracts from the Liberec discussion:

T: You've got the state boasting about economic figures, how the economy is prospering, how we've got lots of exports rather than imports, how everything's functioning as it should, but the problem is, a particular section of people, whether it's firms or entrepreneurs, keep hold of that money for themselves, and it only gets through to the working class [Z: ... which is the majority ...] awfully slowly. For us, the level hasn't gone up in the last three years. I'd say it's gone down. The official figures say that we're getting better, but unfortunately that's not what people are seeing.

Z: They say that wages are going up, but whenever someone gets into my car they're complaining about how little money they've got ...

T: Exactly ... the average wage is meant to be CK18,000 ...

Z: But that's too high because they take the average from the highest strata, not overall ...

T: ... You have to be a director or something, where the wages are completely different. I don't know how it is in the west, but I think this difference in wages like we've got here is really bad.

R: They raise the price of everything, but they'd never align the wages that normal people get. [...]

V: Now Ireland for example, that was a really poor country and it got into the EU and look at them now, they're doing well. They're rich now. [T: Wait ...] Even those who work in factories ... I went there to pick apples ... the rents are high but they get by ok. They're even able to buy cars. You're not going to get a car here.

R: Here you have to save your whole life in order to buy a car ...

T: There's a programme on television now, 'Here in Europe' [*U nás v Evropě*] – I don't know whether you've seen it – where they show how families in Europe live. They showed Austrians, now they've shown French. They get an income of CK150,000 per month, and 28,000 goes on food alone. Those are sums which you don't see here, they're really somewhere else. And leases and rents on a tenement flat are €1500, that's CK40,000, that's only a quarter of the 150,000. Here, to get a lease and a tenement flat, it's more than your wages ...

R: Yeah, you wouldn't have enough even to mortgage. [T: ... It's just wrong ...] They don't give you loans, nothing ...

Z: Here no-one gives you anything if you haven't got enough to give security for it. [...]

Author: You were talking about Ireland ... what's the comparison ...?

V: It's impossible to compare them, it's impossible ...

T: To compare with the Czech Republic ... I think it's impossible to compare any west-European country with us. We can compare ourselves at most with the old eastern bloc, like Poland, Hungary, Slovakia ... [Z: ... Though all of them are starting to overtake us ...] They're all starting to have it better, all the eastern countries. Of course, Belarus and those countries certainly not, but the Poles and the Slovaks are starting to draw away from us. [R: I think so too.]

Z: Even though they have lower ... [T: ... A lower standard of living ...] ... the crown is a bit stronger than theirs ...

T: But generally, I go to Slovakia, I've got family there, and I know that the Slovaks have a standard of living which is even lower than ours, but again the numbers say that it's better. I think the better the numbers are, the worse it is for ordinary people.

Here one finds several references to the transnational context. But before examining them, let us look at what happens a little later in the discussion when Václav picks up his reference to Ireland again, and once more draws the opposition of Tomáš and Zdeněk:

V: They got into the EU and look where they are today. I've been there, I know. [T: But to compare Ireland with the Czech Republic ...] I'm saying, I've been there, you understand, and I'm comparing it with here in Czechia. [T: But it's different ...] It's very different! ...

T: If you think they're doing so well because they're in the EU ... [Z: It's not that ...] It's not that. [...]

V: I'm saying, I've been there and what they're able to buy with their wages and what people here who work in factories buy ...

T: You don't need to go to Ireland, it's enough to go to Germany, France – states which are really ... [Z: States which are right next to us ...] ... all those western countries. Whether the Irish have it a bit better than let's say the Spanish or the Portuguese or those states, you can't compare them in economic terms, those are massive differences compared to when you go to the east, to Poland, Czech Republic, Slovakia, Hungary and further down. There's plenty of countries you can compare with each other – the Swedes, the Finns, northern countries ... you might think there'd be a lot of poverty there ... [Z: Gets a bit cold there from time to time ...] but they're amongst the most advanced countries. ...

Z: Except they've had 50 years to work with and we've only had 10 years ...

T: Of course, but what's worse is that those ten years haven't been positive ... [Z: ... yeah, yeah ...] In fact, we're mostly complaining about these last ten years. If things were always improving it'd be fine, but if we look at the 1990s, it was one great fraud here ...

Z: Whoever had sharp elbows, he ladled it in and then went off to sunbathe.

T: Now it's stabilised a bit, but the gap I'd say is twenty years. If western Europe stood still then I'd say it'd still be twenty years before we're on their level.

In these passages one sees two kinds of positioning taking place. On the one hand one sees repeated contrasts with the economic conditions projected onto western Europe, where it is assumed certain familiar problems do not exist, or exist in reduced form. Income levels in western-European countries are assumed to be far higher in relation to the cost of living than 'here', and factory workers live comfortably and can buy cars. Economic corruption is implied to be much less of a problem in these countries, whereas 'here' the story has been of 'one great fraud'. 'Here' the subjects are unlikely to get a loan when they need one, with the implication (voiced later) that in western countries loans are easier to secure. Overall, the economic gap with those countries is as much as several decades, and differences *between* those countries are played down (see Tomáš's comment that 'whether the Irish have it a bit better than let's say the Spanish or the Portuguese or those states', the 'massive differences' are with the east). All participants seem agreed on this point. Even Vladimír, who presents his interventions as comparisons rather than contrasts with western Europe, seems just as keen as Tomáš and Zdeněk to highlight how fundamentally things are different there. It is explicitly rejected that membership of the EU makes all these countries alike.

On the other hand, in a second act of positioning, other countries in central/eastern Europe are mentioned as places more worthy of comparison, in particular Poland, Hungary and Slovakia. These are places that one 'can compare' with the Czech Republic. They are linked together explicitly by Tomáš as 'the east' and 'the old eastern bloc', and implicitly by the contrast-based references to the west-European countries on the one hand and 'Belarus and those countries' on the other. There is some agreement that 'the Poles and the Slovaks' are starting to do better than 'us', but also the sense that there are 'ordinary people' in Slovakia who have a standard of living comparable (though lower) to 'ours', and who may be victims of deceptive official statistics just like 'we' are. This evocation of places worthy of comparison with the home environment is very much of the sort one might seek as the basis for a political bond. What is problematic from a European perspective of course is that the scope of comparison, while transnational, is rather less than coextensive with the EU: an east vs west division is emphasised. This, as will be seen, is quite typical of the patterns of positioning one finds in the *Economics* domain.

Over the course of this chapter, we shall look at the three domains *Economics, Society and the Law* and *Relations between Peoples* in turn, analysing them for the appearance of subjects, opponents (adversary and enemy), comparable environments and counterparts. The emphasis will be on the common features of the texts across the three country-groups, though inter-country variations are highlighted where marked.

Collective positioning in *Economics*

A) The political subjects and their opponents

The formulations of subjecthood noted in the Liberec discussion recur widely across the groups when problems to do with *Economics* are articulated. 'Ordinary people' is an expression one finds in several of the discussions. A second recurrent formulation appears in the following extract from the Norwich discussion. In focus are the problems associated with supermarkets reducing their prices by importing goods from abroad. Malcolm is using Bill to make a point about prices:

> M: If Bill here made his own shoes and they were £5 more expensive than the ones that Asda buy in ... Asda, all these supermarkets, are our great friends [sarcasm] aren't they, buying all this cheap produce. What they're doing is, they're crushing, they're crushing people like us, and we don't ever win ...
>
> B: ... The little man, no, he never does, does he ...
>
> M: ... Because the simple fact is, if the little man doesn't have the money he can't get in our taxis, can't afford to go out. If they don't go out, can't afford to get a taxi ... [Les: It's an ongoing thing ...] Yeah, so what I'd rather do is I'd rather buy Bill's shoes for £5, £10 more, knowing that I was helping a little man ...
>
> B: Yeah, go to the corner-shop.

Here the main formulation for the subjects is 'the little man'. He comes in various guises: examples seem to be the taxi-driver ('people like us', who have 'noticed a down-turn in our trade'), the person who can no longer afford to get in the back of a taxi to go out, the small producer such as Bill would be if he made shoes, or – as emerges a little later – the workers for small producers who end up doing longer hours in worse conditions for less pay, or without a job at all. The formulation is a rather passive one, and the little man is very much a victim – he gets 'crushed', he never wins, and has a vulnerable family to look after. He is a David who never gets the better of Goliath. He is also local – you would find him in the corner-shop – suggesting his reality and relevance to 'people like us'. The little people need to look out for each other, hence Malcolm's willingness to buy from Bill. Notice that the formulation appears here in the singular as 'the little man', just as individualised formulations were seen in the extracts cited earlier from Liberec. This is not always the case – 'the little people' is another term heard – but where used it can be said to underscore the vulnerability and passivity of the subject.

'The little man' and 'the little people' are common formulations for the subjects in the *Economics* domain.[12] In a similar fashion to Malcolm, Ulrich in Würzburg talks of how the lack of work in the city affects 'us small guys' because 'the little people' in the city generally no longer have enough money to go out, take taxis and give tips. Oliver summarises with a comment based on a simple binary opposition: 'what's happening is the little people are being burdened more and more with costs while the big guys are being relieved of them. The gap's going to widen too.' Amongst the Czech groups, a binary opposition of rich and poor people, or rich and 'normal people', or even just rich and 'people', is common, and a polarisation of the two is stressed. As Tomáš in Liberec puts it, 'the middle is disappearing'.

The little people lack economic advantages.[13] They live in the *real* world as opposed to the unreal world of numbers. 'What is money at the end of the day?' asks Malcolm. 'It's only figures on a computer screen isn't it. ... Obviously ... when someone gets in the cab we take money to pay our bills, cos that is the real world. Everyday-person-view world. But when you go on a global thing, it's only figures on a computer screen, it's only gold bullion.' 'The western world really only hears what is presented, how those eastern states are going up economically,' says Tomáš. 'They really don't realise, because they come here and see we have shops full of goods, but that's completely misleading.

---

[12]Nor are they new: historians identify them as a common trope already in late nineteenth-century Europe (Hobsbawm 1989: 89).
[13]Amongst the Czech groups this includes the option to emigrate: Tomáš in Liberec suggests 'someone who has education and knows different languages can go wherever they want'. To Germany, to Austria – 'to those states', adds Zdeněk. 'We can go to Russia', says Tomáš dismissively.

If they think Czechs are going out and buying smoked salmon, well they're not.'

When the subjects are cast as the 'little people', 'ordinary people' or 'normal people', it is in contrast to those with money. 'The rich', private companies (such as Asda above) and 'shareholders' are commonly used as points of demarcation. Bill in Norwich describes shareholders as 'different people to us', and points to the hotel chain Travelodge to illustrate a fellow subject being cheated of her money by the rich: 'they pay minimum wage, and yet you stay there at £70 a night, and they fill up the hotel and you've got some poor girl there who's on £3.50 an hour. So where does the money go? Shareholders, rich people at the end. Always the same.' Across the groups, large corporations are singled out as one of the main opponents. Peter in Kassel demarcates the subjects against 'the high-up guys' (*die Hohen*), and observes: 'everyone keeps harping on at the little man, "you must have less holiday, you must get ill less often, you must accept less money ...". The companies are earning billions, they're earning more and more, and they don't want to surrender any of it. They say "yeah, we've made a profit of only 150 billion this year, so we need to lay off another 600 ... no, 6000 people."' As he adds a little later to Hans' agreement, 'today companies just want to sell things and everything else is irrelevant to them. And the loser is always the little man.'

We have seen then that the subjects may be cast as the little people in opposition to the economically more powerful who are able to dominate and exploit.[14] A second formulation, also recurrent, sees the subjects as those who *contribute* or who are economically productive, in contrast to those who just 'take'. The formulation 'working people', which carries the connotation of those who undertake their share of labour, is common amongst the British groups. When Alan from the Swansea group talks about the rising costs for running a taxi, he explains: 'we've had to put our prices up. The insurance has gone up, the fuel's gone up, that means we're passing it on to the working man like us.' This formulation based on the idea of contribution is a more active one than the 'little people', and one with which participants readily associate themselves. In Norwich, Les talks of how 'all

---

[14]Note this pattern extends across the groups and is to be found amongst the British as much as the Germans and Czechs. Lamont notes a similar pattern amongst her French interviewees, but finds it to be much weaker amongst her American ones (Lamont 2000: 239).

our money goes in the pot, and it's all shared out with people that are taking it.' The rich are occasionally cited, but also, particularly amongst the British, those in a weak economic situation who live at the expense of the state. Malcolm expresses his anger at the neighbours two doors up, 'the ming-mongs, scumbags. She doesn't work, she's got two kids by two separate fathers, and neither contribute a penny.'[15] At the same time, they 'know the system', and know how to 'take, take, take' from social security, leaving it to 'bleed'. Bill draws much approval from his fellow participants when he summarises: 'The ones at the bottom get it, the ones at the top have got it, and us in the middle are subsidising both.'

That the subjects are those 'in the middle' is a motif found more than once in the British discussions. It evokes a sense of reasonableness (the subjects are not one of the extremes), also that they have opponents both 'above' and 'below' them on the economic ladder. 'You see, we're caught in the middle, people like us,' says Bill, 'because you've got all the scumbags who make life a misery, and you've got the rich at the top, who make your life misery. Basically us in the middle, we subsidise everybody and we pay the penalty for everybody. You know, the rich don't see the scumbags, the scumbags don't see the rich, but we get penalised.' Les agrees: 'do you know, it's always the working people that suffer the most. Always.' The 'working people' are not what one might call proletarians (or the working *class*) stationed at the bottom of the hierarchy: they are positioned between those above who have the money but do not contribute, and those below who have neither the money nor a willingness to contribute. One does not find the term 'working people' with the same frequency amongst the German and Czech groups, nor do these groups refer quite so trenchantly to the 'scumbags' below them – this tripartite scheme is not found.[16] But a distinction between contributors and non-contributors, or productive and non-productive, is certainly used.

On a number of occasions the opponents are cast in national or ethnic terms, with immigrants and minorities marked off and criticised for not contributing. (Note that the criterion of evaluation here is that

---

[15]The word 'ming-mong' can be read as ascribing idiocy and pathos; it does not have a racial aspect.

[16]A similar distinction is noted by Lamont when comparing how American and French workers position themselves in economic terms: the French tend to draw weaker boundaries towards the poor 'below' them than the Americans – (Lamont 2000: 239).

of contribution and productivity; criteria to do with cultural otherness and collective security we shall come to when looking at *Relations between Peoples*.) The idea of national funds being drained comes through strongly in the Lübeck discussion: 'when a Turk comes here,' says Jochen, 'he brings five Turks with him. The children, the wife, perhaps the grandparents ... And all that adds nothing to the GNP [Werner: yeah]. And they're not even allowed to work in the first period, are they. So that means they get social benefits, or Hartz IV.[17] And naturally that puts a burden on the public purse [*die Staatskasse*], through taxes. So to that extent it's not going to pan out well in the long run.' It is always the contributor who is directly affected: Matthias in Erfurt notes how 'they come here and then bring their whole clan with them and they too have to be all given social insurance and the state has to pay for all that ...'. Harald interrupts him: 'Not the state, you!' 'Of course, from my taxes!' The tax burden, here and elsewhere, is treated as falling equally on all the contributors: that some might – legitimately – contribute more than others is a notion rarely voiced.

Only certain immigrants and minorities are demarcated as opponents in the *Economics* domain: 'eastern Europeans' are a common reference-point across the groups; 'Turks' recur in the German discussions in this context, but not for example 'Arabs' or 'Muslims' – terms found later in this chapter. Immigrants from east-European and central-Asian countries are highlighted by the participants in Ostrava and criticised by Zbyněk because 'they don't know how to work ... they're not hardworking'. When the participants in the Norwich group want to speak positively about immigrants, they adopt the same criteria of contribution and productivity: 'If they're decent people and they're prepared to work, that's fair enough,' says Bill. 'It's a great thing because [then] there's more money,' agrees Malcolm. 'My view on them kind of people,' says Les, 'is that anybody can come here providing they do their bit. Like we have to do. And pay their bit, and not take.' Immigrants are by no means debarred from the status of subjects in this domain – providing they fulfil the duty to be productive and to contribute. As Matthias in Erfurt puts it, 'in a pizzeria an Italian

---

[17]Hartz IV was the name given to a batch of changes to the German labour market proposed to the German government in 2002 by Peter Hartz, a Volkswagen executive, and which started to be introduced around the time of these interviews. The changes included reductions in unemployment and social-security benefits, and new restrictions on eligibility.

belongs, and in a kebab place a Turk belongs. If he works for his money then that's ok. [...] If they work for their money then they should be allowed to work, to earn themselves a living and to live here in an orderly fashion. [Harald: Exactly].'

The assumption that those who are currently opponents could be encouraged or coerced to make their contribution is important. It suggests they are not positioned as 'beyond redemption' – their opposition to the political subjects is not an *essential* one, but one based on contingent habits of behaviour. One may perhaps be uncomfortable with Matthias' easy reliance on certain category associations to position immigrants as legitimate, and one should not forget the performative role of such statements – they position the speaker as tolerant and fair-minded, and thus have a local function in the discussion – but it is nonetheless an expression of tolerance.[18] Even where there is a stronger adversarial dimension, these groups are treated as a cost rather than an existential threat, and it tends to be emphasised that if such people pay their contributions (taxes, health insurance, and so on) they are acceptable, but that they should not be allowed to refuse work and live off the state. This is true likewise for the rich and the unemployed. Calls are not made for their expulsion from the country or their imprisonment: their behaviour is treated as oppressive or as a drain on resources, but they are grudgingly accepted. In this sense, the opponents in this domain are best thought of as 'adversaries' rather than 'enemies'.[19] Adversaries are unlikely to be welcomed into the home environment, but if they are already there they may be tolerated. Of course, on the basis of interviews alone one cannot explore how such discourses might be applied in individual cases: one can imagine that a Turkish-German man might be treated as 'working for his living' when serving Matthias a kebab, but as 'piling in here' when spotted at the airport in the passport-

---

[18]Note also there is little demarcation based on race or colour here. Gamson, in his study of lay discourse in the US, notes the ease with which 'black means poor and white means rich' (Gamson 1992: 103). One can imagine that when boundary-formation draws on physical markers in this way then acts of othering are much stronger and fundamental: there is less likely to be the sense that those who face economic problems, or those who rise above them, 'could have been me', and perhaps a stronger likelihood that those positioned as opponents are treated as enemies.

[19]The marginal case would be the 'ming-mongs and scumbags' Malcolm in Norwich identifies, but they are a feature mainly of his interventions alone, and mark an overlap with the *Society and the Law* domain which will be considered below.

control queue as he returns from vacation. The important thing, to begin with, is the availability of a discourse by which to legitimise his presence.

B) Comparable environments and counterparts

As these passages indicate, the extent to which the political subjects and their opponents tend to be constructed in territorial terms is limited. Certainly no speakers talked of economic problems facing 'us Europeans'. But nor were there many problems described as affecting the 'British', 'Germans' or 'Czechs' in broad, undifferentiated terms: the 'people like us' tend to be demarcated with formulations such as 'the little people', the 'people in the middle', or 'those who contribute', while their opponents tend to be evoked with formulations such as 'the rich', 'shareholders', 'big firms' or, mainly amongst the British groups, 'those at the bottom'. It would probably not be an abuse of the material to suggest these are all class-based categories. National categories *are* sometimes entwined with these, but in several cases as shorthand for a narrower group of 'people like us'. They may be applied to demarcate opponents, as seen with regard to unemployment, where concern is expressed about 'cheap workers' from eastern-European countries – the East starting, for the Czechs, a little further east than for the British or Germans. But in these cases it is not the nationality itself which is taken to be problematic but the behaviour with which it is associated. For most problems to do with *Economics*, nationality is just one, relatively minor, element in the repertoire of demarcation.

One problem-area which *was* articulated predominantly in national terms was the finances of the EU. Amongst the British and German groups there was recurrent, dissatisfied talk of 'us British' or 'us Germans' being the major contributors. Even in this context, however, the subjects would sometimes be cast not just as 'our country' but as a broader grouping of similarly economically-developed European countries. A succinct description of EU finances is provided by Jochen in Lübeck: 'The ones who profit are the poorer countries with the low GNP. And the industrial countries, they basically have to step down from their level, surrender their achievements.' Later he says, to the full agreement of Werner: 'As an industrial country, we can't expect anything there [from the EU]. They always try to make it palatable to us with the argument that our economy will then also profit because these countries can then buy things here. I don't know though whether that argument holds.'

This explicitly EU dimension will be returned to in Chapter 6, but the main point to note is that when other European countries are mentioned in these discussions, it tends to be less as rival *actors* and more as the *environments* in which problems arise, either where conditions are assumed to be comparable to the home environment or where they are considered quite different. Although the economic problems discussed tend to be described as affecting the subjects in a quite local home environment, a broader context is evoked through the application of transnational comparisons. These tend to be connected to problématiques such as prices and wages – i.e. the most quantifiable problems – but also (mainly in the German discussions) to consumer spending patterns, loss of social-security benefits, bureaucracy, and even macro-economic policy. Such comparisons tend to be made with other nearby countries in Europe, this meaning different things according to the groups in question. As noted, in the Czech discussions the comparisons on economic problems are with countries in central and eastern Europe. Conversely, the comparisons made in the British and German discussions on these problems tend to invoke countries of *western* Europe. The positioning is rather the opposite in other words, with a strong division between eastern and western Europe emphasised by all. In the following extract, the Swansea group makes a series of typical comparisons between the home environment (Swansea and Britain) and comparable environments (various places in western Europe), in response to Dean's question 'why is British fuel a lot more expensive than in other countries?':

Luke:	Well, why … why is it 40p, as an example, 40 odd pence I think in Europe for a litre of fuel, interest rates is 2% …
Alan:	Well it's cheaper in Ireland and that's only across the water isn't it. It's cheaper in Ireland.
L:	Cos they're all in the euro. [...] They say things have gone up in Europe, they will go up in Europe because they were a lot cheaper than in Britain anyway. Things can't go up a lot more in Britain, they can't put beer up £4, £5 a pint, people would never be able to afford a drink or whatever [...]. About eight to ten years ago over in Spain things were dirt cheap. Now it's a very reasonable, very similar price to over here. So all those countries that were cheap, they're not happy because they've joined the euro and their prices have gone up. [...]
D:	You know, we say that we're more expensive than other countries in Europe … France is a lot more expensive than here. For everything. I don't say so much property, I don't

know, fuel is similar to ours, but you know food, and drink, it's quite expensive.

Marvin: They say in Dublin and everything else as well.

D: You know, you go to Paris and you're talking 4 or 5 pound a pint. Go to London and it's three pound, three pound fifty …

Notable is how the participants entwine the experiences of people in Swansea and Britain with those in Ireland (and Dublin), Spain, France (and Paris), and 'Europe' generally. On the one hand people living in these 'comparables' are reported to be experiencing the same problems as those in the home environment; on the other hand people 'here' are held likely to encounter some of the problems (e.g. '50-year mortgages') already apparent elsewhere. A high level of detailed knowledge is on display, suggesting these comparisons come naturally to the participants.

Near the beginning of the extract one finds the notion that proximate places ought to be similar, at least as regards prices – 'it's cheaper in Ireland and that's only across the water'. This idea is found elsewhere. The groups do not always match one another in the comparisons they make: while Dean from the Swansea group downplays the cost of living in Britain, the Norwich participants suggest Britain is 'one of the most expensive places' because VAT rates are high. But even if they voice different opinions, they agree on the places relevant for drawing comparisons – other nearby European countries – and there is clear recognition that certain economic problems are common to people in all of them. Interestingly, comparisons with North America and other industrialised parts of the world are rare in this domain for all the groups. Occasionally the US is invoked as a contrast, as a symbol of the future and the extremes. But one does not find comparisons drawn with the US on day-to-day things like prices and wages.

The notion of there being *counterparts* in other European countries comes through at various instances in the text. Bill in Norwich, for instance, comments that 'if we've all got the euro, all of Europe including us, then everything's got to be the same prices, like your petrol abroad, your petrol here, your fags, blah blah. And I'm pretty sure, whatever government is in this country would never give up the revenue off cigarettes, beer and fags. So we'd be getting the same wages as our European counterparts but we'd be paying more, so our standard of living would go down yet again.' There are conditions 'here' and conditions 'there', for 'us' and for 'our counterparts', and it would be the intervention of the national government which would prevent their proper equalisation. Meanwhile in Reading, Malik and Derek compare the differing reactions of the British and French to the problem of rising prices. The sense is clear of an 'over here' and an 'over there' where people are faced with essentially the same difficulties, even if they respond to them differently: 'You watch though,' says Malik, 'over there, right, they're going to have riots. They don't have it. ... It's weird how most things, we just take it lying down over here. Like, the French, they won't. They'll have a revolution, get the guillotines out ...'. Derek chips in: 'Yeah ... Stop the boats, stop everything ... every single thing ... yeah ...'. Malik continues: 'But no matter what happens over here, you know, goes up another 5p, 10p, pound, "oh yeah, OK ..." Bit like sheep here in that sense aren't we, plod along ...'.

The assumption that there are comparable environments where the same kinds of problem are faced is quite clear, and with this transnational dimension introduced there seems to be some basis for a bond supportive of a European polity. That the range of comparisons tends to be less than coextensive with the current EU, with an east-west distinction within Europe highlighted to indicate places of fundamental contrast as well as comparable environments, represents a challenge to such a bond, a point Chapter 6 returns to. Such a bond would also be compromised if the passive overtones of this formulation of the 'we' were accompanied by a more general sense of fatalism regarding the possibility of addressing these problems (a question explored in the following chapter).

Collective positioning in *Society and the Law*

A) The political subjects and their opponents

In the domain of *Society and the Law*, the key problems emerge as crime, anti-social behaviour, increasing egoism, and a general decline in 'standards'. The common thread is the attention given to rules, and how they should be approached and maintained. In this domain, the subjects are best characterised as those who play by the rules and stand up for them. They are honest citizens. They are contrasted with those who break the rules (especially major rules), and in particular with those rule-breakers who are armed with excuses and do not have to face the consequences of their actions. They are also distinguished from those who are unaffected by such behaviour, or those who fail to enforce the rules properly, with the resultant unfairness a source of frustration.

One sees these patterns in discussion of crime (i.e. the breaking of legal rules), to which much attention was devoted amongst the British groups in particular. A phrase sometimes heard is that 'it's one rule for some and another rule for others.' 'We've had enough of general yobbery,' says Bill in Norwich, and responding to the perceived vagaries of criminal sentencing he makes a plea which is typical: 'you know, enforce all rules the same. Basically, we all abide by them don't we.' The subjects are the ones who are willing to take a stand, and who look out for each other: 'If he [Bill] ever called me,' says Malcolm, 'don't mind what time of morning it is, even if I have to put my daughter in a blanket, I'll come and help him. Because we need, as a society, to start standing up.' If the subjects themselves ever break a rule, it is likely to be an honest mistake and probably a minor rule, perhaps even a bad one. The subjects are those who expect – and were promised – a system of rules based on clear principles and fairly enforced. The subjects are perhaps passive and vulnerable, particularly since they may be unable to rely on the protection afforded by the institutions of law enforcement, because punishments may be light and barely served.

The opponents are, naturally, the offenders themselves. Emphasis is on the repeat offender, the criminal who, in Malcolm's words, is 'burgling houses over and over and over and over again': not someone who has simply made a mistake (anyone can make those), he is someone who involves himself in a new crime as soon as he walks free. He tends to have excuses on his side, like a 'hard upbringing', but his principal characteristic is that he never learns. As will be seen in the next chapter, one often finds the assumption that such behaviour can be corrected if caught at a young age with education. Opponents in this domain can be thought of as adversaries to the extent that they can be encouraged to mend their ways, but insofar as some will always be criminals and will need to be removed from society for the safety of the subjects, as enemies. 'Everyone's allowed to make a mistake, yeah,' says Malcolm, 'in with the wrong crowd blah blah blah, whatever excuse it is, they're allowed to make a mistake. Second time, "tut-tut, you should have learnt by now but go on, I'll give you one more chance, this time you're getting five years". And then, the next time, "three strikes, you're out, ten years, hard labour, no remission, nothing, you're being done for it, learn your lesson." Get them off drugs for ten years. You know, whatever.'[20]

---

[20]Those who 'do the crime' will have to 'do the time', as the English saying has it – a perspective which allows for the possibility that punishment may be followed by reintegration into society.

A similar pattern of positioning is evident when discussion focuses on the breaking of social rather than legal rules. The subjects are set up as the public-spirited people who play by the rules of proper behaviour, but also the ones who stand up for the rules. Their opponents are the transgressors, but also those who are indifferent towards the transgressors. Peter and Dieter in Kassel take the example of their colleagues on the taxi-rank who throw their cigarette butts out of the window, and who curse you if you tell them to pick them up; complicit in the problem are those who distance themselves and say 'that doesn't affect me!' Hans agrees, and argues that for that reason 'it's important that everyone's aware that it *does* affect them.' A passage from the Erfurt group, in which the social and the legal are entwined, gives a fuller flavour:

Axel: ... I was on the tram, there were two small children around seven or eight years old, it was around 3pm. They were making a lot of noise on the tram, like they do. There was a woman there and she got really worked up about it. And then her mobile phone went off and she had a conversation, but *so loudly* that the whole tram could follow. And she was the one complaining about two small children making a bit of noise. That's simply bad manners and you need to tell these people that. You need to open your mouth and tell them that either children are not allowed to make noise or they must leave off ... Each person ... everyone must start with themselves.

Harald: Sure, that's right. But also everyone's got to have enough education and intelligence so that they don't do certain things when they're not within their own four walls. In private they can do what they like.

Uli: It depends how old people are ... old people don't do that kind of thing.

A: I know of a guy, his mother was a teacher and his father was a professor, and what does he do all day long? He burps and belches.

U: Consideration for other people, that's what it's about really ... [H: yeah, definitely], whether it's mobile phones or someone burping ...

A: Or if I push to the front on the rank because colleagues are slow in moving up. [H: It's a whole load of things ...]

U: Consideration for others ... [H: yeah, yeah ...], whatever
           you're doing ... Or giving up your seat on the U-Bahn
           for a grandmother. [...]
H: It's no longer valued any more. It's a vulgarisation
           (*Verrohung*) of society, it can't carry on ... [A: That's
           it.]
Matthias: You see it with boys, the older ones, when they get in
           the cab, you get a twenty-year-old sometimes, he puts
           his feet straight up on the windscreen. That's just not
           right. I'm doing my work ...
H: The respect for other people's work isn't there any
           more. [M: No ...] There's no regard for other people,
           no regard for property ... [M: All gone ...] All gone. You
           sit on the tram and the person opposite has his feet on
           the seats ... [M: It's not right ...] It's really not right.
           [A: And what do you do?] Well, I tell him to take his
           feet down!
A: And there's too few people willing to do that. Too
           few. This goes back to the legal system. That case in
           Halle or wherever where the guy was killed, the guy
           who showed moral courage and asked whether the
           music could be turned down and then got knifed to
           death.[21] And what did the judge do with the defendant?
           [H: He freed him.] He freed him. And there, I mean, the
           judge himself needs to be put in ... [H: Put in court ...]
           put in court.

For all the participants, and clearly with some centrality, a series of
problems are evident here, linked by the notion of falling standards.
Hypocrisy, rudeness, inconsideration and indifference are all given
emphasis, as well as the insufficiency of protection from the law. It is
treated as beyond dispute that too many people are ignorant of the
rules of social conduct, that there are certain things one does not do
when outside the four walls of one's home. There is no determinism:
each individual has a responsibility to act properly, and even those
from the best backgrounds (child of the teacher and professor) can

---

[21] The case involved a man objecting to his neighbour playing loud Nazi music,
leading to an argument in which the former was fatally stabbed. The judge reached
his verdict on the defendant two days before this interview.

fail in this. Harald positions himself as one of the subjects, offended or irritated by the person on the tram who puts their feet up and willing to do something about it, and unlike the passive majority. There is even a word with which to capture the proper behaviour of the subject in this context: 'moral courage' (*Zivilcourage*). The positioning of the opponents seems to be more of the adversary- than the enemy-type. These people need to be shown the errors of their ways, they need to be reminded of what civilised behaviour entails, with the implication that they are not 'beyond hope' and that there is still the possibility of engaging them.

The criterion of playing-by-the-rules, whether legal or social, is liable to be deployed against immigrants and minorities. Luke in Swansea 'know[s] of a copper,[22] he says they're too scared to arrest the blacks, because the blacks will turn on them and say automatically "he's racial"'. Moreover, these minorities 'know it, they're making full use of that'. Amongst the German groups, 'East Europeans' and 'Turks' in particular are liable to be viewed as corrosive of the social and legal rules, as having excuses to protect themselves from the consequences of their behaviour, and their behaviour is to be assessed according to stricter standards. In a discussion about the criminal tendencies of those from Turkey, the Balkans and eastern Europe, Hamid in Lübeck (who describes himself as of Iranian origin) argues Germans have greater licence to break the rules because 'that's their homeland!' Jochen agrees that if he were living in a foreign country he would keep a low profile: 'I'd start with simple ambitions [*dann würd' ich erstmal ganz kleine Brötchen backen*].' Likewise, the criterion of playing-by-the-rules is applied in the Czech discussions to the Roma ('gypsies').

In the Czech and the Erfurt discussions there is a clear link made to the opponents in the *Economics* domain – the corrupt rich, the kind who are able to escape justice and are relaxing somewhere on a beach in the Bahamas. This ability to escape the consequences of behaviour is, in the Czech discussions, indivisible from the question of economic power. Miloš in Ostrava explains: 'Here the legal system supports those who steal 100 million – they've got lawyers who they go halves with, he pays the judge and everything, and they have 50 million for themselves, they lose 50 million but that's not going to hurt a businessman. That's the legal system. And if you steal 10,000, they lock you up. That's how it is here. Or at the minimum you get some kind of penalty

---

[22]'Copper': a policeman.

to pay. Someone small gets it, someone big doesn't.' The honest citizens break more minor rules, but are more likely to be punished.

B)   Comparable environments and counterparts

Quite in contrast to *Economics*, transnational comparisons for problems to do with *Society and the Law* are almost entirely absent. The problems of criminal behaviour take place on the streets of the city, perhaps under the gaze of a CCTV camera, and problems of rudeness and selfishness are described as taking place in trams, theatres, taxis, and on the pavement. Experiences are sometimes generalised as being symptomatic of conditions in the country as a whole, but hardly ever do participants raise the question of whether similar problems of crime and bad behaviour are found abroad. In some discussions the US is mentioned in this context, as the extreme of the broken-down society, where the streets are dangerous and where criminal sentencing is absurdly harsh. Such contrasts are presented as curiosities however, without any suggestion that it really matters what goes on in the US in this respect. Probably relevant to this is that – as explored in the next chapter – most of these problems are explained in terms of factors exclusively within the city or the home country, such as the mentalities of local actors. This seems to diminish the relevance of the experiences of those in other environments.[23]

Where speakers do draw a comparison, it is more likely to be cross-temporal than cross-spatial. The past, as the era of effective discipline and a clearer delineation between right and wrong, is invoked as a point of orientation. 'We used to get scrubbed and the cane at school,' says Malcolm in Norwich, to Bill's agreement. Les joins in the reminiscence: 'I used to get the bloomin' cane, knuckles and everything! I learned, I learned properly! I feel sorry for teachers today, I really do.' 'Years ago everyone was afraid of the local bobby [policeman], weren't they,' adds Gary. Likewise Sebastian in Kassel on the increasing reluctance of individuals to help one another: '40, 50 years ago, after the war, you always said 'we' and you helped each other. Now it's 'I'.' Of course, cross-temporal perspectives can be found regarding

---

[23]Corruption is the one problem generally not given a local emphasis (it takes place unseen, and away from the lives of ordinary people) and which sometimes provokes a few transnational comparisons. Perhaps this is understandable given it is a problem heavily entwined with the *Economics* domain, where as we have seen a transnational dimension is readily evoked.

problems of *Economics* too, but they tend to have the flavour more of contrasts than comparisons. That the past was quite different in economic terms is treated as normal (technology was less advanced then, economies were less developed, etc.), whereas what is more remarkable is that contemporary conditions in nearby countries should be different. For problems to do with *Society and the Law* on the other hand, that the past was different is treated as anomalous: conditions 'then' and 'now' are pretty much the same, and human nature cannot have changed. But that experiences should be different, or alike, in other countries is attributed barely any significance at all.

Collective positioning in *Relations between Peoples*

A) The political subjects and their opponents

Whereas the subjects were identified fairly easily for the two domains looked at so far, for the *Relations between Peoples* domain further interpretation is required. Perhaps given the open identification and judgement of peoples – which is central to most of the problems articulated in this domain – has come to carry a stigma in liberal democracies due to associations with racism, speakers generally do not make explicit their assumptions concerning with whom they see themselves as sharing problems.[24] Insofar as there is racism, it is 'euphemised' (Lamont 2000: Chapter 3).[25] Indulging however in some interpretation, one may say that the common-sense subjects for each of the countries studied are the national majority, often ascribed connotations of peacefulness and good sense, and implied as being white (though the subjects themselves are 'not racist'). Of course, not all participants would have included themselves in such a description (some were non-white); the argument is rather that this would be commonly recognised by the majority if not all participants as the dominant assumption to be engaged with, the background against which any expression of opinions and arguments takes place.

---

[24]Note this ambiguity may have consequences for the hostility displayed towards opponents, since the threat posed by 'them' may seem all the greater insofar as 'we' are amorphous.
[25]That issues of racial colour can be unspoken yet still powerful is one of the contentions of – and one of the great challenges facing – scholars in the field of 'critical whiteness studies': see e.g. (Dyer 2000).

A passage from the Swansea group takes us straight to the heart of matters:

Marvin: Like I said, I'm not racist against blacks, but I'm frightened of, you know, the Arab people, the fanatics, the ones who're living in this … the way they've been brought up as youngsters … to me they're a threat, like … the way they live and that …

Alan: What was that fella in Clyne Park, look how long it took to get him off the street, and he was slagging people off left, right and centre. Threatening he was going to kill us and everything, know what I mean?

Luke: They only got him off the street in the end because he was behind the terrors, and there's a big thing now …

A: But if you put your soap-box there and started gobbing off like that about Pakistanis and that, you'd be in and gone. […]

L: Careful what you're saying now, there's a Paki behind over there …

A: Bollocks. [pause]

L: Such a thing, you've got to say that … You know, in Swansea now, in a local pub, and you've got to watch what you're saying. Going back to that. Shouldn't have to. And you're scared. Scared … You know, you mention one wrong thing and you're going to be up in court.

M: You imagine how they feel, when they come over to this country, they must be frightened themselves. Got to be, haven't they.

L: Well why come over then?

M: Well, rather come over here than live out there.

Dean: Why do you feel that they feel threatened over here?

M: Well they're bound to, aren't they.

L: No I don't think so. I don't think so one little bit.

M: Because they know so many people are against them. And they do know it, don't they.

The problem is that of 'intimidation' by outsiders. Clearly this is a different problem from those found in the *Economics* domain (although Alan's reference to asylum-seekers might easily have taken the discussion towards a problematisation based on the 'burden' motif), and it differs from those found in *Society and the Law* in that the threat is perceived to be a group threat based on group difference, rather than an individual threat based on an individual's choosing to break the rules. The subjects which emerge in this passage are the 'white people' who feel 'intimidated' and who are being prevented from saying what they want to even in their local pub in their own city. ('It's as if we're becoming the minority,' says Alan later.) Note there is no debate about this: Martin, who expresses sympathy for 'them' and challenges the arguments of the others, does not contest the reference to intimidated whites; the clash of opinions takes place at a secondary level, on the question of whether 'they' also feel threatened and to what extent they have a right to feel threatened. The opponents are cast by Marvin as 'Arabs' or 'fanatics', and Alan (quickly followed by Luke) connects 'Pakistanis' to them. What links them is their tendency to threaten the 'people like us'. When, a little later, the group talks about the Iraq war, their discourse is remarkably similar: 'It's going to take years to clean it all up,' says Marvin, 'because as I say, at the end of the day they're fanatics from a very very young age and it's been drilled into them ... They've sat down in school and read books, "this is this, that, this world we live in is a load of shit, it's not the right world, we shouldn't be here ...".' 'They've been brainwashed haven't they,' continues Luke. 'You know, that they're going to a better place when they die, and they can't wait to die. And they're prepared to die.'

The discussion in Swansea was particularly explicit, but many of these discursive patterns occurred more widely. Across the interviews, 'Arabs' and 'Muslims' are cast for this domain of problems as the principal opponents of the subjects, with the latter understood along the lines of the peaceful and sensible white majority. These are opponents very clearly positioned as *enemies*. They present an existential threat, (note Marvin's comment that he is 'frightened' of them, and the multiple references to 'intimidation') and they are uncompromising. The religious element is often underlined. While 'Pakistanis' are mentioned briefly in the Swansea discussion, and 'Turks' occasionally in the German discussions, the category of 'Muslim' is much more common. They cover their faces and they do not speak 'our' language. As will be seen in the next chapter, the idea that mutual toleration is possible with such people tends to be rejected, and unlike for *Society and the Law*, there is general pessimism about the possibilities that education might hold: the differences are held to be essential.

A favourable interpretation would be that when speakers use terms such as 'Muslims' or 'Arabs' what they are positioning themselves against is not *all* Muslims/Arabs but only those especially 'fanatical' and uncompromising in their behaviour. If one could say that only the *extremes* amongst these categories are positioned as enemies then one could draw the conclusion that things are much as they should be: tolerance, after all, can be regarded not so much as a good in itself but as dependent for its value upon that which is to be tolerated, and speakers who express intolerance of the fanatical are perhaps simply speaking up for tolerance. Such an interpretation is hard to sustain however, since one sees little attempt to make distinctions of this kind: rarely for instance is there talk of a 'milder majority' of Muslims who might be engaged to combat the actions of a 'dangerous minority', and in the few cases where such distinction is made it tends to be to suggest that the majority is in league with the minority. Furthermore, the occasional direct references to race seem to run counter to the making of distinctions: they serve rather to emphasise the unity of the opponents. Here is Ulrich in Würzburg on the subject of relations with 'Arabs':

> They want to destroy the whole western world. Europe in many respects, but above all the arch-enemy the US. That's the ultimate arch-enemy for them, and ... I'm definitely very critical of these people. I mean, the Arab mentality, it's not everyone's cup of tea. It's just a rather different world from ours. It's the same in Britain or France. If I meet an Italian or a British person or a French person, that's my mentality, I've got no reservations with them, or an American, it's all basically the same for me ... [Ralf: yeah, yeah] But these people I do find completely different ... [Oskar: A different culture ...] Completely different. And ... I have the feeling that Germany is being more and more overrun, with all this scavenging going on at the moment. Everyone comes in and everyone tries to extract the most for themselves. Now there's simply no more left, it's like a huge winter sale here in Germany ... [R: Yeah, yeah ...] That's how it looks to me. Everyone just comes, especially from the east. From Britain no-one comes [R. chuckles], or from France, or Italy. But all these lot come here and want to suck the country dry until there's nothing left. That's how it looks to me. Little by little. So, I don't see ... I say to my son too, 'Son, Thomas, if you can, go abroad later. Because here it's going to get much worse.' I'm quite serious. I don't know how it's supposed to be sustainable. There'll be one great mishmash, each group with its culture and each wanting to install its religion. After a while you just don't understand it at all.

The group as a whole agrees that 'Arabs' (again, seemingly elided with Muslims, given the references to religion) represent 'a different culture', and Ulrich is by no means the only one to invoke the category 'the western world' to describe the subjects. Innocence and vulnerability are alluded to with the introduction of Ulrich's son Thomas; the Arab mentality, by contrast, is an aggressive one, bent on destruction. They have an intrinsic mentality constitutive of who they are. The way Ulrich speaks dismissively of an imminent 'mishmash' in Germany, characterised by a plurality of cultural and religious groups, suggests he understands 'the west' in its true form to be culturally and religiously homogeneous; a reference to race is conspicuously absent, although one feels it is not far away – race, one might say, is being euphemised as religion, culture and 'mentality', allowing the subjects to maintain the aura of reasonableness. What to make of Ulrich's reference to 'the East'? One interpretation is that half-way through this passage Ulrich begins to draw on the discursive resources of the *Economics* domain: note how his reference to those who 'try to extract the most for themselves' is reminiscent of the opponents of the subjects in that domain – those who take but who do not contribute – and note the explicitly economic metaphor of Germany as the site of 'a huge winter sale'. As will be seen in the next chapter, the motif of 'the cheaper East' is a common one for talking about problems in the *Economics* domain, and is therefore a natural digression from what is here the main act of demarcation based on culture, religion and race.

Individuals occasionally seek to counteract these dominant acts of positioning, a fact which deserves to be highlighted so as to weaken any determinist implications. Harald in Erfurt, for example, in a discussion of whether mosques should be allowed in the neighbourhood, is emphatic in his defence, despite persistent objection from Matthias: 'One has to tolerate another culture. It's a simple fact that they're there, you can't wish them away, and you can't do away with them using laws and regulations either. They're different cultures and anyone who wants to go to a mosque ... [M: But it can't be right that the state builds the mosque ...] On the contrary... [M: ... That can't be right ...] One has to tolerate it ... [M: Yes but ...] ... one has to tolerate it if they want to build up their own culture here.' Such expressions were rare however, and tended to be made by individuals alone.

As well as against 'Arabs' and 'Muslims', the subjects may be demarcated against the extremes within the ranks of the national majority. In the German discussions, for instance, it is underlined that the subjects have nothing to do with the events of the Third Reich, nor with today's skinheads, and nor do they wish to be associated with the excessively tolerant. The political subjects are the reasonable middle. In the words of Ulrich in Würzburg: 'it's a problem here in Germany with all the Muslims and stuff we have. They've simply come over here and now they want to enforce their culture exclusively and they're unwilling to toe the line at all. And the problem is that in Germany we tend to go in either for blind racism, with our skinheads who go around smashing everything up, or we have this complete deference towards foreigners, "our dear foreigners", this super-tolerance, which is equally bad. So I'd want to see things change a little – and I'm no racist [laughs], I simply don't understand it.'

Germany's past is a crucial element in the construction of the subjects in those discussions. It informs the notion that the subjects are barred from talking openly about the problems they face. One sees it at several moments in the Lübeck discussion. Hamid, recognised by all present as being of Iranian origin, at one point makes a strong statement which seems to make the others uncomfortable: 'But the Jews have the money! It's clear, the Jews have the money. Look, who's the head of Deutsche Bank? A Jew. All the power in the world, it's held by Jews ...'. On its own this is just a provocative utterance, but what is interesting is the reaction which follows, more indicative of collective assumptions: after a few silence-breaking chuckles, 'Hamid, you've got the advantage that you can say something like that!' says Jochen, referring to Hamid's 'foreigner' status. 'Yeah,' says Werner, 'just what I was going to say. We're not allowed to say such a thing.' Elsewhere in the discussion, Jochen talks of how 'many people' (it seems he knows a few) are dissatisfied with being associated with the acts of previous generations of Germans: 'Anyway, a lot of them aren't even alive any more, the ones who were involved in it back then. Hardly a person left. Subsequent generations should remember what a calamity it was, but that they're always labelled as scapegoats and that accusations are made again and again and so on, that's going too far for a lot of people. Because they say: "I had nothing to do with that. My great-grandfather, he lived it, but me ...".' Hamid makes a comment similar to his other one: 'even today the Germans have to live under that. Every year this whole stuff is wheeled out, again and again. Weeks are spent on it, and think of how much money flows from the whole thing. Every year ...'. After a pause, Jochen replies with: 'Hamid's opinion as a foreigner is sometimes noteworthy. A German's opinion on that couldn't be any better could it, or couldn't be any different.' (Niklas, it should be added, explicitly dissociates himself in both these episodes, saying whether or not he is 'entitled' to say such things, he has no wish to.)

In the Czech discussions, the delineation of the subjects is fairly weak, mainly because there is less discussion of such problems. At times one almost gets the impression the Czech participants are rejecting any sense of subjectivity in this domain. Michal in Plzeň, for example, says 'I think the Czech Republic is pretty uninteresting for terrorists,' and when responding to the 'Peace and War' card says 'that's something which doesn't affect the Czech Republic much, because no-one here really engages in that, we don't shoot each other across the table.' Notable in a passage from the Liberec group, aside from a repetition of this theme, is the way the presence of Czech soldiers in Iraq is treated as a rather ridiculous notion. As Zdeněk says, 'Our society is struggling to accustom itself to having professional soldiers.[26] We're not used to it. How many times do young boys get into the car and it turns out they're professional soldiers ... When I look at them I think 'Fuck, I can't believe my eyes!' Tomáš confirms that 'it's something which is beyond our borders.'

Despite this weaker sense of subjecthood, many of the same discursive patterns can be found in the Czech discussions as in the British and German ones. Muslims, despite their relatively minor presence in the Czech Republic, are treated as a particular source of difficulties. Zbyněk in Ostrava emphasises: 'Muslim is a different nature from Christian ... Shiites, Christians, they're all different. So therefore problems arise. There'll be problems here in a while like the problems around the world generally. Already they want to build a mosque, because a lot of them go to the spas. That's what they want. And they don't know how to compromise, Muslims ... that's the Muslim for you ... It's a different mentality, different upbringing, different everything.' Whereas the key idea to describe eastern Europeans, which we saw when looking at the *Economics* domain, is 'they don't know how to work and contribute', and one of the key criticisms made of certain other groups, as we saw when looking at *Society and the Law*, is that 'they don't know how to behave properly', here one of the key criticisms of Muslims – the main opponents in *Relations between Peoples* – is 'they don't know how to compromise'.

B)   Comparable environments and counterparts

The motifs used to denote opponents in this *Relations between Peoples* domain are not applied to *all* peoples mentioned, in particular not to

---

[26]The Czech army was fully professionalised in 2004 with the ending of compulsory military service.

those who seem to form part of 'the West' – for example, when participants talk about 'the French', 'the Italians', 'the Americans' etc. While these are sometimes described as having 'national characters', it tends not to be assumed so readily that these are fundamentally irreconcilable. As Ulrich from the Würzburg group says above, with the agreement of Ralf and Oskar: 'If I meet an Italian or a British person or a French person, that's my mentality, I've got no reservations with them, or an American, it's all basically the same for me.' Likewise, the possibility that disagreements amongst such peoples might lead to war is generally ruled out. As Ralf puts it, 'the only conflicts which are left are far away from us, and here in Central Europe, in Europe, in the EU area we have a very peaceful shared existence. I think that's very important, that's a historical step forward. Germany-Britain, the bombardment in the Second World War, this hard enmity is gone, gone once and for all.' War, says Pavel in Plzeň, 'is today a problem of the Third World. Africa, there are always wars of some kind there. In South America there's nothing. In North America of course not at all, nor in Europe.' Michal supports him: 'yeah, in the south they have wars with each other, they have civil wars.' When opponents are constructed within the West for problems in this domain – which is not often – they tend to be positioned at most as adversaries. Also, a distinction is more readily made in these cases between peoples and governments, with aggression sometimes ascribed only to the latter.

Instead, when other European countries are referred to, it tends to be as places of comparison rather than as actors. Unlike the *Society and the Law* domain, a broad range of comparisons is evoked with regard to problems in this domain: transnational ones are common, at least amongst the British and German groups. A white national majority is at least one of the features shared by the countries which the Swansea group describes as facing the same problem to do with 'invasion' – Australia, France, Germany, America, Finland and Switzerland. A similar passage from the Würzburg discussion draws in references to London, England or Britain, the Netherlands, France, the US, and 'the whole of Europe'. The concept of 'the west' or 'the western world' is widely deployed (cf. a passage from Ulrich above), and with its connotations of order and reason it plays a role similar to that which 'civilisation' would have played in an earlier historical period. But the religious element should not be eliminated, given how commonly it is deployed to heighten the sense of difference. Rather than seeking a meta-concept for these locations, it is perhaps best again to think in terms of a series of concepts sharing a family resemblance. The white-majority countries, the west, the Christian world and the peaceful world would be core concepts in this; the 'colonial powers' (mentioned only here) and 'liberal democracies' (mentioned nowhere) would be very much subsidiary ones.

One might think the experience of the Third Reich, whose *sui generis* nature is keenly appreciated in the German discussions, would render transnational comparisons difficult. A passage from Lübeck suggests it merely problematises them:

Werner: Whoever disputes the Holocaust and claims that ... that there was no annihilation of the Jews and the rest, then they're completely far-right, they're beyond credibility. Because we can't deny that, the Holocaust took place. But I think, in the meantime sixty years have passed in this country and there's far too much banging on about it today. In other countries where there've been similar problems (not to the same extent) it's handled quite differently. If I look at France for example, Le Pen, who's emerged as a right-wing, more or less right-wing radical figure ... In France it's never been the same problem as it's been here with the NPD or the Republicans ...

Jochen: Even to mention the past ... because of the past we have, it's particularly difficult for us to be far-right, or to develop in that direction. It's particularly difficult for us, that's certainly clear. [W: yeah]

Niklas: And it's important that one deals with that. And that one draws the lessons of it, and ... avoids that radicalism, that one should always keep what happened back then at the back of one's mind, and meditate on it ... how one discriminates ...

J: Because there's never been anything comparable to the Holocaust in history, you really can't compare it with France or Le Pen, it's a completely different level ...

W: I didn't want to compare them in that respect, I just wanted to point out that Le Pen, for example, he was against foreigners, against Moroccans and Algerians who've come to France, and ... that ... in France he was able to say it, but if we here in Germany say 'OK, we want to have fewer Turks here ...' or 'We want to have fewer Iranians,' or whatever, then immediately we're neo-Nazis. No politician would say that here.

Here one sees Niklas, not for the first time, intervening to disrupt a portrayal of the Germans as victims. Germany is held to be distinctive in the extent to which open criticism is tolerated, and Jochen and Werner subsequently affirm that the Holocaust cannot be compared; but Werner still maintains that France is comparable to the extent the French share the same problems associated with immigration as the Germans.

Amongst the Czech groups comparisons with experiences in other countries are much rarer. The home environment is considered a peaceful place where open conflict does not occur – as doubtless the British and Germans would agree, were it not for the arrival of immigrants from outside. Whilst the Czech groups certainly do not imply a strong boundary between eastern and western Europe in this domain (unlike in *Economics*), they do distinguish between big states and small states, and doubt is expressed as to whether certain problems experienced in the former can be expected in the latter. 'Why would there by terrorism in the Czech Republic?' asks Michal in Plzeň. The Czech presence in Iraq is acknowledged, but treated as trivial next to the deployments of Britain, France and the US, who thereby make themselves targets for terrorism.

Overview

This chapter has developed the concepts 'political subjects' 'opponents' (adversaries and enemies), 'counterparts' and 'comparable environments', and has used them as the basis for a reading of the source material designed to elaborate the second element of a political bond. Of interest in this regard has been the imaginary of interpersonal relations evoked in these discussions, the extent to which its hostilities are tempered, and the extent to which it bears elements transnational in scope. A recapitulation of the main acts of positioning found is in the table below.

It is a discursive repertoire rich and complex, but not unpatterned. To render it in the stark, uncompromising square boxes of a matrix inevitably risks conveying an exaggerated sense of uniformity and overtones of determinism. Once more one encounters an important tension: discursive practices are patterned, yet any attempt to express that pattern will inevitably be incomplete and procrustean, since speakers may sometimes diverge from it, and since new patterns are always being generated. Any basic notion of free will must allow that individuals may want to reject the 'we' that other participants construct (as we have seen some do, especially as regards *Relations between Peoples*), and that speakers may venture into discursive territory which is not rule-bound, where patterned ways of speaking are less apparent (as with problems to do with *Quality of Life*, to which Chapter 6 returns). One can furthermore expect that in the period since these interviews were conducted, these patterns will have somewhat evolved – the economic crisis emerging in 2008 has perhaps changed the customary evaluations made of economic conditions in certain countries, and thus perhaps the inclination to make comparison with them. While practices of cross-spatial comparison are likely to remain similar in form, their content may change with developments over time. The same point holds for the demarcation of opponents: times of crisis are likely to add new formulations to the already rich set discernible here.

It is also worth reminding that these interviews were conducted with interlocutors drawn from a restricted set of occupational, gender and racial backgrounds. As indicated in Chapter 2, too much social science proceeds from the strong assumption that biographical facts are determinative of people's interpretations of the world; while this study was structured differently for the reasons indicated, still one may acknowledge some of the variations which differently-composed groups might have produced. Individuals higher in the socio-economic scale may have a wider set of travel experiences abroad, perhaps prompting transnational comparisons on a wider set of issues. Those from ethnic minorities may be less inclined to construct 'peoples' than those from majorities, since they may be all too aware of the negative depictions and uncompromising attitudes this may lead to and more concerned to present themselves as individuals. Females may be less adversarial in their representations of the political world, as well as better placed to see distinctive problems ignored by males. Nevertheless, as an indication of prominent discursive features rather than an effort to render these comprehensively, an overview carries heuristic value.

Perhaps one of the key points which emerges from this study of collective positioning is the importance of taking seriously the oppositional dimension when conceptualising the collective bond. The problems of these three core domains are articulated not in detached or consensual terms but with a strong sense of 'we' and 'they'. In

	Economics	**Society and the Law**	**Relations between Peoples**
Political Subjects	Active formulation: the contributors, the working people. (More) passive formulation: normal/simple/ real/little people/ persons, without advantages; the people in the middle (esp. in GB groups).	Those who play by the rules, or who break only minor rules. Those who stand up for the rules.	The peaceful and sensible majority, generally with (white) racial connotations. *Variation*: these problems less discussed in CZ groups
Opponents	The oppressive – the rich, private companies, shareholders. The non-contributors: scroungers (GB), the corrupt (esp. CZ); 'cheaper' workers, esp. from eastern Europe. Status: adversaries rather than enemies, to be encouraged to contribute their share.	Criminals, anti-social egotists, incompetent/ soft judges and police; certain minority groups. *Variation*: different minority groups mentioned: mainly those of Turkish or Balkan origin in D groups; esp. Roma in CZ. Status: mixed. Adversaries if they can be educated, enemies to be imprisoned if not.	As enemies: uncompromising fanatics, often with religious difference emphasised. Esp. Muslims. As adversaries: the overly tolerant (inc. soft politicians); powerful peoples and governments within the West, esp. the US.
Comparable Environments and Counterparts	Nearby European countries of a similar level of economic development. *Variation*: for GB & D groups these are countries in western Europe; for CZ they are central-/eastern-European countries.	Virtually no transnational comparisons. Occasional comparisons drawn with the past.	Other western countries – states of Europe, US, Australia and others. *Variation*: amongst these, for CZ groups mainly other small states.

Summary of Collective Positioning
(Abbreviations: GB – Britain; D – Germany; CZ – Czech Rep.)

articulating a political common, participants construct and orient themselves towards certain social groupings while positioning others as hostile to these. There is no reason to suppose this is purely an artefact of the interview format – after all, it was *problems*, not people, that participants were encouraged to talk about, and it was generally to abstract issues rather than social groups that the topic cards made reference. And yet, as they discussed these matters of common concern, quite clear boundaries came to be marked out between those who shared in these problems as 'people like us' and those whose position on them was different, either generative of the problems or contributory in some way. The importance of conceptualising the collective bond such that one can accommodate this adversarialism seems clear – yet this adversarialism should be understood not as entailing a single, privileged Other, but a range of others varying according to the problem at hand (Lamont and Molnár 2002: 8).

Conversely, the difficulties attendant in conceptualising the collective bond either in terms of shared values or in terms of diffuse feelings of trust and solidarity across the citizen body also seem to emerge. Note for example the absence, almost total, of the invocation of 'Europeans' as a subject position. There is virtually no problem-area – with the possible exception of the marginalised problems of *Quality of Life*, to which we shall return – where it is assumed that 'we Europeans' hold a common perspective and are affected by problems alike. Unemployment, for example, is not treated as a problem for 'Europeans' in general, as an affliction which all share a common purpose in seeking to overcome, but as a problem for 'the little people' or 'the ordinary people', where these exist both in 'our country' and in other European countries, and where in both they are at the mercy of a range of economically more powerful actors. Problems of social atomisation and increasing egoism likewise are treated not as abstract and undiscriminating developments before which all are equal, but as hitting in particular those people who both 'play by the rules' and 'stick up for the rules'.

Of course, the prevalence of this kind of positioning does not imply that a broader sense of the common good is altogether missing: the calls are generally for 'fairness' and for a restoration of 'the middle', not for the absolute ascendancy of 'people like us'. This is important, insofar as non-universal forms of subjecthood always risk descending into parochialism and indifference towards the majority. But it is generally assumed that this pursuit of a better state of affairs would have to unfold in circumstances where a set of opponents are blocking the way, and with whom some form of conflictual encounter would be necessary. In the face of this tendency to adversarialism, those arguing for a more consensual *values*-based bond would perhaps have to argue that it is the discussion of political problems itself which opens up these divisions, and that they may be closed and consensus restored by shifting the focus elsewhere, to the values that bind or to practices of cooperation. Such a move is difficult though, since it would imply a diversion from one of the essential concerns of a political community, perhaps even the paramount one, which is the contemplation and amelioration of problems which have been articulated as public rather than private in nature. To overlook them would be to remove the 'political' from political community.

However, what also emerges in this chapter is that certain acts of collective positioning incompatible with a political community characterised by liberal tolerance are made with some degree of regularity, and with regard to one domain of public life in particular. When problems of *Relations between Peoples* are raised, there is frequent evocation of *enemies* – those whose very presence is treated as illegitimate. 'Muslims' represent the category most commonly thus invoked, though one can imagine that in other periods other terms would perform the same role – the specific referent of the positioning act is contingent.[27] With emphasis on the irrationality, aggression and intransigence of the other, there is a strong tendency to construct essential attributes which are unsusceptible to change and which do not permit the possibility of compromise.

At first glance this pattern seems to open up a significant line of critique against a political bond as a promising conceptual response to the question of the common. When proposed as an ideal in Chapter 1, it was contrasted not just with existing civic approaches to the collective bond but also with culturalist approaches, which it was suggested were liable to be exclusionary or repressive. Having noted that a significant body of problems invite acts of positioning likewise exclusionary and uncompromising, have not the same dangers one wanted to avoid reappeared, severely weakening the vision's appeal? The objection seems unconvincing. The crucial point is that, by speaking analytically of

---

[27]Lamont brings this point out clearly in her study of American and French working men: the racial and class boundaries drawn are quite different for the two groups, with the implication that 'nothing is inevitable' about how such boundaries are drawn (Lamont 2000: 6).

problems, one holds out the possibility of change, since different kinds of problematisation and ways of understanding these problems are possible, and indeed – as will be seen in the next chapter – a plurality of discursive motifs concerning their origins and nature are already in circulation. A problem-oriented perspective, speaking for instance of problems such as group conflict or the unwanted exposure to foreign cultural symbols, holds out the possibility that opposition is based on substantive disagreement, and that compromises are possible if those problems are addressed or redescribed. Thus the possibility of some form of political action, based on fostering an alternative and more appropriate set of discursive practices, is recognised and a critical stance can be maintained. If, by contrast, one takes a *cultural* bond as one's ideal, one is liable to accord too strong a degree of permanence and acceptability to the acts of positioning one finds, acquiescing in the assumption that they are constitutive of the we-people and that opponents are constitutively different. Normatively unattractive formulations for the 'people like us' become, from this perspective, much more difficult to shake off. The question of discursive change will be dealt with in more depth in Chapter 6, but it is as well to highlight the advantage of treating problems, not cultural markers or beliefs about such markers, as the reference-point for collective positioning.

Furthermore, problems to do with *Relations between Peoples* constitute only one aspect of the political common, and the acts of positioning they give rise to are but a subset of a wider set of discursive practices. These discussions indicate the importance of taking seriously the issue-context in which positioning occurs, for it varies from one domain to the next. That there is plurality of this kind has normative appeal, since it implies multiple possibilities for *inclusion* as well as exclusion. It prevents the emergence of one over-arching axis of conflict, a stark, Schmittian opposition based on a single category of 'us' and a single category of 'them', of the kind that might lead to the fragmentation of the political community. Instead, the construction of opponents is always specific to a particular set of problems, and there is always the possibility (the realisation of which is a practical matter) that those 'really-existing people' who come to be positioned as opponents by association with one criterion can be repositioned as 'people like us' through association with another. Those positioned as economic adversaries may be 'redeemed' as rule-abiding folk, and those positioned as opponents regarding the deployment of religious symbols may be repositioned as sharing the same predicaments in the domain of *Economics*. Such plurality inhibits the possibility of equating individuals with a single type of adversary. As generic categories, adversaries may be fought at a political level while individuals encountered in everyday life are regarded as more complex amalgams, and therefore as deserving civility. In this way a plurality of concerns and ways of speaking has the potential to bind together, in a web of overlapping conflicts, those who take up these discursive practices.

What then of the specifically transnational dimension? Comparisons extending to people and places beyond the home environment are a significant feature of these discussions.[28] The scope of comparison varies across domains. Whereas for problems to do with *Economics* they are drawn rather more narrowly than the contours of a European polity, and for problems of *Society and the Law* transnational comparisons are mainly absent, for problems to do with *Relations between Peoples* they extend considerably beyond the boundaries of any putative European polity to something one might describe as 'the West'. The inclination to make comparisons across a broader space is likely to be a function in part of how these problems are understood, and we shall see shortly how the patterns traced correlate with others to do with the explanation of problems. Related to this is the importance of how the opponents are cast: where they are seen as an assortment of local criminals there is scarcely any inclination to compare across a wider space, whereas where they are regarded as something like a transborder unity (e.g. 'Muslims', large private firms), the comparisons are made more readily.

Notice that there is little evidence to suggest comparisons are prevented by a claim to exclusivity, by the idea that 'our experiences' could not possibly be replicated elsewhere, either because 'our nation' is of special status or because its historical trajectory is too distinctive. The instance of German speakers drawing comparisons with France

---

[28]One of the few other studies to look at transnational social comparison likewise finds it to be a meaningful idea: (Delhey and Kohler 2006), in an investigation of levels of life satisfaction, report that upwards of 75% of survey respondents in the four territories studied (Turkey, Hungary, Western and Eastern Germany) were willing to make cross-national comparisons in addition to those with friends, neighbours and co-nationals when invited to assess their own standard of living. The findings are limited by the fact the possible range of comparators was set by the survey designers in advance (as Switzerland, Netherlands, Sweden, France, Poland, Spain, Italy, Hungary and Germany – countries exclusively European, in other words) and by the single dimension of comparison ('living conditions'). Nonetheless they support the general argument for taking transnational comparisons seriously.

on far-right extremists is an important case in point. Nor need one suppose that a major barrier is the fact counterparts will rarely be face-to-face groupings for the subjects. The idea of non-face-to-face groupings is a familiar one after all, not least following Benedict Anderson's famous conceptualisation of the nation as an 'imagined community' (B. Anderson 1991). Instead one may assume that if comparisons are not more frequent it is in significant part due to limits on the necessary knowledge resources. Comparisons seem most evident when they can be made on the basis of personal experience – the price of a beer or a house, the cost of a mortgage, or a personal encounter with relatives living abroad. The extent to which predicaments can be quantified is another important factor: it is the numerical issues, in *Economics* especially, which tend to provoke comparison. Such comparisons could easily be extended to income levels or taxation systems – but this is information less easily discerned through personal experience, and the knowledge resources would need to be made available. Such is one of the arguments for a transnational, median-income poverty line.

These points remind that how comparisons are drawn is something susceptible to contestation, for the comparator is never self-evident. Changes in the prevalent comparisons may be politically desirable, since comparisons reflect and help to sediment ideas of what is acceptable and what should be done differently. Drawing comparisons for problems of intergroup conflict with other countries in 'the West' serves to entrench the notion there might be a racial basis to them; failing to evoke others as comparable environments (Turkey, India or China, for instance) compounds this and encourages them to be seen as unitary actors. These points will be revisited in Chapter 6.

The variety of self-positionings one can observe in these discussions, some of them very localised and others evoking a much wider political space, combined with the merely sporadic appearance of explicitly territorial categories, suggest reasons for avoiding the traditional nation-state idiom, where the emphasis is on a single national 'identity' or a coherent hierarchy of nested identities (Wagner 1996). Merely adding a European 'level' to the scheme seems too neat, especially if to denote a higher-order, generalised sense of unity. Instead one has the possibility of something more complex, of a poly-dimensional political association in which different contests are played out in different domains, potentially with appeal to multiple sets of institution. If a European polity were to fit comfortably into this vision, it would require that a European context be invoked more frequently, and on more problems, than has generally been found in this chapter, where it has been noted the context is more often a local one, a semi-European one, or a broader-than-European one.

It would also require a conducive set of assumptions regarding the worth and plausibility of political projects. Organised collective address of the problems of the political common needs to 'make sense' if a European polity is to be validated in these terms. The mere identification of political adversaries and a concomitant sense of injustice can be of only limited political significance unless accompanied by narratives to do with how these adversarial relations arise and the extent to which they can be addressed. It is to these issues of the explanatory and agential context that the following chapter turns.

5
The Credibility of Political Projects

In a community one could properly call political, rather than a cultural community with political features or a thinly tied assembly of individuals, the noteworthy allegiances would be those inspired by the sense of shared predicament. We have explored this claim in terms of the allegiances of citizens to other citizens. A similar proposal can now be made on the related question of allegiances towards the institutions of the polity. Attachments to these institutions would depend on them and their demands making sense to people in problem-related terms, expressed in the appreciation that they provide significant opportunities for the pursuit of common purposes. This need not prompt the image of citizens devoted to the fulfilment of all goals by political means: nothing so grand is intended. But there would need to be some sense that political institutions can answer to at least some of the concerns of 'people like us'. This is what one wants to express by referring, as the third element of a political bond, to the credibility of *political projects*. Seeking to address common problems in an organised, collective fashion would need to be treated as a sensible and feasible proposition. If the sense of shared predicament in the face of common problems is what could bind citizens to their 'counterparts' further afield, it is a sense of the worth of a political project which could both augment this and couple it with allegiance to the institutions of the polity.

In this chapter these ideas are developed further by exploring two kinds of assumption in the empirical material: those to do with what is relevant for the explanation of problems, and those concerning the extent to which they are amenable to organised address. Both allow one to think more clearly about what it is for a political project to make sense to people. The kinds of explanation commonly given for problems are important because they express expectations concerning the parameters within which political agency can be effective. How problems are explained opens up certain possibilities for their remedy while closing down others. Furthermore, where there is a lack of explanatory resources altogether, this may have the consequence – even if the problems are taken seriously and the desire for change stated – that they are treated with a sense of fatalism that puts in doubt the worth of organised action (Gamson 1992: 6). By looking at the repertoire of explanations for problems to do with *Economics, Society and the Law* and *Relations between Peoples*, we can establish some general guiding principles regarding what kinds of political project will be received as appropriate. Then, by looking directly at the patterns of assumption concerning the possibilities for action, we may identify more specifically what tends to be expected in terms of organised address for each of the three domains. By the end of the chapter it should be clear at a theoretical level what may be meant by referring to the credibility of a political project, and more empirically what kinds of commonly-made assumptions one finds concerning politics as a problem-solving process. How Europe and the EU connect to these patterns will be the subject of Chapter 6.

Explanatory motifs and the possibilities for action

Perhaps one's first inclination when thinking about the concept of explanation is to treat it as a matter of reported causality.[1] Explanations in this perspective involve an account being given of the reasons for which a situation has arisen. By way of example, one can take the instance of a 'particularly hot summer'. Someone treating this as a problematic situation and wanting to account for it might supply a reason as follows: 'This has been a particularly hot summer because of the build-up of CO_2 emissions.' It is a straightforward example, and the element of reported causality is quite clear: it is the fact of a build-up of CO_2 emissions which is being treated as the cause of this summer's hotness. The statement acts neatly as a reply to a 'why' question. One could, if one wanted to, extend the analysis by considering the underlying idea

---

[1]The discussion here naturally excludes explanation as a puzzle in the philosophy of science. Further, within the field of lay explanation, it draws less on psychological approaches such as *attribution theory* and more on those emerging from ethnomethodology. A useful overview is (Antaki 1988).

or *warrant* (Toulmin 1958) that build-ups of CO_2 do generally cause hot summers, and indeed the possible reasons for maintaining that this is so (the *backing* for the warrant), for instance a newspaper article which describes consensus opinion amongst scientists as holding this to be true. This type of logical analysis of isolated statements has an attractive air of the methodical, and with carefully designed utterances it works well to highlight the cause-attributing aspect of explanation.

There is more to explanation, however, than the mere presence of reasons and reasons for accepting reasons. Issues of language usage and context are crucial. In the example above, the explanation is constituted at least in part by the assumption that this was indeed a particularly hot summer in need of explanation, with the consequence that it becomes important to explore what is commonly understood by the notion of a 'particularly hot summer', and likewise what one understands by 'build-up'. Definitions (conventions of usage, that is) are as much a part of explanations as reasons are. Furthermore, there is the assumption not just that build-ups of CO_2 emissions cause hot summers, but that this is the most *relevant* fact in play in this particular instance: as opposed e.g. to changes in wind patterns or solar activity, or as opposed – more disruptively – to the possibility that the problematic situation was in fact indoors, that it was a particularly hot summer due to a failure of the air-conditioning. Assumptions about relevance are critical. Thus a good portion of the explanation lies not so much at the surface level of the utterance in the explicit expression of reasons, but in the assumptions of appropriateness embedded in the utterance and in the way one reads it, where these are matters of social convention and discursive context (Draper 1988: 16). When looking not at contrived and idealised utterances such as the above, or those generated in a tightly-constrained experimental environment, but at spontaneous group discussion such as forms the research material here, one may have particular grounds for adopting a conception of explanation looser than that of reported causality. As we have seen, in the group environment points are often made jointly by more than one participant, based on multiple interventions, and ostensible contradictions even within the single intervention may appear as a consequence of the deployment of different types of discursive resource. To restrict oneself only to the identification of consistent reports of causality may be to exclude a large body of illuminating material.

Charles Antaki suggests that 'perhaps the safest thing is to take no strict line on what will count as an explanation beyond the very general principle that it be *some stretch of talk hearable as being a resolution of some problematic state of affairs'* (Antaki 1994: 4). While 'resolution' is rather strong, and one might prefer to speak of the *response* to a *problematisation*, the spirit of the suggestion is sound. The guiding notion of explanation in this chapter will be likewise a quite general one, oriented broadly to what one can call patterns of assumption concerning what is relevant to understanding. This is by no means to overlook the reason-giving aspect of explanation – reasons and their absence are an important part of what we shall examine – but one should avoid a strict emphasis on these alone. Faced with the contrapuntal rhythms of everyday conversation, the term 'explanatory motif' is probably more suitable than 'explanation'. Unlike the study of reason-giving in its ideal form, the examination of patterns of assumption is not a simple question of analysing what follows a 'because'. Assumptions are not flagged up by a clear set of syntactical markers, and it does not pay to focus too rigidly on the grammatical structure of utterances. As an interpreting actor, the analyst naturally does not put an equal emphasis on *all* assumptions identifiable in the text, but highlights some in particular as these correspond to the theoretical concerns of the research.

While in principle one can select *any* passage of text and usefully analyse it for explanatory motifs, those explored in this chapter have been chosen for their richness – that is, for the presence in concentrated form of motifs dispersed more widely through the material. Many such passages appeared quite naturally in conversation, as participants articulated and talked through the problems under discussion. Free-flowing conversation provided many opportunities to study reported causality, the ascription of characteristic traits to people and situations, the evocation of reference-points, and the usage of key concepts. In addition, during the interviews themselves, certain interventions from the researcher were designed to elicit assumptions concerning the facts relevant to the problems at hand. Some were quite direct, including questions such as 'how do you explain that problem?' or 'why does that problem arise?'; some were more indirect, exploring related issues such as the attribution of responsibility with questions such as 'who is to blame for this problem?' These questions are ambiguous on the criteria of what is relevant, and so – given no response can include *all* the possibly relevant factors – participants would have to discriminate between the relevant and the less so. This produced material fertile for analysis: one then studies whether, for instance, connections are drawn primarily to local factors centred on actors and mechanisms within the home environment, or whether they are made to broader processes assumed to play out at a transnational or global level. By examining the reference-points evoked, one is able to explore the spatial context in which the problems of each domain are assumed to unfold. Alternatively, one might find that such questions drew puzzlement or uncertainty in response, implying the unavailability of explanatory resources with which to handle the problems in question. On occasions one finds interesting instances of the *non*-attribution of responsibility, when it was conceded that an actor's conduct had led to a problematic state of affairs, but they were not blamed on the grounds that they had no choice.

Consideration of the repertoire of *explanatory motifs* acts as a prelude to looking at what *possibilities for action* are assumed to exist. That something *should* be done about the problems of the political common is implied in the urgency and sometimes indignation with which they are articulated. That something *can* be done is a separate issue. Problems affecting people like 'us' could be cited with a strong degree of involvement without this necessarily being matched by the sense they might feasibly be addressed.[2] As with explanatory motifs, one looks at the assumptions embedded in the flow of discussion, as well as at responses to direct interventions from the researcher designed to elicit the taken-for-granted. Probing questions included 'can that problem be avoided?', 'can anything be done about it?', and 'what kinds of action can be taken?' Where the possibility of action was affirmed, of interest then would be the agent deemed appropriate to leading it.

Chapter 6 will look specifically at how the EU is invoked in these discussions. Here we shall be making a preliminary set of distinctions concerning a) whether possibilities for action of any kind are recognised, and b) if so, which of three different approaches tends to be emphasised. A useful sensitising framework is Perrin's threefold distinction between expectations of agency centred on *government*, the general *public*, and the *private individual* (Perrin 2006). The first involves the expectation that government officials can adopt policies to tackle the problems in question, and may be judged according to their willingness and success in pursuing these. The second involves society-focused collective action such as the formation of social movements, the organising of boycotts, or the use of media to communicate to a wider public.

---

[2]One can of course imagine that, were such scepticism to be practised over a substantial period of time, it could lead to the normalisation of the problems involved to the point where they are treated as 'facts of life' and thereby deproblematised.

Both such approaches entail organised collective action, and offer a potential rationale for the polity as either the apparatus by which desired ends are sought or the space in which groups of citizens may coordinate for common purpose. Conversely, a *private* approach involves moves to *avoid* problems rather than a coordinated effort to resolve them: it is closer to Albert Hirschman's concept of 'exit' (Hirschman 1970). This last perspective, which supposes certain concerns can be addressed only by individual adaptation, offers few resources for making sense of a polity in terms of the pursuit of political projects intended to address common problems. The governmental method has a clear role to play, in that the expectation of purposeful governmental policies immediately suggests a longer-term project that enacts these. The public/societal method is of some relevance too, in that societal action suggests communication with those assumed to share in the problems in question, and thus may contribute further to the integrative acts of collective positioning that were looked at in the previous chapter. Thus when possibilities for action *are* emphasised in these texts we shall be alert to which of these three categories of action seems to best capture the kinds of proposal being made.

Economics

A)   Explanatory motifs

One of the first things to note about problems to do with *Economics* is that they sometimes elude explanation. They form a large proportion of the discussions and are discussed with considerable urgency, but there is often a sense of mystery concerning their origins. Particularly for problems with a numerical dimension, such as rising prices, a widespread lack of explanatory resources seems evident. The participants from the Swansea group are not untypical as they struggle to explain a rise in fuel prices, house prices and mortgages: 'Now how can they justify this in Britain,' asks Dean, 'not just in Swansea, in London or in other cities, the purchase of a house can go from, for example, from £50,000 to £200,000 in two years. It's ludicrous ... more debt, more stress, more everything ...'. The author took the opportunity to intervene with a question: 'Why are the prices going up so much do you think?' Dean again: 'Why has it gone up? ... I don't know, I can't answer that. Maybe cos five or ten years ago the cost of shares went up and everyone thought "oh this is a good bet, let's jump on it", and it all went back then and they all lost thousands of pounds. It's the same what happened with the properties. Whether it'll start coming down

I don't know. [...] But you know, everything's got to come to a head, hasn't it ...'. Dean's reference to shareholders adds a further element to the mystery, an extension of the pattern, but does little to make sense of it. All he has to guide him, it seems, is the very general notion that things 'come to a head', and perhaps that what goes up must come down. With similar uncertainty, when the Norwich group reports long-overdue improvements in the economy, these are accounted for on the grounds that luck inevitably changes. 'With life,' says Les, 'I mean, you know as well as I do, with life itself, where one door shuts ...' Bill anticipates: 'Another one will open.' Who does the opening and closing is unclear: the doors seem to swing on their hinges.[3]

Although explanatory motifs can be sparse for *Economics*, they are by no means absent. Importantly – the second point to note – where they appear they generally refer to processes broad and transnational in scope. They invoke a whole range of factors extending far beyond the home environment where the problems are met. Of course, local factors are not disregarded – there are certain themes which one sees with some frequency. We have already seen that a link may be made between a country's economic well-being and the willingness of people to contribute to the system, and that the problem of unemployment is explained at least partially in terms of the (un)willingness of individuals to devote themselves to finding a job. As Malik and Derek in Reading put it, 'there are those who won't work, and that don't work' – 'and who won't never work!' Excessive and wasteful bureaucracy, ill-judged regulations, and corruption (both in the private and public sectors) are further motifs which refer principally to factors centred in the home environment. What is interesting, however, is how these local aspects can be explicitly connected to factors much further afield. A passage from the Würzburg group displays this broader spatial

---

[3]Note that while Dean's intervention in Swansea acknowledges that an explanation for such problems may exist though he cannot give it himself (perhaps one of the 'they' mentioned can), the interventions of the Norwich group suggest not only that they themselves can offer no explanation, but that potentially no explanation exists because the sequence of events is arbitrary. While the first position need not produce the fatalist assertion that the mechanisms of change are beyond control – one can imagine the view that 'it's not our business to know, but someone in power ought to' – the second does seem likely to generate this. Either way, one may suppose that vagueness on the drivers of change undermines the capacity to identify modes of political action able to influence such mechanisms and the willingness to link these with public policy.

dimension clearly, with all participants emphasising the transnational when exploring the reasons for unemployment and the decline of industry, and citing a similar set of contrasting countries:

Ralf: I wanted to say something more on the subject of work, something which seems important and one hears a lot in this context: globalisation. Very much linked to unemployment because it's possible for companies to go abroad relatively easily and simply to say – which wasn't quite so easy before – 'we're going to the Czech Republic, we're going to Poland, the jobs are cheaper there, the labour in Romania etc. and ... we'll do our manufacturing in China, Taiwan, it's cheaper everywhere.' Globalisation's the keyword, I'd say, another of the causes of high unemployment ...

Ulrich: Yeah, and it'll get worse too. After a while, even among these cheap countries, the Czech Republic becomes too expensive again ... There are countries which do it even cheaper ... [R: ... Yeah ... India, or Russia ...] ... So one of these days a worker is going to be working all day long for a handful of peanuts ... The gap between rich and poor is getting bigger and bigger ... [R: mmm, mmm]. I often think that some day – unless new factors come into play, you never know what may happen – that some day you'll have the massively wealthy and the utterly destitute ... on one side of the city you'll have the rich all living together, and on the other side you'll have all the poor, passively going about their lives ... [Oskar: Like back in the Middle Ages ...] Yeah ... [O: Up in the castle ...] Up in the castle all the rich will be living ... [O: And down below ...] the plebs ...

R: Yeah, just like in the Middle Ages. Really sharply polarised, so that there's no middle layer any more. It's already going in that direction, it's already looming here now. Rich and poor are drifting further and further apart ...

O: And it's going to intensify too, because for example in China another 200 million people are waiting for jobs. The costs and the wages aren't going up yet because they still have 200 million people who want work. The wages aren't going up. In ten years ... who'll still be producing here then?

U: Right now in Germany we have this problem of wage dumping. With the lowest wage ...

R: These are splendid times for employers, it's clear, because they can really extort the employees. I mean, what's going on here in Würzburg with Siemens-VDO, you know ... [U: yeah], 'either you work longer hours and take home lower wages – wage dumping – or we go abroad', they want to go to the Czech Republic I think ... [U: yeah]. And that's the pattern with a lot of companies, isn't it. That they can say 'we're going abroad,' or to individuals: 'if you don't want it there are five others behind you, another ten at the job centre, they're all waiting to take over your job.' That's simply how it works today ... for the companies these are splendid times. The employers, the companies, they're rubbing their hands ... employees have never been so properly extorted here before.

The motif of the 'cheaper East' pervades the discussions in all countries.[4] As Peter in Kassel notes: 'VW, Mercedes ... every car company has gone abroad somewhere. And it carries on – now they've gone to Poland, then the wages in Poland become too expensive so they go to Lithuania. And further and further if there are people working for two euros ...'. The further east one goes, the cheaper the conditions become.

Sometimes one feels that these comments have an orientalising flavour and that the logic of the *Economics* domain is being mingled with that of *Relations between Peoples*. An association is sometimes made between the cheapness of price found in these relevant contrasts ('the cheap countries') and a cheapness of value. But while there is arguably an intersection of domains here, with multiple evaluatory logics being applied, it is worth highlighting how a more purely economic language can reassert itself. The Lübeck group, for instance, in a discussion of employment and working conditions, begin by talking of how immigrants from the east are willing to do:

Niklas: ... The jobs that the Germans don't want to do. [Werner & Jochen: yeah, yeah ...]

---

[4]Perhaps events since the time of interview (2005) will have encouraged new tendencies to look westwards as well – the role commonly ascribed in public discourse to failings in the US market for 'sub-prime mortgages' as a cause of subsequent financial upheaval clearly suggests the possibility. The important observation would remain the same: speakers assume developments in far-away parts of the world to be decisive for experiences faced closer to home.

Hamid: It's still the case – Germans don't want to do every kind of job. That's still the case ...

J: The Poles, for example, they work in the fields a lot, for farmers on the land. You hardly see a single German there, because they don't want to do it.

N: The work is too difficult ...

Just, however, as one thinks that the point is about to be made on the basis of intrinsic cultural differences, reasons of an economic kind come to the fore:

W: The work is too difficult and also, for the going rate here it's very badly paid. Compared to the Polish rate it's very good. There was a report on TV recently, about how job agencies – mainly over in the East, in Mecklenburg etc. – how they hire workers through a subcontractor in Poland because they'll work for 5 euros an hour, whereas here they'd have to pay a German worker 8 euros. So ... and 5 euros per hour is very, very little.

The Czech groups, though they are geographically to the east and are sometimes mentioned as such in the British and German discussions, are no different in deploying spatially wide explanations based on the motif of the 'cheaper East'. Tomáš in Liberec links unemployment to the movement of industry away from the area: 'all the jobs that there were under communism with the textile industry, the seamstresses, we had so many of them here and all kinds of businesses, they're no longer around, that's why there's unemployment. If someone trained as a seamstress and all that came to an end in the Czech Republic, clothing's imported from China and the seamstresses don't have any work here, then it's logical that she's going to be on benefits.' Developments taking place within the home environment (the Czech Republic, and the region therein) are presented as dependent on events outside in places of relevant contrast such as eastern Europe – which for the Czechs begins east of the Czech Republic and includes Belarus, Latvia and 'those places', as Michal in Plzeň puts it. They are also presented – more distinctively – as being strongly bound up with conditions in *western* Europe, with the German economy in particular highlighted.

B) Possibilities for action

This repertoire of explanations and explanatory motifs has important implications for the credibility of political agency. With economic affairs within the home environment treated either as a matter of puzzlement, or deemed heavily dependent on the outside world, the possibilities for action are assumed to be quite constrained. Although several participants suggest the government or state can encourage individuals to adapt to the situation by giving them the appropriate incentives to 'get off their arse' (Luke's term) and to follow the job vacancies – a mixture of *governmental* and *private* means by which to react to problems – very few positive proposals for organised action emerge in the course of the discussions (in contrast to at least one of the other domains). The fact that many of the explanatory factors extend beyond the home environment is something that most likely accentuates this. Generally speaking, only where explanations contain at least some more local elements are they accompanied by proposals for action.

A weak sense of governmental agency is widely expressed on the question of industrial decline and unemployment. Several of the British groups point out that, while the country still has coal mines with coal in them and while in theory these could be reactivated, in practice this is unworkable because imported coal will always be cheaper. As Derek in Reading says, 'Wales and Yorkshire, still full of coal-mines, I mean, the coal's still down there ... [Malik: But I think it's cheaper ...] ... cheaper ... [M: ... to come from Poland ...] It's cheaper, yeah ... [M: It's what you just said, it's cheaper to bring the coal, import it from Poland, than to have guys digging it in this country ...] That's right.' 'That's how it is with manufacturing as well,' says Malik. 'All the little kids wanted to be coal miners. But coal mining died. They can't say "I still want to be a coal ..." No, you got to go and find something else.' For Alan in Swansea, 'a lot of it is out of this government's control. Like HSBC, the bank, they took all their call-centres to India. [...] Because it's cheaper to employ them over there and set up a new call-centre than keep them over here.'

Similar scepticism about what politicians can achieve in response to economic problems comes through strongly in an extract from the Würzburg group. Ralf refers to the 'job summit' between Chancellor Schröder and CDU leader Angela Merkel, which had taken place a few weeks before the interview, in which the heads of the two major political parties met in an attempt to find solutions to the unemployment crisis:

R: There was this attempt recently with the summit a few weeks ago, where the government met with the opposition to try and regulate ... to intervene, so that corporate taxes – which are already low – are lowered even further to encourage companies to invest more and so create more jobs.

Oskar: Yeah, well the pressure comes from outside, because neighbouring countries like Austria, they've already got a tax-rate of 19% ... the Netherlands is lower too ... In Bavaria the problem at the moment is that companies are moving abroad because corporate tax in Austria is lower than in Germany. 19% compared to 25%. So we have to trail behind and ultimately at some point it'll probably all level out across Europe ... the prices, the taxes ... [R: Mmmm, mmmm] and so on. There's this slow process whereby it all levels out ...

R: Yes ... but ... to come back for a minute, the taxes are lowered – the corporate taxes – and what happens then? The companies accept it all gratefully and skim off the tax benefits, but they don't create any new jobs. [U: yeah] That's how it's probably going to go ...

Ulrich: It's about nothing but profits. And if they can make more profit then they will. So I just think, in these big companies, with all the shareholders and bosses, it's just about creaming off more and more, as always. [...]

O: It all hinges on the global market and shareholder value ... [U: yeah]. Whether it's Deutsche Bank or Daimler Chrysler. They have to measure themselves against Toyota or Citibank. It's global competition, and if they become too weak or if their investment returns are too low then they get a slap on the head from their shareholders who say 'Toyota's got 100 billion, Daimler Chrysler's only got 20 billion,' or whatever, 'you need to put the pedal down, because otherwise ...'

Oskar's interventions explicitly emphasise the influence of outside factors on decision-making – 'the pressure comes from outside', and the competition is 'global'. Governmental decisions (e.g. the lowering of corporate taxes) do have consequences, but the emphasis is on their negative consequences (the loss of revenue without the creation of jobs), and those with the real decision-making power are assumed to be the companies. Subsequently, the group reaches a consensus on an assessment made by Oskar that politicians are just 'puppets' when it comes to the economy.

Another motif is that while yesterday's politicians might have had the opportunity to prevent these problems, for example by choosing not to privatise industries, today's politicians are powerless and it is *too late* to alter the situation. The Kassel group emphasises that the government is unable to control the movement of companies: 'That doesn't work any more,' says Peter, 'it's simply too late ...', says Hans, 'in the past ... in the past ...', chips in Dieter, 'we've got no chance now. The train has left the station.' In the wake of technological change, unemployment is here to stay. 'The car companies began it,' says Peter. 'Along came a new machine and it replaced 10 workers, then along came the next one and it replaced 100 workers. [...] So, now we have a minimum of 6 million people, probably 7 million ... we'll never get unemployment back down again. [...] Our economic development no longer allows us to employ so many people.'

Inevitability is one of the dominant motifs of the *Economics* domain, unsurprisingly given the thinness of explanatory resources one sees. Emblematic is the supposed inevitability of price rises. As Derek in Reading says, 'It's a never-ending thing, innit ... the petrol goes up, everything goes up ... no matter whether you think you're bread and butter don't, it do ...' 'Everything goes up,' confirms Saeed. State debt, spoken of as another major constraint on a government's ability to pursue policies favourable to social security, is talked about in similar terms of inevitability. Notice how spatially wide explanations for problems can feed into scepticism about the possibilities for action: in this passage from the Kassel discussion, it is explicitly pointed out that while state debt is a surmountable problem when national economies are fairly independent, in today's world they are entwined, and so the traditional options for managing the problem are unavailable:

H: It's traditionally been the case here in Germany that the state intervenes a great deal. And now what's happening is that this state involvement is being reversed quite sharply ... [D: yeah]. That means that the social safety-net gets bigger and bigger holes in it. In other words, more and more people are now falling through the net and getting into circumstances which are very painful for most of them.

P: Fine, but then you get back to the point that the state is taking in less and less and so it's able to give out less and less. [...] I mean, ultimately what this comes down to – and we haven't said a word about this yet – ultimately it's about our debts, our state debts. [H: That's a very interesting dimension, definitely, because ...] Our state debts increase every day, we need to pay more and more interest on them, the state has less and less of what it takes in at its disposal, and at some point ... I mean, the balance ... We've been building up debts since Adenauer was Chancellor, since back then, despite the fact that our pension funds are being emptied by them ... [D: Kohl ... by Mr. Kohl ...] And basically, no matter what we're talking about here, it boils down to these state debts. And as long as they're still there, until we've got rid of them, we can't really make demands of the state. Whatever amount goes into these debts, that's how much less we get back.

H: So the question then is, why are the debts so ...

P: Because the state ... because the state supported everything ...

H: Not just that but because it also didn't pay enough attention to making sure that money comes up from below again. Because ...

P: A normal company would have gone bankrupt decades ago, but not the state. I really don't see ... I can't see where they get the money from. Where does the money come from? Even the rich oil countries are supposed to be in debt. Where does the money come from? [H: Imaginary, as they say ...] I mean, every day we have less and less ... the state has less and less at its disposal ... [...] And everyone who gets voted into government says 'yes, we want to remove the debts.' That goes on for a year and then next year they're twice as high ... [D: Exactly] That's ... at some point there's going to be a collapse.

H: It's going to happen sometime. It can't carry on.

P: Yeah, and then what happens? Currency reform. Very simple: currency reform. [...]

H: And that's exactly the point, today it's no longer so easy to bring about currency reform. That doesn't work any more, because this interlocking, this international interdependence is far too extensive to allow such a thing.

The sense of powerlessness here, born of the presumption of the state's financial constraints, is linked to the feeling of mysteriousness – what is it that keeps the state afloat, where does the money come from? The idea that most things cost too much for the public purse, and the absence of positive proposals for changing this – e.g. raising the top rate of taxation – is characteristic of discussions across the country groups. Amongst the Czechs in particular, it is regularly emphasised that the state has little money at its disposal and so its ability to act strongly is limited. As Zbyněk in Ostrava says: 'The public purse doesn't have enough in it to give money out. Infrastructure is inadequate for a good transport system. We've got so few motorways, really slow railways, and air transport is inappropriate for a small country. There's never enough money there, it'd gobble up everything.' That state debt is not quite analogous to private debt, and may permit greater scope for choice between competing options, is something that speakers overlook or ignore.

There are added reasons for pessimism about the possibilities for governmental action voiced amongst the Czech and Erfurt groups. One of these is the sense of dependency on the economies of western Europe, as highlighted in the Liberec passage above. Uli in Erfurt expresses this perspective: instead of casting the home environment as Germany as a whole, he casts it as the former East, and highlights its dependence on the West: 'in the East we're practically dependent on the development aid of the state. We're not lifting out of it though by way of capitalism, because that's messed up our whole economy. So we'll forever be dependent on the development aid of the state until the economy at some point recovers – but that'll last forever.' A second basis for these groups for a low sense of agency in *Economics*, different to the other German and British groups, is the inclination to see the state as blighted by corruption and incompetence. Public officials are accorded little trust when handling large amounts of money, and so their interventions in the economy are generally regarded with suspicion. Miloš in Ostrava tells a story, familiar to all in the group, of how an Israeli firm charged with constructing a stretch of motorway was given a contract so generous that the state lost huge sums of money. The error is presented as typical of financial incompetence, and is seen as compounding the fact that government policies are already constrained by weak finances.

Positive proposals, other than individuals 'getting off their arse', are not entirely absent. Participants in the Kassel and Erfurt groups are both very much in favour of the idea that any firm leaving Germany has to repay whatever subsidies it has received. Harald in Erfurt suggests how one should treat such firms: 'if someone has a need to enlarge his company and thinks he has a better chance abroad then he should go – but without a cent from here. That's how it should work, and not how it works now, with threats like "if you don't want us then we're off." If I was Chancellor I'd say, fine, let's have a tête-à-tête then, bring me your passport, we'll put a stamp in it here: "Not wanted in Germany – go!"' Similarly, Bill in Norwich argues that 'if you move your business lock, stock and barrel then as far as I'm concerned you're gone. You shouldn't import them things back over here, you should ban it. Don't let them sell it on our market.' Some speakers, pointing more to a *public-cum-private* approach, recommend that consumers exercise discrimination in their purchasing – Malcolm finds general agreement on this point: 'You go to Comet,[5] right. Now, what happens is, when a new product comes out, like a DVD player ... I paid £185 for my DVD player three years ago: now you can get them for thirty quid. But you could always get them for thirty quid! They make the money ... they overprice them because everybody wants something that's brand-new. If people would stop being so bloody stupid – me included – would stop being so stupid and turn around and say "hang on a second, we're not going to be fooled into any of your marketing crap any more," we'd have them for thirty quid'. [Les: But people won't do it, will they. [Bill: They've got to have one first, haven't they.]

To the extent this is a problem of consumer ignorance, the possibility is maintained that something can be done about it. Advertisers are blamed for encouraging people to take on debts they cannot manage, with Peter in Kassel characterising the madness like this: 'Everywhere it's being suggested to us: "You need this, you need that, you need the newest computer, you need the newest bedroom, you need the newest kitchen, this oven's got air circulation, it's not just a grill, you can stick your head inside and use it as a sunbed!"' Compulsory schooling in basic day-to-day economics is therefore put forward as a worthwhile policy, to prepare people to 'think twice' before they buy. However, to the extent that the problem is not just to do with the mentality of actors within the home environment (consumers) but is to do with economic processes extending further afield, the possibilities for action are constrained again. Furthermore, organised action of a *public* kind such as a collective boycott is sometimes cast in doubt with an expression of scepticism regarding the willingness of others

---

[5]An electronics retailer.

to show firmness. Even if people like 'us' were to take the lead, the rest would probably not follow.

Having expressed considerable doubts about what can be achieved collectively, either through governmental action or society-led approaches, it is perhaps no surprise that Les and Bill arrive at arguably the least agential of possible remedies to their economic problems: the luck of the lottery. 'If I had a £5000 cheque fall on my back every so often, I'd be bloody over the moon,' says Les. Their notion of the possibilities for action is limited to making alterations to the probability that one pulls out a winning ticket. 'What annoys me with the lottery,' says Les, 'it was made for the working class, why do we have to keep bunging money for all these bloody 'good causes'? The good cause is the people who are bloody playing the game!' There is a tragic note, given the willingness to adopt a collective category of subjecthood, in their calls to limit the size of the largest prizes and charity donations, and to 'give more to the lower numbers'.

Society and the law

A) Explanatory motifs

For problems to do with *Society and the Law*, explanations are found more easily – there is less of the uncertainty that encircles those of *Economics*. Just as we saw in Chapter 4 that transnational comparisons are rarely made in this domain, so one finds that most explanatory motifs focus on actors within the home environment, i.e. mainly within the city itself. To the extent that wider factors are invoked, these may be connected to the country as a whole, but tend not to be connected to the world outside, and explanations hardly ever include places of contrast abroad. The sense of political space is, in this sense, much narrower. Problems such as crime and society's response to it are generally not placed in a transnational context.

One might instinctively respond: how could this be otherwise? Are not the problématiques in question – crime, anti-social behaviour, the decline of the family – *essentially local* in nature? Yet one should be sceptical of the notion that there are essentially local problématiques, and one can quite plausibly think of broader explanatory ideas not used. The decline of religion would be one (a natural one given the countries studied), and it would be entirely feasible in principle for a discussion to frame law-breaking, antisocial behaviour and the lack of community feeling as being due to the fact that 'no-one fears God any more'. Such a perspective would then enable the problems articulated to be treated as consequences of transnational processes of modern-isation experienced in many human societies – a perspective implying a much wider sense of space. But this is not found. Nor does one find discussion of technological change and its implications for the atom-isation of society or the decline of the family, another potentially wide-ranging, transnational perspective. Instead the focus is narrower. The exceptions are the links made between immigration and an increase in criminal behaviour, and the borrowing of explanatory motifs from the *Economics* domain, especially amongst the Czech and Erfurt groups. Both of these open out a wider sense of space, albeit largely by associ-ation with the logic of other domains.

Considered crucial across the groups for people's willingness to abide by the legal and social rules is the way they were brought up as chil-dren. A bad upbringing, both in the family and in school, is the main explanation given for irresponsible behaviour. Tomáš in Liberec com-plains of the inadequacy of the school curriculum in preparing children to live harmoniously in society: 'The curricula in schools are badly designed because education – moral education, how people should behave in society – is something they really don't teach at all in schools. That's a problem. They're always having to read articles or whatever, but how reality works, how the laws function, they just don't take that into consideration at all ... [Radoslav: How life works ...] They don't prepare children for that at all. They have to learn that for themselves later, and either they end up on the right side of the line, they achieve something and they're intelligent, or they end up on the wrong side and they're just rogues.' Likewise, those who *have* been taught well at school 'know the difference between right and wrong', argues Malcolm in Norwich. Problems set in when both the household and the school experience a decline in disciplinary standards. Dieter in Kassel empha-sises the importance of upbringing and role models when talking about the development of 'moral ideas': 'it's a matter of education, of the personal development of the child. There needs to be proper guidance there, from the school or the parents.'

The importance of upbringing is affirmed by Harald in Erfurt in a similar fashion – 'here's where life begins, if you like: in the kinder-garten' – but with a twist corresponding to the changes experienced there since the fall of communism: 'You can still notice the difference today between people who grew up here in the East and people who grew up in the West. Let's take the same age-group, that's probably the best way to compare. Here you got an all-round education at school, and you took an interest in things yourself because various things were forbidden. Because whatever was forbidden, that was something you had to know about. "Why is it that here I'm not allowed ...? What's different over there ...? How's it going to hurt me if I go over there?" OK, and in the other education system, in the western one, it was more "This is what you need to know for your life and that's it, no more." Because whatever goes beyond your knowledge, well there's some other person who knows it. You don't need to look beyond the edge of your plate.' Uli agrees: 'They bred nerds, one-track specialists.' Education is seen as defining people's horizons and their morality.[6] For Harald, what is important for the enforcement of rules is not so much institutions and structures themselves as the morality of the people within them. One might regard this as an assertion of the moral/social over the legal: 'I always say, with all the things that are on the cards here, at the end of the day it's always a person who does it or causes it, it's a person, not some law. If that person says "I don't want to," then he's decided it. He's given the option to do it or not to do it, he always has that. ... And so it all goes back to education, to the kind of morality which is given to individual people. That's where it all really begins.'

Besides these influences on the willingness to follow the rules, the conduct of those charged with *enforcing* the rules is another key explanation given for problems in this domain. Problems arise insofar as they fail in their duties. Magistrates and the police – particularly amongst the British groups – tend to face criticism. They are regularly described as being fussy, immature and having the wrong priorities. Malcolm in Norwich speaks fondly of the days when a policeman would just have said '"oi, cut that out", slap across the head, end of story'. Derek at Reading, that night he found a burglar in his house (Chapter 3), found the police too casual, and they were 'over-powered with paperwork'. Malik, from the same group, supports Derek's narrative, and later augments it with a different perspective based on a television programme he has been watching called *The Secret Policeman*. Asked to describe it, he explains 'it's just about the treatment of ... like for example, like the

---

[6]Also from the same group: 'In GDR-times people were more sophisticated in the head than they are today,' says Axel, 'because today it's only consumption which counts – everyone with his chair, his table, his bed, his TV, which has always got to be better and better. Whereas before, this community ... the public-spirited way of thinking, it was all a little bit different.' Uli picks this up: 'The people from the old West Germany, they have a horizon that extends up to the garden fence. "My little world, nice high fence and whatever's outside I don't care about."'

police, right, one of the things – just showing their racist side, basically, you know ... They would, say, stop 50 Asian guys and black guys, and then, right, they'd have to stop a couple of white guys and say "alright, I'll let you off John, let you off Paul", just for the stats, you know. So "no, no, it's not all Mohammed, Mohammed, Mohammed and Winston, we've got John here, and we've got Peter and Paul here ...".'

The conduct of those who enforce the rules is highlighted amongst the Czech groups with added dimensions – notably the significance of mentalities inherited specifically from the communist period, and the financial weakness of the state. The motif of the corruptness of the older generation, morally tarnished by its association with communism, is a recurrent one (and one that can exist in parallel with ideas about the greater public-spiritedness of people under communism). In Liberec, Zdeněk and Tomáš agree that one of the reasons why the police are considered heavily susceptible to corruption is that they were brought up to have a 'completely different attitude', in conditions where different behaviour was normalised, and that there is a need to wait 'until that generation dies out'. The assumption of corrupt values is made of officials in all forms of public office, including the judiciary, the police and the law-makers. Weak state finances compound the problem by lowering rates of pay and increasing the temptations of corruption.

The explanatory motifs traced so far assert the relevance of factors domestic or local. Very occasionally, a transnational dimension is also raised. The notion of a declining 'threshold' as regards willingness to engage in criminal activity is associated by both the Lübeck and the Würzburg groups with the arrival of immigrants from outside the home environment. The principal places of contrast here seem to be eastern Europe and the Balkans.[7] Explanations based on *economic* factors are particularly in evidence amongst the Czech and Erfurt groups. As suggested in Chapter 4, in the discussions of these groups in particular, elements to do with *Economics* and *Society and the Law* are entwined. When explanations for social and legal problems are given an economic dimension (the inability of the poor to get access to good-quality education in schools; the decline of standards in the household due to the precarious economic circumstances of parents, and the decline of

---

[7]Places which have arguably long occupied an ambiguous status in the western imagination as a kind of 'Other within': for one treatment of this theme, see (Todorova 2009).

standards in schools due to the emigration of teachers) this opens out a wider sense of space through association with the *Economics* domain. Otherwise, however, the explanations remain local. Insofar as the Czechs habitually associate criminal behaviour with minorities, it is with the 'gypsies' (not, for example, with the Vietnamese, one of the country's largest minorities), and the gypsies are treated generally as a domestic problem – they are not recent arrivals from the outside world, and cannot be connected with a particular sponsoring state. To point to them is again to rely on a 'domestic' explanation for crime.

B) Possibilities for action

As noted in Chapter 3, the notion that something *should* be done about the problems of this domain is clearly expressed. A sense of injustice is strongly evident when the British groups talk about vulnerability to crime and the lack of adequate protection, when the German groups discuss various forms of antisocial behaviour and the weakness of the public's response, and when the Czech groups talk about institutional corruption. The sense that something *could* be done varies somewhat, but is generally more pronounced than for *Economics*. One sees calls both for government-led approaches and for initiatives originating from 'society' as a whole. All of these possibilities for action are connected to national or subnational actors, consistent with the fact that explanations tend to be limited to factors within the home environment. Indeed, and significantly, it may be that there is a stronger sense of agency here than in the *Economics* domain precisely because the sense of space is rather narrower.

One of the reasons it is stronger relates to the emphasis placed on upbringing. To the extent that misbehaviour is associated with the distorted values and attitudes of individuals, better education – whether at school or in the home – presents itself as a convincing remedy. Axel in Erfurt argues that 'certainly more money and time need to be devoted to the future of children', and children should be encouraged 'to develop their own opinions and to know roughly what's right and what's wrong.' Matthias makes an allusion to an event three years earlier when a pupil from the local Gutenberg High School went on the rampage, killing seventeen people: 'the connection (*Zusammenhalt*) between the parental home and school teachers, it's no longer there like it used to be. I can still remember when I was at school, my schoolmistress and my father used to meet at least once a week [laughs from the others] ... No but really, if it was still like that today then what happened at the Gutenberg *Gymnasium* would definitely never have happened.' Harald adds his agreement. The British groups talk a great deal about 'nipping bad behaviour in the bud'. If people can be caught 'from the word go', then it seems there is a real chance of bringing them up as honest citizens. It is, one may say, an assertion of the importance of civic education, and it persists despite the scepticism of certain state institutions such as the police.

Education, while emphasised across the groups, is treated as a long-term approach, and changing the behaviour of adults is viewed as more difficult. Especially for those groups which consider crime a major problem, education needs supplementing in the short-term with better enforcement of the rules. The potential of punitive action to tackle crime is a second *government*-led way in which agency is affirmed. It is true that there is much ambivalence expressed regarding the organs of the law such as the police and magistrates. The participants in Swansea are keen to describe themselves as 'always the target' for the police, and we have seen Malik in Reading reading a television programme as informing him about 'the police's racist side'. But a degree of reflex cynicism – or healthy scepticism – coexists with plenty of calls for action. Stronger sentencing is an obvious one: a principle of enforcing the rules harshly on 'true criminals' and gently on those who have been caught out for a minor thing also seems to have an instinctive and widespread appeal. Worth highlighting is that these calls for stronger law enforcement are sometimes set in the context of the national political system. A political party is needed which is willing to 'enforce all the rules the same'. Note Malcolm's use of the word 'promise' here, and his reference to his own political involvement:

M: We were promised three strikes and you're out, weren't we. And that was one of the reasons that I've voted for this government, yeah, we were promised three strikes and you're out, and I think the reason why we've all picked on this subject is because at the end of the day it is the most important subject. We would pay more of that [Taxation] to get better that [Legal System]. [B: Definitely.]

L: We would yeah, that's right. I mean, who's worrying about paying more of this [Taxation] when everything else comes into play? D'ya know what I mean? And this is where the Liberals score, don't they. Because their policies, what they're coming out with now, is what people are going to be thinking about. The Conservatives, I mean, they're not that bad but at the end of the day who's going to produce the most for everybody's safety?

The expectation that something *should* and *can* be done is evident in the tone of disappointment and the willingness to see higher taxation, as all three participants affirm. Les's reference to British political parties is hard to read – the Liberal Democrats do not traditionally score well on law-and-order issues as he suggests, but the reference could be to their position on taxation. Either way, his last sentence conveys a sense of expectation: the ability to guarantee safety on the streets is one of the key criteria for assessing the worth of politicians. The possibility of transnational forms of action is undiscussed; the problems are national or local and need to be dealt with as such.

The possibility of *public*-led approaches is raised in several of the groups. If people will stand up for the rules – rather like Harald did when demanding that that person take his feet off the seat – then there is the possibility that society can be made a better place. There are two difficulties cited with this however. First, few people may be willing to take a stand – timidity before the transgressor is a pattern emphasised. Second, it is quite likely one will be ignored. Dieter in Kassel says: 'Think of our stupid colleagues, they chuck their cigarettes out of the car here, onto the rank where they're standing, in other words their immediate environment. And if you approach them and ask them, if you say "Listen, you've just thrown your cigarette butt out, that's littering" ... "Yeah well the street-cleaner needs work, doesn't he." That's ... when you think how stupid that is ... Are you really going to expect that these people can develop, that they can change ...?'

Confidence in either a governmental or a public-led approach only goes so far, and ultimately the only solution may be immediate, *private* action to extinguish the problem. Just after the passage above in which the merits of different political parties are considered, Malcolm's next comment twists things in a rather different direction: 'And I tell you, I've already had this conversation with you Bill, it's only a matter of time before there's vigilantes.' If education fails, if individuals continue to break the rules and politicians are unable to get a grip on the problem, then 'people like us' will need to resolve things on the spot. 'Whoever's in power,' says Bill, 'we all look to the government and the council for what we want ... [Malcolm: Yeah ...]

but they seem to have abandoned us.' The only alternative is to take a stand:

> B: What you want is a political party which speaks like us. Someone who was actually committed to what they say. I mean, they give you all this 'I'll do this' but when they get there they become one of the brothers in Parliament ... [M: [of B] I'd follow him.] Cos we all want the same things, don't we. We want fairness across the board, but you don't see it, you don't see it.
>
> M: He's like me, he wants ... [B: Fairness, don't we.] We had a really good discussion one day, didn't we. We were actually talking about vigilantes. He had problems with scumbag neighbours, I had problems with scumbag neighbours ... [B: We all have ...] ... You sort mine, I'll sort yours.

Nor should such talk necessarily be dismissed as posturing. A later passage of conversation finds Malcolm recounting an incident to do with noisy neighbours where the police refused to act and where a solution was achieved – 'and I don't mind telling you this on tape' – only with the intervention of 'two mad, big, muscley, bouncer Geordies,'[8] old acquaintances of his from Newcastle, who explained to the miscreants 'if you ever fuck with him again we're going to kill you.' This is clearly at the radical end of expressions of agency; agency which avoids formal channels of authority and which can hardly be described as organised. It is a small brick through the window of our conceptual scheme, yet it is consistent with the general sense that problems to do with criminal or anti-social behaviour are soluble. There is none of the sense of inevitability one finds in the *Economics* domain. They can be tackled, one way or another.

The assumption of agency is in some ways weaker amongst the Czech groups. A call for more psychiatric help for criminals when they come out of prison runs up against the major barrier to action which is distinctive of the Czech discussions, the lack of state finances. This is the counter-argument raised whenever the usual points are made about improving the education system or the quality of law enforcement.

---

[8]Geordies – people from Newcastle.

'The biggest problem is the lack of finances,' says Tomáš from the Liberec group. 'Whether it's how much goes on healthcare, on the police, on transport, on the legal system ... the money problem is the biggest one.' Without better wages, the quality of the police force will remain low and the likelihood of corruption will be strong, but no change can be expected 'if the state doesn't take in enough money to be able to give out.'

There is another restraining factor, and this links to the second major problem, that of corruption. Whereas the British and the western-German groups treat the legal system as a means of rooting out corruption (insofar as they are concerned about corruption at all), for the Czech groups the legal system – stretching all the way back to the law-making process – is instead seen as one of the primary *expressions* of corruption, the locus rather than the solution. Corruption is considered a barrier to all kinds of institutional response to the problems of law and order. Rather than as a defender of the public interest, the legal system is liable to be considered one more means of advancement. In the face of loopholes and the ability of those at the top of the hierarchy to circumvent the law with the help of a sharp lawyer, what matters then is not the legal constraints but the personal morality of the individuals who hold office. And their morality, of course, is the morality of society more broadly. Tomáš and Zdeněk in Liberec both argue it is impossible to point the finger of blame at individuals, that the problem is with the society from which these individuals are drawn: 'it's the upbringing, it's the morality of those people, but that's how the whole of society functions,' says Tomáš. This brings us back to the notion of a whole generation which has been tarnished by its association with the old regime. Is it considered possible to change their mentalities and behaviour? The assumption seems to be that it is not. 'People brought up completely differently,' is what Michal in Plzeň calls them, and all one can do is 'wait until they go off into retirement and a new lot comes along.' Zdeněk and Tomáš likewise assert the need to wait patiently 'until that generation dies out; the main thing is to educate the new generation differently'.

To summarise, the sense of agency in this domain, while still qualified, is stronger than in the *Economics* domain. Especially amongst the British and German groups, education and law enforcement are widely assumed to be convincing *governmental* approaches – though the government involved is the national one, and there is no sense of a transnational context here.

Relations between peoples

A) Explanatory motifs

Problems in the domain of *Relations between Peoples*, such as conflict, threat and intimidation, provoke two main kinds of explanation. Neither of these implicates the political subjects themselves, since they are generally assumed to be peaceful people. The focus is on other peoples: one set of explanations is based on other peoples seeking to compensate for what they lack – in particular, power and resources; another set is based on these peoples expressing what are perceived to be their essential characteristics, for example an unwillingness to compromise. Conflicts arising from the first, e.g. over the control of resources, are presented as rational and may sometimes involve western governments. Those understood to be of the second kind, whether involving terrorists or intransigent minority groups within the local environment (and this link is made), involve at least one party considered in some way irrational.

The military intervention in Iraq (2003–) is discussed at least partly in power-political terms. The West is seen as contesting power with the 'Arab-Muslim' people, as symbolised by individuals such as Saddam Hussein or Osama bin Laden. The latter, as they challenge for power, present a threat which the West then has to act against. Marvin in Swansea on Saddam: 'Well I think it was right to be done. Right to be done. Cos he's a threat and always will be a threat, and I think the longer he'd been left in power … You know, obviously they didn't find nothing then, but in time he could have quite possibly made a nuclear bomb or whatever. He is a threat. [...] If he'd had a chance of making a bomb he'd do it. I think the Iraq war was right, myself.' 'It's all to do with power, isn't it,' he says a little later, which suggests a conclusion to Dean: 'You know, at the end of the day, the most powerful country in the world is America. So at the end of the day, cowardly as it may be to say, I'd rather be with America than against America. [murmurs of agreement]' An indication of a power-based perspective is found when the Plzeň group discusses the strength of the Czech army: Michal suggests it is 'paltry compared to other states', and 'compared to the rest of the world it was much stronger before the Second World War, and we still couldn't beat off the Germans.' Robert points out 'to say to the Americans "don't do that!", if the Czech Republic says that then of course it won't have any effect.'

Who has the power is deemed one of the keys to understanding relations between peoples. A global contest for power and resources is posited, with complete consensus, by the Kassel group when accounting for international conflicts:

Hans:	I think the crunch with this whole thing is that the distribution of resources here on Earth is very varied, that most wars take place due to this distribution. Whether it's basic economic goods like oil or other raw materials, or as is going to happen also with water, which some day is certainly going to have to be divided. Doesn't affect us so much yet, but it may certainly hit us later. Perhaps very soon.
Dieter:	That'll come too. ... With oil we're probably already there ... With water it's coming. [...]
Peter:	It's always a matter of distribution ... [H: yeah]. Wars happen because things are wrongly [*falsch*] distributed. But that's completely normal. If I have something, why should I give it up to you? Tell me. That's just how it is, isn't it. And you say 'why don't you give me some, you have a lot, you don't need it all.' Yes, but I say, 'sure, but why? Bad times might come, then I'd need it.'
Sebastian:	I think with war and peace it's more that certain countries want to keep their position of power ...
D:	Yeah, that's exactly what he's saying. Simply to hang onto their personal or country-specific advantage and secure their position ...
P:	Or, then there's these wars which in Africa ... a lot ... that some general launches a putsch and is brought to power ... [D: ... Power, power! ...] And then we're back at the same stage like when we had Hitler who killed the Jews and ... in the one case the Tutsus [sic] get killed, in the other case the others get killed ...
S:	Sure, but these African wars, for example, the Americans aren't very interested in those. [P: Right, because there they can't ...] Yeah, because they can't extract anything there.
P:	And probably soon the cost of the raw materials, even if they could get something out there, it'd be too expensive to ship it over to America ... [S: ... No raw materials in Africa ...] Yeah, exactly. [S: ... That's how it is ...]

One sees two kinds of explanation of conflict here, one explicit and one implicit, and relevant to different kinds of war. The first is the structural one to do with relations of power: if resources are distributed unequally, there will be wars as those in possession try to fend off the challenges of those without them. These wars are presented as rational or 'normal', and they may involve western actors such as the US. The second is a more essentialising explanation: wars in Africa are not necessarily about resources because there may be none there, rather they are more to do with meaningless violence (like that of Hitler against the Jews – though the point is not developed). Note the phrase 'some general', as though the occurrence were so common that the details were unimportant.

Some conflicts then are driven by (rational) considerations to do with the distribution of power, some by (irrational) proclivities to engage in war, and presumably some by both. Insofar as the West is generally assumed to be peaceful (with the possible exception of the US), these conflicts would take place just in far-away places of contrast;[9] yet what happens *there* is seen to intrude on life closer to home, integrating the sense of space. Axel in Erfurt gives one indication of how, raising the example of Rwanda, which he and Harald agree is an archetype: 'it's the best example, it's *the* example ... [H: Definitely, the very worst ...] Rwanda, where these Tutsis and Hutus ... [H: Hutus and Tutsis] ... Hutus and Tutsis, where they got in each other's hair and basically slaughtered each other ... where this Canadian General said – said to the UN – that we need to act immediately ... Politicians were told that we need to act, we need to keep them apart. Otherwise we get a huge refugee problem, that's the consequence of murder and slaughter and whatever else.' Peter in Kassel indicates a different way developments may impinge on the home environment, based on aggressive intentions:

For me ... Not in the near future but sometime in the future the great bogeyman [*Feindbild*] is going to be the Chinese and the Muslim. [H: yeah] ... In any event it's going to happen that the Chinese bursts out and attacks. I think there's no way around that. And the Muslims all over the world, they're all peaceful like we said but you see what happens everywhere with their attacks and all. The Muslims, they're

---

[9]Or in the past. At Würzburg there is talk about Spain and Portugal as having been 'imperialists' – 'they divided up the world' and Oskar makes here a rare explicit mention of race, perhaps made easier by the fact that the events in question are historical: 'to put it simply, the white race wanted to dominate other races. To make gains for itself and to exploit places like Africa.'

in every country, and some day they're going to take over – this is my opinion – they're going to take over world supremacy. Because the potential is there. This belief is there – this fanatical belief is there ... So there's enough potential for war, there's enough for the next hundred years. Question is, how long will it all survive? Until someone, some kind of madman presses the button and everything goes up. Pakistan – all you need is for someone who's a bit hysterical to come to power and some day he presses the button. China overwhelms Taiwan – the Americans have said they'll defend Taiwan, what would they do then? [D: yeah].

Aside from contingency (represented by the notion that a madman, or someone in Pakistan, could come to power and press the nuclear button), there are two main explanatory motifs evident here. There is the motif of power relations (the struggle for world supremacy); and, entwined with it, the essential character of the contrasting people (the 'fanaticism' of Muslims who are trying to take over countries). The passage is reminiscent of the comments made by Ulrich in Würzburg noted earlier, where he suggests 'they want to destroy the whole western world.' When these people come to live with 'us', they bring their irrationality with them, and their behaviour is simply the expression of their natures. The same sense of irrationality was evident in earlier passages from the Swansea group, where Arabs were referred to as 'fanatics from a very, very young age' who have 'had it drilled into them.' To be sure, these explanatory motifs are quite rudimentary – indeed, this may be part of their appeal. To declare perplexity at 'their' motivations is one way to express moral superiority, as though their minds are too evil for people of our nature to grasp. But the incomprehension seems more than merely tactical: it is one of the few vocabularies available to speakers with which to explain why conflict arises.

With (slightly) less alarmism, the Lübeck group expresses clear consensus when discussing the problem of 'Germanness' being undermined: it is to be explained in terms of the unwillingness of other peoples – Turks in particular – to make the effort to integrate. Jochen worries that his grandchildren are 'going to be living as a minority' – he senses it is only a matter of time. Niklas, ever sceptical of the willingness of his fellow participants to talk in the logic of this domain, explains the same problem of uneasy relations between peoples with reference to an economic argument: 'the worse the economy goes, naturally the worse the rivalries between Germans and immigrants

[*Ausländer*[10]] become. Because a lot is pushed onto the immigrants, they're blamed for the fact that there's so few jobs. It's a problem.' Niklas, however, is rather on his own with this argument. The problematic point tends to be presented not as that other peoples have different traditions and ways of living (to object to that would be 'unreasonable'), but rather that those peoples are unwilling or unable to compromise on their differences. They seek to impose their customs and way of life on the inhabitants of the city. It is part of the motif 'they're more racist than we are,' a favourite of the participants in the Swansea group, as if to say '*they* are the ones with irrational prejudices'. The explanation for uneasy relations is fixed on the minority.

We have also seen amongst the Czechs an explanation of conflict based on fundamental difference. Zdeněk in Ostrava spoke above of Muslims not knowing how to compromise, of it being their 'mentality' and of their having a 'different nature to Christians'. That there were not more examples amongst the Czechs of threat and conflict being explained in these terms could be down to several things. It could be that the number of interviews was simply too small; it could be that, having heard of western media criticism – particularly around the time of EU accession – of Czech attitudes towards minorities, the participants interviewed were wary of presenting themselves in these terms to a British researcher. Certainly Robert of the Plzeň group several times tried to reverse the interview by asking the author about race relations in Britain. Perhaps just as likely, however, is that the lack of exposure (at the time of interview – the situation may change) to unfamiliar groups who might conceivably be thought of as constituting a collective threat provides little opportunity for a discursive repertoire of this kind to be deployed.

In studying explanatory motifs, special attention has been paid to the sense of space which tends to be evoked, to the territorial spread of factors deemed relevant to understanding the origins of problems. Both of the principal explanations traced for *Relations between Peoples* – the one based on power and differences of power, the other based on the characters of contrast peoples – imply a wide sense of space. In the first case this is quite evident: one sees evoked a world of peoples with more or less power who try to improve their positions. The second, one

---

[10]*Ausländer* is a complex term to translate: 'foreigners' would be more appropriate in some contexts, and 'immigrants', while suitable here, is imperfect to the extent that speakers may also be referring to the descendants of immigrants.

might think, is a perspective which is *non-spatial* or *deterritorialised*, since it is based on characteristics rather than structural features. Yet on the contrary, one feels it is highly spatial because these peoples, and the conflicts which they give rise to, are associated with particular parts of the world. Africa, the Middle East and (though mentioned only a few times) China are of significance, and the peoples who are encountered within the home environment and comparable ones are explicitly associated with such regions in the sense of them being 'from there' or 'belonging there'. The sense of space is, again, very wide.

B) Possibilities for action

Rarely in these interviews does one encounter the idea that relations between peoples can be improved through dialogue or mutual understanding. We heard Hans in Kassel make this suggestion in Chapter 3, but it is certainly uncommon. A few individuals amongst the German groups (Niklas in Lübeck, Ralf and Oskar in Würzburg) call for German language lessons to be made compulsory for immigrants: 'with integration', says Oskar, 'it's up to politicians to take them by the hand and say "here's a language course for you to take"'. The sense that these should be obligatory – not just offered – may be read as implying however that the emphasis is more on enforcing conformity to 'our' practices than on establishing the means for dialogue. The absence more widely of progressive ideas is most likely because conflict between peoples is seen to be out of the hands of the political subjects: as generally peaceful people, it is not they who are responsible, their behaviour is merely reactive. Those whose aggression is understood as a challenge for power and resources are subverting the status quo and the problem is of their own making; if a western country like the US is the active party, this tends to be treated as a greedy government looking for money and oil, little to do with the subjects themselves. When antagonism is attributed to the *character* or *nature* of other peoples, their intransigence or irrationality, again the subjects are positioned as those responding to rather than initiating the problem.

In neither case does the notion of 'dialogue' get very far. *Public* approaches to overcoming these problems, and those based on individual action, are scarcely mentioned. Admittedly, the research was conducted at a time of much talk in the media about a 'clash of civilisations', a term which could easily act as an organising concept for those inclined to see conflict as inevitable. The term was not used in these discussions, though a comment by Dieter in Kassel encountered earlier has a similar ring: 'this whole thing with the takeover by

Muslims – or them achieving parity I should say, there won't be a takeover – they're everywhere and they install themselves everywhere and ... I'm not against *Ausländer*, but this way and means by which it's all happening, I find it really unhealthy. And there's not going to be war between countries any more, instead war takes place between people(s), who live side by side but who have completely different cultures from each other ...'. Whatever the impact of one particular discourse of the moment, the fact remains that conflict tends to be normalised, across all the groups. There is the fatalistic sense that clashes, if not already in progress, are only a matter of time. Of course, this should not be read as evidence in support of a 'clash of civilisations' or 'clash of peoples' thesis: our focus is on common-sense assumptions, and it is a quite separate question whether one would want to buy into the common-sense position that conflict between peoples is unavoidable.[11]

A recap of the material confirms this assumption of the inevitability of conflict. 'Unless you can zap people for thinking,' says Malcolm, 'you will never ever have peace.' Radical contingency is one aspect: we have heard Peter in Kassel suggest that 'all you need is for someone who's a bit hysterical to come to power and someday he presses the button.' Or as Pavel in Plzeň puts it, 'just like 11th September, two planes struck a sky-scraper and the next morning there was suddenly a war going on, in Afghanistan.' The scarcity and unequal distribution of resources is another determining aspect we have seen. Then there is the problem that the attitudes of certain peoples are not conducive to harmony. All such assumptions clearly limit the perceived range of possibilities for action.

There are some however, with slight variations between countries. For the British groups, dealing militarily with high-level threats when they arise is one necessary course of *governmental* action. Tackling the threat means eradicating it rather than engaging with it, a job for the country's armed forces. Malcolm at Norwich, with the backing of Gary and Bill, says the Iraq war was 'a necessary evil, we had to go in there, we had to do something,' as a response to the attacks on the US of 11th September 2001. The logic of the 'war on terror' is accepted

---

[11]Also, at the micro-level, these repertoires are deployed unevenly: only when a situation is problematised and conflict is foregrounded are they likely to be invoked, a fact that allows plenty of exceptions to be made.

unproblematically. 'There's only one thing, there's only one thing I ever, ever agree with in the whole of the Bible – I think it's the greatest book of fiction ever – what it is, is "an eye for an eye".' In this domain, action is not guided by rules but by what has to be done to show power and to remove the threat. 'Now at the minute, the biggest war we got in the world at the moment is terrorism. Now we got the greatest soldiers in the world, the SAS ... They could have murdered these terrorists in their sleep, they know where they are ... Do away with them! I don't want to hear about it, I don't want to know about it, just do it. [...] If I get on an aeroplane, yeah, say next week, and two years later it comes out, in Ally McNabb's book or whatever, that that same aeroplane didn't blow because the SAS went in, dragged these dirty, stinking, cowardly, murdering bastards out their beds and put a gun in their heads and blew their stinking rotting brains out, yeah, am I going to complain about that? Am I hell!' In this approach of cutting out the threats, there are no rules to follow. 'War is war, isn't it,' says Marvin at Swansea, 'simple as that.'[12]

A second *governmental* approach raised in several groups is to reduce the mutual exposure between peoples. One way to do this is to take a tougher line on the number of outsiders let into the environment. As noted above, the Swansea group credits other countries in Europe, and Australia, with being firmer. Such a policy, as one can imagine, is favoured not just for the benefits it can bring for the problems of this domain (reducing the unwanted encounter with those held to be intimidating and uncompromising) but also, in the logic of the other domains, as a means of cutting crime and reducing the economic 'burden'. Malik in Reading suggests: 'say for example the war in Bosnia, and then the war in Afghanistan, yeah? Now, once everything's been sorted out and it's no longer a war zone, now these people that have come over here as political asylum, can't they be like sent back? You know, not in a horrible way, deported or anything, but another country

---

[12]This emphasis on no-holds-barred military action against salient threats is generally found less amongst the Germans or Czechs. The deployment of their troops overseas is presented as a radical move out of keeping with national tradition. Certain Czech speakers also emphasise the limits of their state's capabilities: 'we're so meaningless,' says Pavel in Plzeň, 'from our position our country's unable to influence things,' says Michal.

that likes England, that aren't well off, do something over there, make it better for the people ...'. The proposal is presented as an act of charity. Derek 'know[s] what he's saying'.

At Swansea, such a move would no doubt be welcomed, though there is some concern about feasibility. The chief obstacle is taken to be the softness and craftiness of the national government. According to Derek and Alan at Swansea, the government does not act against immigrants because 'everyone's afraid to step on them'. Amongst the German groups one also finds calls for the national government to be stricter on how many outsiders are let into the country, with the success of such calls likewise qualified. The motif of weak and sly national politicians is widely present, in the German case entwined with the discourse on the country's history. An interesting discussion of this appears in the interview in Lübeck, following on from a passage mentioned earlier dealing with the ability of (mainly Turkish) immigrants to speak German:

Jochen: ... Politicians here, they immediately get a lot of hostility if they talk about foreigners. It's such a hot subject, so dangerous for the politicians, that they really don't want to touch it, and if they do then they generally run into problems because ... because it's immediately assumed that they're xenophobic, radical-right, fascist etc. [Werner: yeah, exactly ...] and that's not always the case. If one speaks objectively about foreigners ... you're not immediately a Nazi just for raising the topic. But a lot of Germans – a lot of those I've spoken to – think that there is a problem with immigrants, and they'd quite like to have a party here in Germany that was a little bit more to the right, that draws up laws ... [W: yeah] ... that clamps down a little harder – but without going too far to the right ... [W: Into the brown corner ...] ... exactly, without going into the brown corner, not into the brown corner. Take that Schill Party for instance, they got 20% straight off in Hamburg, and they were to the right, located a bit more to the right, but from the very beginning they distanced themselves from the brown corner ... They said 'Security is important to us, we want people to still be safe on the streets at night.' And that's what people want ...

Niklas: In reality they were brown though!

J: Yeah but like I said, people would like to have a party which was further to the right than the CDU. But they're afraid of becoming a slave to these pied pipers, the skinheads, the brown neo-Nazis ... [N: yeah] ... And that's always a thin line of course ...

In two connected moves, politicians are treated both as contributors to the problem articulated, and as being insufficiently willing to address the problem, out of touch with what 'the people' think. The extremeness of their tolerance is matched by the extremeness of neo-Nazi hatred. A very similar point is made by Ulrich in Würzburg, for whom 'the reasonable middle is lacking in this country at the moment'.[13] The sense of inadequate representation on these problems is very similar to that found amongst the British, though it is assumed to be a distinctively German phenomenon.

Overview

The observations of the chapter may be summarised in table form:

	Economics	Society & the Law	Relations between Peoples
Explanatory Motifs	Sometimes lacking. Alternatively very broad, stretching beyond Europe – global price & wage inequality, the 'cheaper East'.	Generally local – mentalities & conduct of local actors; declining levels of discipline; weak institutions of enforcement.	Generally broad, stretching beyond Europe – global inequalities of power and resources; intransigent impulses of opponent 'peoples'.
	Variation: in CZ, 'the East' starts further east (e.g. Ukraine).	*Variation*: in CZ + Erfurt, references to communist past as further source of problems.	*Variation*: less discussion of these topics in CZ than GB and D, though similar motifs appear.

---

[13]The day before this interview, Chancellor Schröder had called upon Germans to acknowledge the lessons of the twentieth century in a speech commemorating the sixtieth anniversary of the liberation of the concentration camp Buchenwald. Cf. Appendix.

	Economics	Society & the Law	Relations between Peoples
Possibilities for Action	Governmental: Little. Sense of inevitability; global price/wage inequalities assumed conclusive; 'too late' to act.	Governmental: Some. Improve schooling; stronger law enforcement.	Governmental: Little. Conflict largely inevitable. Can reduce exposure, e.g. with immigration controls.
	Variation: in CZ + Erfurt, references to constraining effect of weak state finances and economic dependence on western Europe.	Variation: in CZ, references to constraining effect of weak state finances and corruption.	Variation: occasional reference in GB (not D/CZ) to use of military force where necessary.
		Public: Some. Ostracisation of rule-breakers – if others in society willing to 'stand up'.	Public: Not mentioned.
	Public: Little. Boycotts mentioned, but problems of identifying who to target, and getting others to cooperate.	Variation: in CZ, need to await new, uncorrupted generation.	Private: Not mentioned.
	Private: Some. Individual adaptation (e.g. acquiring new skills); enlightened consumerism where feasible.	Private: Some. Better home education; personal action (inc. vigilante-style) against rule-breakers.	

Summary of Views on the Credibility of Political Projects

Juxtaposing the findings like this, the differences across domains become clear. One sees that one domain of problems – *Economics* – is characterised by a combination, on the one hand, of general uncertainty about how to account for the emergence of problems, and on the other hand, when explanations are supplied, by the construction of a wide spatial context in which the determining factors lie far from the environment in which the problems are experienced. To simplify just a little, it tends to be suggested either that problems arise for reasons mysterious, such as the strange tendency of prices to rise faster than earnings, or that they arise due to developments on the other side of the world. Although the transnational dimension is of potential significance for a European polity, neither perspective in its current form lends much credibility to a political project designed to tackle such problems, since neither perspective invites a clear sense of what could be done and by whom. It is little surprise then that one finds considerable scepticism about the possibilities for action.

The pattern is rather the reverse, however, as regards *Society and the Law*. Here one does find a fairly clear set of explanatory motifs, and rather than invoking reference-points which are far removed these tend to be mainly local. Problems arise due to factors close to home. This more readily available set of explanatory resources, and the tendency to evoke a narrower spatial context, seems more conducive to the credibility of a political project, and indeed one does find a reasonably positive set of assumptions about what can be achieved to alleviate these problems.[14] The most commonly heard proposals (education and stronger rule-enforcement) do not point in any obvious way towards a European polity, though would be compatible with one were certain powers of decision-making decentralised.

The third domain of problems – *Relations between Peoples* – is notable again for the wide spatial context in which the problems in question are said to be unfolding, and for ambivalence about the extent to which they can be addressed. The tendency to assume problems experienced at a local level also play out on a wide scale is likely to be a contributing element in the scepticism regarding the possibilities for organised address, in that it implies such problems are always likely to cut across polity boundaries. They are neither purely local and therefore susceptible to local address, nor are they purely distant and therefore susceptible to a policy of disengagement and withdrawal. This globalist perspective also separates these problems (and the more local conflicts speakers entwine with them) from particular historical and social contexts, making their origins ever harder to decipher. However, here there is also a distinctive factor involved. As seen both in this chapter and the last, a strong link is made between the problems articulated and the nature of the opponents, with a marked tendency not only to assume that differences between peoples are real and essential, but that dialogue is unfeasible and that conflict most likely is unavoidable. This

---

[14]Some might suspect this is the legacy of acts of displacement by politicians, such that stronger narratives of agency for law-and-order problems are promoted precisely to compensate for narratives of powerlessness on economic issues.

friend-enemy dynamic is not only an assertion of intolerance, but of the impossibility of tackling problems of inter-group conflict. The opponents cannot be engaged in a conciliatory approach to overcoming such problems, for these opponents are assumed to be essentially unconciliatory themselves. They are not included in the solution to the problem; rather, they are pretty much equated with the problem, and the solution depends on their being absented from the home environment. This rather clearly undermines the prospects for a democratic political project in this domain, whether centred on the national level or European.

Both when raising doubts about the possibility of organised action, and when affirming its feasibility, it is principally action by *governmental* means which participants invoke as the reference-point. As we have seen, interventions by the researcher to inquire 'what can be done about such problems?' tended to draw responses that foregrounded the role of 'politicians' (generically, and as individual leaders), of 'the government' (in the abstract, and in the guise of ruling parties), or of 'the state', whether to demand further action be taken, to give credit (occasionally) for certain initiatives, to express concern at a failure to act or the breaking of 'promises', or even just to write off officials as 'puppets'. It is the government, it tends to be assumed, which is the actor of greatest relevance to the remedy of common problems, and it is its *capacity* rather than *entitlement* to act which tends to be questioned. Where the authority of the government is judged weak, we have seen that *private* and *public* means of action may be proposed, whether it be adaptation by individuals to the market economy, or an attempt to get others to boycott certain goods. But these are options of last resort, and references to them are rarer.[15] If the message of much contemporary political science is that politics today no longer takes place through the traditional institutional channels, and that 'civil society' is the principal reference-point for taking action on matters of common concern, this is a message which seems not to have been absorbed by our speakers. Perhaps in contrast to the kind of assumptions to be found in lay discourse in North America,[16] amongst these

---

[15]Other than some isolated remarks about taxi-driver organisations, there are two references in total to NGOs – and these as examples of embezzlement.

[16]Cf. (Perrin 2006; Gamson 1992: Chapter 4), in whose studies public/societal action assumes a more prominent position.

European groups it is the government and the state which is to the fore.

While this suggests that the principle of collective self-rule is still in some sense taken for granted – governments, as the things one votes for, are treated as the most relevant actors to the problems which should be addressed – the unevenness with which faith is expressed in their capacity to tackle these problems is striking. Survey research indicates large majorities in industrialised societies remain favourable towards democracy as an idea, whatever their thoughts about its practice (Hay 2007) – yet what is one to make of such a finding? While the principle of collective self-rule is always deeply complex to institutionalise, perhaps especially in the pluralist context of contemporary Europe, its vitality depends in the last instance on a certain strength of expectation that common problems are susceptible to address. Only then is governmental authority likely to be seen as a positive means to address the substantive concerns of its citizens, and, one may suppose, only then is one likely to see any resolve to ensure it fulfils such a role, that it does not regress towards the mere exercise of state power, with all the possibilities for oppression this holds. As we have seen, for political agency generally, such expectation persists, but within narrow parameters. It is stronger for some policy-areas than others, and one cannot rule out that it may be stronger elsewhere on the European continent than in the places of interview.[17] But too often one sees the spectre of problems without solutions. As sources of collective empowerment, political institutions and civil-society organisations seem to command allegiances which are pale.

Maybe some would argue these low expectations are appropriate. Could it perhaps be that the problems articulated are genuinely little susceptible to organised address, and that our speakers have appraised them accurately? Such might be the argument of those who observe an increasing dislocation between territorialised political authority and

---

[17]In the qualitative study by OPTEM, Britain, Germany and the Czech Republic are noted to be amongst those EU countries where at the time of interview there was a high 'general level of pessimism' concerning the years ahead. (OPTEM 2006: 9). One might infer these are therefore also the 'hard cases' more specifically as regards faith in the possibilities for collective agency. While this is conceivable, one needs to be sceptical of arguments which put a strong emphasis on national boundaries as containers of discursive practice. Note also the discussion of Eurobarometer data in Chapter 6, which suggests the patterns noted in these interviews have wider extension.

the deterritorialised forces of capital and information, and who conclude the latter will escape the control of the former in the foreseeable period (Bauman 2004). It would perhaps be the argument also of those who suggest we live in a 'second modernity' in which the major problems faced are rooted in past efforts at human betterment, and that the promises of 'first modernity' to achieve well-being through mastery and control have shown themselves chimerical (Beck 1997; Giddens 1994). Yet such conclusions would be premature, not least because it is exactly the potential of new political arrangements such as the EU to offer forms of political agency which exceed those available in the Westphalian system, and to combat some of the unwanted side-effects of politics in the nation-state setting. Moreover, even with regard to established state structures, one can convincingly argue that the limitations of existing political arrangements have been exaggerated, and that discourses of powerlessness and decline are little more than vague prophecies with a potential for self-fulfilment (Hay 2007). If our speakers express doubts about the possibilities for political agency, it is not because reality permits this interpretation alone, but because a certain set of perspectives on how one should understand the nature and origins of political problems have been internalised, ones that leave limited scope for purposeful initative.

What has been excluded from the analysis so far is how the EU as such fits into the picture described, what place it takes up in the array of discursive practices traced. Of particular interest, given speakers' emphasis on *governmental* forms of action and their perceived limitations, is the extent to which the EU comes to be regarded as an augmentation of, even a substitute for, governmental agency at the national level, or conversely is assumed to be suffering from the same and perhaps additional shortcomings. Likewise one will want to examine how it is drawn into the patterns of collective positioning identified in Chapter 4. It is to these matters, and to the wider implications for political allegiance in Europe, that the last of our core chapters turns.

6
The Place of Europe and the EU

Though centrally concerned with questions of political community on a European scale, this study has stepped back from the EU as such to explore the broader web of meanings into which it is set. It has avoided treating acontextual 'attitudes to Brussels' or 'feelings of European identity' as the key ideational fact, instead decentring the EU by taking discussion of political problems as the starting point. We have observed a large number of concerns regularly articulated in discussion, amounting to a substantive core around which a political bond might develop. While inferring that a 'political common' finds validation in existing discourse, it has been noted how certain patterns of talk diverge from those one might look for in the formulation of political subjects, opponents and counterparts, and as regards political projects of organised address. Hence the concepts have started to acquire a diagnostic rather than merely descriptive function.

This chapter connects these considerations back to the question of a European polity. The first section examines how and when 'Europe' and the EU are invoked in discussion. These, it will be observed, tend to become entwined with the discursive patterns by now familiar, as the motifs characteristic of political discussion more generally come to be applied to this sub-sector. The EU thus emerges as epiphenomenal, apprehended by its place in a larger scheme. Accordingly it attracts ways of speaking which, while in some respects consistent with the political bond idea, in others serve rather to undermine it. The second section charts the important divergences in this respect, and looks at what would need to be different in discursive terms if such a bond were to have resonance. Discursive practices are likely to be enduring but by no means impervious to change, and it may be that there are existing features which can facilitate such change – 'platforms to build on', as it were. In considering these questions, an explicitly critical standpoint is adopted towards the material.

'Europe' and the EU in discussion

As indicated in Chapter 2, no concerted effort was made to steer discussion towards Europe-related matters until the interviews were near conclusion.[1] In each discussion references to these did appear naturally at some stage, featuring a range of terms, principally 'the EU' (the most common term in the German groups, and amongst the Czechs in the expanded form of 'the European Union', though rare amongst the British) and 'Europe' (used frequently as shorthand for the EU, especially in the British discussions).[2] These references were considerably more common than those to other transnational political arrangements such as the United Nations or to transnational economic institutions.[3] They were significantly *less* common though than references to governmental actors at the national level.[4]

---

[1]The following paragraphs draw on (White 2010c).

[2]The terminology itself is interesting: greater familiarity (perhaps not approval) seems implied by the frequency of the abbreviation 'EU' in the German groups, while the use of 'Europe' by British speakers suggests a more distant relationship. Occasionally one finds other terms too: 'Brussels' (used sometimes amongst the British, generally pejoratively), the 'common', 'internal' or 'European market', and 'the euro countries' (this appearing occasionally in the British discussions to indicate a wider political grouping beyond the eurozone). For simplicity, the umbrella term 'Europe and the EU' is used to summarise.

[3]The UN was mentioned just once, as was NATO, while the IMF, World Bank, WTO and G20 were never mentioned. Note also that not only were such structures absent in name but the *concept* of them (e.g. of global government) was also un-mentioned. These points are worth emphasising given the relatively high profile these institutions achieve in Eurobarometer surveys, where respondents are actively encouraged to express opinions on them (see e.g. Eurobarometer 71 ('Public Opinion in the EU'), 2009, pp.203–4).

[4]In total, 254 mentions of governmental actors at the national level (including 'the government', 'the state', political parties, or individual politicians and heads of state) were counted, and 94 mentions of the EU or related terms (cf. fnt. 2). In addition to this basic difference in visibility, virtually none of the latter kind distinguished between the EU institutions, mentioned Euro-parties or party groupings, or identified EU-related individuals. (These figures are indicative: where one speaker repeated a reference twice in quick succession, only one was recorded; also, judgement was required to distinguish mentions of 'Europe' with political content from those referring simply to a geographical space.)

For the purposes of analysis a distinction can be made between two kinds of reference to the European. The first involves the direct expression of opinions concerning the Union's institutions, decision-making procedures, and the transfer of sovereignty, separate from the context of substantive political problems. An emblematic example would be the complaint made by Alan in Swansea about the money wasted ('£20 million or something') each time 'Brussels' moves from Brussels to Strasbourg. Such opinions, though conceivably an influence on perceptions of agency, are not the focus here, since they were rare and appeared mostly in response to the researcher's direct questioning about the EU late in discussion. Of close to 100 EU-related references in the data, only nine were detached in this way from substantive concerns. Perhaps this relative infrequency is because such references concern phenomena specific to the EU's institutional configuration, about which public levels of knowledge are notoriously low and of which ignorance is often conceded (OPTEM 2006). Even *criticising* the EU on procedural grounds requires a familiarity with its institutions which may rare. Perhaps infrequency also reflects diminished concern. While questions of the mechanisms of integration will properly be of salience to scholars, it seems natural those without a professional interest may prefer to work outwards from problems of immediate concern, and to invoke 'Europe' only where it is assumed to have bearing.[5]

We shall therefore focus instead on a second type of reference to the European, whereby 'Europe' and the EU are woven naturally into the discussion of problems facing 'people like us'. This means, in addition to evaluating the implications of the preceding chapters, looking at how 'Europe' and the EU are invoked directly as reference-points to understand the problems of the political common – both their origins and their possible resolution. In this approach, it is the context of invocation which is crucial: not 'attitudes' to the EU in some general sense, but the political significance which is ascribed. Of course, the EU and its current policies constitute only one possible version of a European polity, and alterations to these policies would probably cause adjustments to its perception. But studying how the current version is cited tells us much about how the discursive patterns explored in the previous chapters intrude. The way the EU is described differs according to

---

[5]The study's focus on substantive problems might be suspected as another reason, but note that one of the problems discussed – corruption – offered clear opportunity for a discussion of the EU in these terms if desired.

the three domains we have outlined, and so they are considered in turn, before returning to the fourth, less clearly delineated set of problems to do with *Quality of Life*. The section concludes by examining how relevant data from other sources undergirds the observations made.

Europe as remote: *Society and the Law*

As may be anticipated from preceding chapters, in one domain of problems – *Society and the Law* – the significance ascribed to the EU is extremely minor. These are salient problems across the groups, representing some of the most important ones 'people like us' are liable to face. There is a clear set of opponents against which the subjects are demarcated – the persistent, serious rule-breakers – and a clear sense of injustice and of the desirability of intervention. But it is the domestic arena which is the focus. Comparisons are almost never made with experiences in other countries: the relevant ones are assumed to be cross-temporal (declining standards, declining discipline etc.) rather than cross-spatial. Problems tend to be explained in local terms, with little reference to outside factors, and although one sees relatively positive assumptions concerning the worth of organised address, these tend to imply roles primarily for the national government and fellow citizens. Significantly, this implies speakers are not blindly cynical about all forms of political agency – government has its role, at least for certain issues. For the *Society and the Law* domain, the concept of the political bond fits fairly well. It is not one conducive specifically to a European polity, but nor would it be incompatible with such a polity, since the possibility that certain policy-areas be in the hands of local authority is recognised in most democratic polities and confirmed by the EU's subsidiarity principle. The expectations associated with this domain could be *accommodated* in a European polity, though with implications for the institutional regime as will be discussed later.

In discussion of *Economics* (especially) and *Relations between Peoples* (to some degree), 'Europe' and the EU are invoked rather more.[6] That a connection is made on both reminds that the meaning ascribed to the EU cannot be reduced to a single register of evaluation, whether economic or geopolitical, a tendency one finds in some of the EU-related literature. It also implies the absence of references on *Society and the Law* is no mere artefact of the interview format, since otherwise one would

---

[6]The prominence of economic perspectives on the EU is also evident in the findings of (Duchesne et al. 2010).

expect similar reticence across the full range of topics discussed. Yet this was not the case: for *Economics* and *Relations between Peoples*, such references did appear. This is no doubt linked to the fact that both are described in transnational terms. Opponents are assumed to have a presence both inside and outside the country, comparisons are made with experiences in other countries, and explanatory motifs include factors extending well beyond the local environment. With this enlarged sense of space, some of the conditions would seem to be in place for a bond consistent with a European polity. But for both domains one finds assumptions and acts of positioning which counter this. While speakers do occasionally raise the prospect of political action at a European level (understood in *governmental* terms, for society-based forms of action at a European level are not mentioned), it is generally with severe doubts attached.[7] Furthermore, references to 'Europe' and the EU are not always references to the (im)possibility of political action, but to the unfolding of problems themselves.

Europe as a symptom: *Economics*

For *Economics*, the patterns of positioning found in Chapter 4, including the evocation of counterparts in other European countries (restricted albeit along an east-west axis), and the construction of opponents as adversaries rather than enemies, are replicated when discussion connects directly to the EU. True to the idea that, in this domain, opponents are not irrationalised and calls are not made for them to be prevented from living side by side with 'people like us', calls for current eastern-European member-states to be expelled from the Union are not heard in these interviews. Rather one hears demands for fairer treatment such that 'people like us' (the contributors, the taxpayers) are not called upon to subsidise 'them' to the degree currently expected, or such that when they come 'over here' to work they receive the same wages and pay the same contributions as would locals. Where opposition to EU enlargement to the East is expressed, it takes the form of a criticism of the timing rather than of the act itself. Peter in Kassel argues that 'all these eastern-bloc countries haven't developed far enough to fit in with us. I think it's all too early. It should have been perhaps in ten years or so ... and above all not this whole mass at once.' Dieter confirms: 'That's the

---

[7]That such references are uncommon means one can set aside the secondary question of according to what principle of authority – intergovernmental or supranational – EU policy-making is envisaged.

problem, yeah. The way it's being done, that's the mistake. You're not necessarily against having the borders removed, letting everyone move around more, that's certainly a good thing. But I think there should have been more thought given to the mechanisms, and perhaps to the consequences too.' Importantly, in this domain and in contrast to *Relations between Peoples*, the differences between the 'people like us' and the opponents are generally not essentialised. Those who do not contribute could in principle be encouraged to do so – to 'pay their bit' – or, if unable, to take less. The positioning is agonistic rather than antagonistic.

Interesting in this regard is how, amongst the Czechs, one finds awareness that some in the west treat them as economically unwelcome in the EU. In an intervention supported by Vladimír and Zdeněk, Tomáš in Liberec responds to a question about the economic consequences of enlargement: 'Britain, France and Germany are all countries which are starting to ask themselves why they should have to fund the poor countries if those countries contribute hardly anything. Suddenly the Germans are discovering they've got the same problems with work, with the labour market, they're all closing in on themselves so that we don't go and work there, even though each of us knows it wouldn't be a problem if they opened up. There'd be maybe a thousand people more there but it's small numbers, those who want to work abroad went abroad a long time ago. And those who can't are not going to go even if they give us work there, because of family reasons and language problems, those kinds of problem.' While there is a clear sense here of feeling opposed, and a sense that the other side's view is misplaced, the conflict is nonetheless framed in the most rationalist terms: there is assumed to be general agreement from both sides on the nature of the conflict, and one sees a willingness to adopt the adversary's perspective. Again, these are hostilities which are tempered.

This may be a rather precarious condition nonetheless, and the emergence of a deeper enmity cannot be excluded. While there is no essentialising of the opponents as irrational, occasionally one observes something close to the essentialising of their economic situation, for instance the poverty of eastern Europeans (though not to the 'dollar-a-day' extent of those in the 'Far East'), and an essentialising of their unwillingness to contribute. Were they thus positioned as being *irredeemably* poor or unwilling to contribute, their legitimacy as opponents might well be questioned. This is by no means the only perspective – references are made to countries once poor but now richer, such as Ireland, Spain or Portugal – but it is one that does arise. Noticeably, one sees little enthusiasm expressed at the prospect of further enlargement of the

Union eastwards, where economic conditions are held to be quite different. 'The problem I see with Turkey joining the EU,' says Werner in Lübeck, 'is that we, that Germany is already the biggest net contributor, and we'll have to pay even more in afterwards, and we'll get none of that back for ourselves. And again that's something which is going to hit us as tax-payers. It means we'll have even less money in our pockets.' Hamid comments that 'one Turkish person brings five Turkish people with him,' and that 'if more countries come into the EU then we can call it a day here.' As we saw in Chapter 4, a zero-sum relationship is posited between the 'industrialised countries' of western Europe and the poorer countries of eastern Europe, and the idea of admitting more adversaries into the community is not welcomed.

Amongst the Czech groups, this positioning towards potential EU member-states further east is replicated. Jan in Ostrava worries that 'the biggest problem for us is going to be if Ukraine comes into the euro [sic], all of those countries – Belarus, Russia, Uzbekistan, the Tartars, whatever ... we're going to be between them and the West, they'll be crossing over us, they'll get to us first, so there'll be problems here.' While it would certainly be too strong to say that the opponents are positioned as enemies – they are not assumed to pose an existential threat, rather they are a 'drain on resources' – it is clear that their acceptance as members of the political community is contested and that the agonistic rather than antagonistic nature of the dynamic is potentially unsteady.

What of the EU's agential capacity? Chapter 5 highlighted the widespread assumption that problems of *Economics* are beyond the control of political authority, and thus the evident scepticism concerning the possibility of a political project in this domain. Fully consistent with the emphasis on irresistible forces at a global level, speakers give little suggestion that European approaches may succeed where conventional ones fail. The EU is very rarely mentioned in these discussions as a means of addressing economic problems which cannot be addressed by national government. Nor is it much blamed for *failing* to act, something which might imply the possibility. Given the underlying understanding of the problems in question, the EU would need to appear as a kind of *deus ex machina*, an unexpected rupture from the narrative frame, in order to be seen as a decisive and positive influence. It comes closest to this in the Czech groups, where credit is occasionally given for infrastructure improvements: Robert in Plzeň notes judiciously that 'it can be said that in the time we've been in the EU the situation's improved.' Michal confirms: 'the Union's contributed to the construction of every bridge here, large and small.' It remains doubtful however whether such EU-led action is seen as an expression of agency rather than a welcome but mysterious change in fortunes. Generally, with most economic problems linked in discussion to global factors far beyond the borders of Europe, little positive role is accorded to a European polity. Motifs of political authority as powerless before global forces are a challenge for the EU just as for state-level institutions.

Indeed, across all groups, various current policies of the EU are often heavily entwined in discussion with some of the key problems in this domain, such that the Union is treated either as an expression or as an exacerbation of them. This can be seen in many instances. Discussion of the introduction of the euro, for example, exhibits the motif of the little/normal people being taken advantage of by the rich or the financial corporations. 'The euro helps firms,' says Zbyněk at Ostrava, since it saves them the costs of the exchange rate, 'but the euro doesn't help normal people.' 'For us it'll all be one and the same,' says Josef, 'we're the small guys, we're really small ... We'll pay to swap our taxi-meters, we'll have new digital ones with euros on them rather than crowns, but that'll be it.' The motif of inevitability is widespread, despite the indignation. At Swansea, Luke reports: 'I picked a guy up at the station, took him to Three Crosses, big massive house at Three Crosses. He works for the government and he's working on the euro at the moment, and he has said that we will definitely be in the euro. Definitely be in the euro within five years, without a shadow of a doubt. He said, if it goes to a referendum, if they say no, we *will* be going into the euro, everything will be fixed. "We will be in the euro", he said, "I'm working on it now."' Thus one of the 'big people' (with a big house) tells one of the 'little people' what is going to happen. The anecdote is convincing to Alan, who has already expressed his concerns about the euro.

Likewise, the EU comes to be absorbed into discussion of problems of price and wage inequalities. When Bill in Norwich refers back to the decline of British industry in the 1970s he cites the economics of the European Community as part of the problem, rather as speakers cite 'the East' more generally: 'We couldn't compete with their coal price. Common Market ... Use our own coal, use our own steel, eat our own fish, our own farming produce first, then you export what's left. You might still have a bit of a coal industry ... If we just supplied ourselves, rather than worrying about exporting first ... If every country did look after themselves first ...'. There is no indication that the EU might be a way of controlling wider economic processes: rather it mirrors them. An extended passage from the Würzburg discussion is useful for illustrating many of these themes coming together. It begins with Oskar lamenting the movement of companies from Germany to eastern Europe:

O: The population is a little sour, to pick up the example of Siemens-VDO[8] again. Germany pays a great deal into the EU pot, a contributing country for new accession candidates like the Czech Republic. The Czech Republic says to Siemens, 'if you set up a company here, then for the first year we'll pay the people ourselves. They'll work for you for free.' Siemens says 'oh, lovely, we can do that.' But in principle it's also a boomerang effect for Germany. We pay for the construction of the East and in return they entice the companies away. And here, the people who actually pay for that … [R: Exactly], they're punished even higher then.

Ralf: … Cutting off the branch you're sitting on … […] Key word is larger internal market, that's why these countries – it wasn't so long ago – were brought into the EU. The door was opened by us, to encourage development, and now there's this boomerang effect. The idea was to build up the markets there. That was the point of the thing I think, the enlargement of the EU – Poland, Czech Republic, Slovenia etc. – to build up new markets there, so that the people there can also, how should I say, boost the economy here, so they can buy the products which are produced here. It was already noted even then – I can remember – in the political discussion that things would turn out as they have now, with this migration to the East. It was known even then, when all this was opened up. It was done anyway though, and now … you asked earlier what can be done about it, it sounds very hard and sad when I say it, but actually nothing. It has its own dynamic, the door has been opened and now it's open! You can't close it any more. So I … the proposals that we could possibly make, they're of a theoretical nature,

---

[8] A supplier of electronics for the car industry. Its plant in Würzburg was due to be closed at the end of 2007 and relocated to Ostrava (Czech Republic), causing significant job losses.

probably nothing will happen. Because the EU will carry on existing in its current form, the contributions and the subsidies will also be paid to the eastern countries just as up till now ... I don't believe that anything will somehow be dismantled there ... and the borders are open ...

O: We hope of course, in the German case, if we've been paying in for years ... have been net contributors for Spain for example, which meanwhile has growth figures much bigger than Germany, we're the tail-light when it comes to growth ... We hope naturally that at some point there'll be a 'return on investment' so that it goes the other way too a bit, so that the Spanish also give up a bit of the cake. That's the hope. And everyone hopes of course that that works out, and that when they lose the Spanish ... and the smaller states, that when they lose they don't just say 'goodbye, we're leaving the EU'.

R: But that's ... if I think back to the past, whenever it was a question of the payment of contributions, there was always a great deal of argy-bargy. They always dug in hard. That's also a very difficult development, that one forces other countries to pay more ... Lots of protest and outcry, and opposition ... Great Britain is a good example there isn't it. It's famously notorious for that.

O: Great Britain has kept itself out, out of the EU ... The Germans and French at the moment are paying not just for unification – the Germans for unification – but also for abroad, for neighbouring EU countries. And that puts a brake on growth of course. ... The British have simply decided against that and have said 'we're not going to be a part of this crap, we see only negative growth there, we're keeping out.' Same with Switzerland.

R: Yeah but Britain ... Britain *is* a member of the EU. [O: They're in politically but ...] Britain isn't part of the currency union ... [O: They have their pound ...] But they're a member nonetheless, of the economic union? [O: Yeah, they're cunning ...] The Irish have the euro, don't they? And they've had a strong economic boom as a result, from what I can gather. [O: They're takers too ...] Yeah, sure, they've profited a lot from it, from these subsidies you mean ...? [O: Exactly] The Irish have ... that was structurally a pretty weak country. [O: A small country too ...

so the growth is naturally greater.] Anyway from what I've heard, the prices have really gone up too. I recently drove a businessman who spends most of his time in Ireland and he said that the prices are now almost higher than in Germany. In Dublin, the hotels etc, the gastronomy, it's all to do with the EU ...

O: Likewise in Greece the prices have gone up ... massively ... [R: ... Mmmm, mmmm ...] Another disadvantage for ...

R: Also in the south-European countries ... Italy's become downright expensive, Spain has gone up a lot ... It's all a consequence of the EU. But I mean ... [O: There are winners and losers ...] Yeah, that's it ...

Author: Who are the losers? Who suffers the most from it, would you say?

O: The population, they're losers. The people who have to pay more for something. For example for a car. A Greek person must now pay more for something like a car. A Greek person, because of the euro, now has to put down more money than before. A winner would perhaps be a guest-worker – someone who can easily go to another EU country, can move there, can start work there immediately, he's a winner. Losers are perhaps the people in the countryside who aren't mobile ...

R: Yeah, and when it comes to countries, I'd say at the moment that *we* are the losers.

Ulrich: Well we always were in the EU. It was always Germany ... [O: ... yeah ...] I mean, the Spanish were the great winners ... [R: Sure, but ...], they're the ones who've been subsidised the most ...

R: But at least earlier we had lower unemployment, we had a good standard of living ... And the social-security system functioned properly, it was all the best, so one happily paid higher contributions and put up with being the largest contributor, but now, as far as the substance goes, nothing functions like that any more, it's all different ...

O: Losers, for example, are people like us. States like Bavaria start to cut their budget. The local authorities receive less, like Würzburg for example. What do the local authorities do? They raise the costs, the fees in other words. Each one of us, in the last ten years, has 50% higher additional expenses, like rent and rubbish collection for example, right? Everything goes up, and the local authorities want to draw in the money again. Each one of us in the last ten years has considerably less money in our pockets. We earn six or seven euros or whatever like before, on average, but the consumption ... the household has really suffered in Germany [R: Mmmm, I'd definitely call us losers ...] Yes, we're losers. The entrepreneurs who are flexible and who go abroad, they're winners; the little man in Germany at least is a loser, because he has considerably less money. We're not able to go out to the pub each week and have a beer and eat good food, that's simply no longer an option. We have considerably less money in our pockets.

Note the pessimistic assumptions here concerning the possibilities for dealing with economic problems in an organised fashion. Ralf's lengthy intervention towards the beginning, concerning the creation of the single market, displays many of the motifs identified in Chapter 5 being applied to the EU. A sense of inevitability comes though clearly. The critical decisions surrounding the single market were taken in the past, and the move to extend EU membership to countries such as Poland, the Czech Republic and Slovenia was made despite informed political discussion of the fact it would lead to the movement of companies and jobs eastwards. Now that the process is in motion it has its own dynamic, the borders have been opened and they can no longer be closed. Concrete proposals about how to tackle such problems could only be 'of a theoretical nature,' since it is unlikely anything will change.

One sees also the motif of the political subjects as contributors being applied in the EU context, with discussion of the EU's finances prompting the 'we' to be constructed in national terms ('the population', Germany as a 'contributing country') and regional terms (Bavaria). The number of different ways found to convey the idea that 'we' are the ones on whom the burden to contribute falls is indicative of a strong sense of injustice here: not only do 'we' pay, but 'we' lose our jobs.[9] The

---

[9]One can also speculate, from a more psychological perspective, that a certain satisfaction is found in emphasising how narrow is the circle of 'we contributors' who bear the burden and who can thereby claim the moral high ground.

adversaries – the 'takers' – are also constructed along national lines as 'the smaller states', 'eastern countries' or (like the Czech Republic) 'the new accession countries'. These are all described as unitary actors rather than as environments. That they are assumed to be in competition with one another is clear – there is the sense that Germany is losing out to its rivals, indicated by the notion she is the 'tail-light' amongst the European economies (the same term is used in the Kassel discussion). Though there is no call for such countries to be expelled from the Union, there is clearly – from Oskar's side at least – little trust towards them, since it is supposed that should these countries cease to profit from the Union they might simply decide to leave it.

Mixed in with this however is a discursive pattern more conducive to a political bond. When the subjects are formulated not as those who contribute but as the 'little people' opposed by the economically powerful, a tendency to draw comparisons and to evoke 'people like us' elsewhere is considerably more evident. One sees here the discussion taking a turn of this kind as it moves away from the problem of EU finances, with comparisons then drawn with certain other European countries regarding economic conditions – prices in particular, due to the introduction of the euro. When this happens, other Europeans are portrayed not so much as competitors but as counterparts facing the same challenges. This sense of shared predicament seems evident in the reference to the Greek person who now has to pay more in order to own a car. This fits well with the positioning of the subjects in this section as 'the little man', who is being squeezed by rising costs and who ends up with less money in his pocket. Here, the idea of a political bond is considerably more plausible than when the positioning is such that the adversaries are national competitors.

Europe as old news: *Relations between Peoples*

When discussion turns to problems to do with *Relations between Peoples*, one finds further reference to 'Europe' and the EU, though with less frequency than in the domain of *Economics*. As we have seen, questions of conflict and the threat of conflict are generally not conceived as domestic to the majority-peoples of 'the West', as these are constructed in discussion. Relations between western peoples are generally assumed to be peaceful: whatever their differences in 'national character', war between them is unlikely. As we heard Ralf in Würzburg put it, 'the only conflicts which are left are far away from us, and here in Central Europe, in Europe, in the EU area we have a very peaceful shared existence'. Differences between European nationalities are minimised, and the idea that they might dangerously threaten each other is not raised. Perhaps understandably then, a role for the EU in coordinating harmonious relations is hardly mentioned. The organised maintenance of peace is unnecessary, it seems, for the very reason that peacefulness is taken to be characteristic. Ralf does credit the EU with having consolidated peace on the continent, but Ulrich from the same group expresses his doubts: 'I don't think the EU helps Europeans live together – economic interests, yeah, but not the ability to live together. I mean, I don't find a foreigner nicer or less nice just because he's in the EU, that doesn't matter. It's got nothing to do with it, I'd say.' Hardly anywhere in the discussions is a positive role as peace-maker foreseen for the EU. The most prevalent form of positioning in this domain, whereby other peoples of 'the West' are treated as 'people like us', seems to render such a role of little consequence.

Nor does a positive role tend to be accorded to the EU as regards those inter-people relations quite clearly problematised. Building up 'Europe' as a global power in military and defence terms so as to manage threats emerging from outside 'the West' – another possible form of collective action, desirable or not – is a proposal heard rarely in these discussions. That 'the West' evokes something broader than Europe probably weakens the extent to which acting at a European level is given credence. Also, the appeal of a collective western or European foreign policy is perhaps diminished by the assumption that the opponents are held to be living *within* the home and comparable environments, not just beyond them. While an association is undoubtedly made between Arabs/Muslims and a certain part of the world (broadly, the Middle East), at the same time they are assumed to be close at hand – perhaps sitting at the next table, or walking the city streets. When the problem is constructed in this way as one of daily exposure, the relevance of foreign and defence policy is much diminished. Furthermore, within 'the West', the power of 'the Americans' tends to be emphasised. When Jochen in Lübeck suggests that 'the bigger Europe becomes, the more weight it has in global politics,' the reaction from the other participants is rather muted. 'Does Europe really have any power though?' asks Hamid. Jochen maintains his point, though rather cautiously: 'No, power probably not, but its weight will increase. So you can't ... from the American perspective it gets more difficult just to ride roughshod and say "what Europe says is totally unimportant to us." [Niklas: Definitely.] Not *totally* unimportant, I said. As opposed to if Germany alone said "I don't like that".' Amongst the Czech groups, the possibility of projecting global power is not even discussed.

The main approach advocated for tackling problems to do with *Relations between Peoples* is, as we saw, the minimisation of mutual exposure. This is something the national government rather than the EU is assumed to have control over (though as we have seen, the effectiveness of the former is somewhat doubted on the grounds that politicians may be too soft to take action). A European approach, either based on supranational regulation or cooperation between those in 'comparable' countries, is generally not advocated: again, perhaps because the problems are already seen to be in the local environment, one sees little of a 'fortress Europe' motif. Alan in Swansea asks: 'If Brussels is supposed to be the centre of Europe and all the politicians are there, why can't they turn round to Germany and say "well look, you *have* got to take some [immigrants]. France, you *have* got to take some ...?" You know what I mean, instead of putting them on the back of lorries and shipping them over here. Surely Brussels, if they've got all the power, should be saying "well *you* got to have some, *you* got to have some", and spread it out, instead of them all coming over here.' The sense that fairness demands similar countries be treated equally may suggest there is the basis for a European approach, but his point is not picked up by the rest of the group, and indeed Andy himself says he 'doesn't have much faith' in the idea. For problems to do with *Relations between Peoples,* the plausibility of any kind of political project centred on a European polity seems weak, even setting aside the issue of normative desirability.

Europe as a nice idea: *Quality of Life*

In Chapter 3 it was noted that there is another body of problems which appear occasionally in these discussions, related to topics such as the environment, hygiene and the quality of services, which can be loosely summarised under the heading *Quality of Life*. These problems, it was noted, once articulated tend to be put to one side, with their importance questioned or with attention diverted elsewhere. However, in those instances where one does find problematisation of this kind – with discussion of pollution or food-safety standards, for example – 'Europe' and the EU are invoked with some frequency.[10] For such problems, the 'people like us' would be a fairly inclusive category: potentially everyone is affected by environmental pollution, by the purity of the water supply or the meat which goes into sausages. Where

---

[10]The number of such instances is admittedly small (around ten or so, across all interviews), so generalisations must be cautious.

EU regulations are mentioned, they are presented as well-intentioned and probably appropriate: at Kassel, all participants speak approvingly of the EU legislation they say is designed to deal with fine-particulate pollution, the environmental problem of the day. In the Plzeň discussion, all participants note that the environment in the Czech Republic has improved considerably in recent years (reference is made to reductions in factory emissions, improvement in the quality of buses and their exhausts, and the disappearance of dirty old cars like the Trabant and Tatra), and there is general consensus that the adoption of the EU's standards accounts for this. Robert, with Pavel's agreement, makes an explicit link to EU accession: 'if we hadn't been obliged to change, who'd have bothered?'

These problems to do with *Quality of Life* tend to be marginalised however, and with them the potentially positive role of a European polity in dealing with them. This is true even amongst the Czechs, where discussion of such problems – probably for the very reason of recent adaptation to EU norms – is the most common. One sees something of this in a passage from Plzeň, which begins with Pavel responding to the question whether he was in favour of the Czech Republic joining the EU:

Pavel:	... Now I'm no longer as sure as I was before, but back then when it was happening I was in favour.
Michal:	I think in the future it's going to be a good thing but for now there's nothing in it ... [R: What do you mean, nothing?] For us right now there's nothing good in it.
Robert:	What do you mean? ... We've just been talking about the transport improvements and stuff ...
M:	Yeah that's one thing but a second thing is all the new stuff which they're implementing: the registration office ... pubs need to have toilets, kitchens, everything. You've got to buy a 10,000 CK walkie-talkie for the car ...
P:	Exactly, yeah, this is why I don't see it like I used to any more ... [M: Right ...]
R:	Fine but how can you say you don't see anything in it when the quality of services is going up? The quality of everything is going up.
P:	Because I have to buy a different walkie-talkie ... Ok, that's one thing, another thing ...
R:	In any case I've heard they're dividing the radio band into quarters so a lot more people can use it. It's all about

improvements. The others don't have the right frequencies ... [P: I know, but ...]

M: It's an improvement but you don't notice the improvement. Where do you notice it?

R: Where? ... Well, right now the band is so mashed up that ... it's not separated out ... [P: That's true, sure, but ...]

M: OK so let's talk about the toilets here in the pub. What I notice is that it smells lovely and everything's pretty, but the snag is the landlord has to install some photocell on each urinal and for each one he has to pay 70,000 CK. The quality improves, but at the expense of the one who has to pay for it.

P: Our walkie-talkies are a trivial thing, it's true. But another thing for example are the butchers. Today you're not allowed to have the producer and the slaughterer together in one place like in a classical abattoir, so the classical butcher has to cease business. Schneider,[11] he's ok, he's got a slaughterer there and a producer there ... [M: Is he ok?] Isn't he? Relatively, compared to the average butcher ... [M: Which was the one that closed? The slaughterhouse ...] One of them closed ... But Schneider ...

R: You're both talking about whether it's better for you yourselves ...

P: Yeah well how *is* it better for me if I liked that particular sausage, if all the hygiene norms come in and ... It's been eaten for decades and it's never hurt anyone ...

R: Of course but you notice it in the quality. In the toilets for example, if you go to a pub and you've got one tiny piece of soap ...

P: Fine but that's just a detail I think, the old toilets would've been fine if someone looked after them. [M: Right ...]

R: No ... now you've got liquid soap ... the regulations ... [P: Fine but that's ...] Those are norms ...

P: Those are things which cost hundreds of crowns ...

R: Those are things you encounter every day ...

---

[11]A local meat-processing plant.

M: The services improve but at someone's expense – someone
            somewhere has to pay for that improvement.
R: Yeah of course. It's a demanding investment.

One must be careful with such a passage not to overstate the link being
made to the EU and its policies: for the Czech groups, EU accession
probably symbolises wider processes of 'democratisation' and 'liberal-
isation', functioning as much as a *signifier* for a whole range of developments as their assumed *cause*. Nonetheless, there *is* a linkage being
made here between the EU and daily life, and one way to read the
exchange of views is as a contest over the 'meaning' of EU accession.
On the one hand it is presented, mainly by Robert, as improving the
quality of various 'services', from radio signals to toilets to sausages
(i.e. addressing problems to do with *Quality of Life*), while on the other
it is presented, mainly by Pavel and Michal, as engendering new costs
for the little people (i.e. creating further problems in *Economics*). In the
one view, the benefits are general, and one should not ask simply
'whether it's better for you yourselves'; in the other 'the quality
improves at the expense of those who have to pay for it.' While the
debate is unresolved here, Robert has to argue strongly to prevent the
supposed collective benefits being crowded out. Insofar then as it is
problématiques such as these which tend most often to prompt a
favourable reference to the EU and its policies, this positive basis for
allegiances to the EU is undermined by the doubt cast on the seriousness of the problems at stake. The kind of positioning and the relatively strong sense of agency are conducive to such allegiances, but
the problems involved amount at most to a quite minor part of the
political common.

The findings in context

The observations of this chapter have been grounded in the original
data produced by this study. Is there confirmation to be found in existing sets of data? In Chapter 2 we made some cautionary remarks about
Eurobarometer polls, both on account of their focus (they contain little
which corresponds for example to our examination of collective positioning, or to the origins of political problems) and due to the limitations of the polling method generally. These concerns rule out a
systematic cross-check of our results. Nevertheless, careful inspection
of Eurobarometer datasets from autumn 2004 (the time of the first
interview) to summer 2010 reveals findings clearly supportive of what

has been argued so far. As an indication of the wider relevance of our account, the main points can be summarised as follows.

Note, to begin with, how the survey data suggests perceptions of the EU's relevance vary according to issue. For those we have categorised with the heading *Society and the Law* – e.g. issues of urban security and crime prevention – Eurobarometer records that citizen expectations tend to focus on the national government (Eurobarometer 62, 2005: 34). Europe is perceived as remote. Problems meanwhile to do with *Economics* – those generally regarded the most salient – are seen as in principle a proper concern of the EU, but also as those for which today's EU offers little in the way of remedy. Citing EU averages, Eurobarometer records that 'unemployment is the main concern of European citizens', yet that 'the verdict on the European Union's actions to combat unemployment is fairly critical: 25% of respondents think that the European Union plays a positive role in this area', while the figure for rising prices is just 21% (Eurobarometer 62, 2005: 26).[12] The EU's achievements tend to be rated more highly on issues such as environmental protection (52% express satisfaction here) and foreign and defence policy (53% and 52%) yet as the survey authors note, such issues tend to be less salient (Eurobarometer 62, 2005: 26). As our study has brought out, they relate either to second-order issues of *Quality of Life*, or to increasingly taken-for-granted issues of inter-state peace. The numbers giving approval to the EU on other, more salient aspects of *Relations between Peoples* such as immigration are again much lower (29%). On the issues that matter, the EU is little regarded as a convincing source of remedy.

Can one account for this with reference to a sense of fatalism concerning what public authority can achieve on these issues? The data is ambiguous, since Eurobarometer question-wording tends to invite the feasibility of agency to be assumed. That tackling unemployment is something the EU should regard as one of its highest priorities is a point which, when prompted, sizeable numbers of respondents are willing to affirm (e.g. Eurobarometer 66, 2007: 167). But while a desire for active measures on a salient issue seems evident, their perceived credibility is

---

[12]The question (Q34) was: 'And for each of the following issues in (OUR COUNTRY), do you think that the European Union plays a positive role, a negative role or neither a positive nor negative role?'

left unquestioned.[13] The same applies for immigration, on which it is said 75% of citizens consistently favour a common European policy, though again the proposition to which responses are solicited is a 'should' rather than 'could' one (Eurobarometer 67, 2007: 168, QA39.3).[14] Still, a discrepancy between hopes and expectations does occasionally appear in these datasets: one sees it explicitly when citizens are asked in Eurobarometer 71 (2010) to evaluate the likelihood that certain expressed goals – on gender pay equality, the environment, solidarity in society and work-life balance – will be realised by 2030 (significantly fewer expect it than hope it). Fatalism on matters of globalisation, understood primarily as 'the relocation of certain companies to countries where labour is cheaper', is also widely evident, with Eurobarometer 63 recording (p.59) that 'the globalisation process is often perceived as irreversible'.

Whatever the role of such views in shaping broader attitudes to the EU – Eurobarometer is of limited help here – the fact comes through strongly that the EU ends up commonly being seen not just as an inadequate remedy to certain key problems but as a factor in generating them. As survey 62 reveals, larger than the percentages of those who see the EU's role with regard to unemployment and price rises as either positive or neutral are the percentages of those who see it as negative (Eurobarometer 62, 2005: 26). Consistent with this is that the stand-out 'fear provoked by the building of Europe' is the transfer of jobs abroad, something of which 74% of respondents recorded themselves 'currently afraid' (Eurobarometer 62, 2005: 141; similar figures are found in the surveys thereafter); note also the link commonly made

---

[13]See (Eurobarometer 66, 2007: 167), QA26: 'From the following list of actions, could you tell me what should be for you, the three actions that the European Union should follow in priority?' N.B. not all Standard Eurobarometer questions of this sort allow an emphasis to be placed on tackling unemployment: see (Eurobarometer 67, 2007: 178), QA41: 'European integration has been focusing on various issues in the last years. In your opinion, which aspects should be emphasized by the European institutions in the coming years, to strengthen the European Union in the future?' Respondents are given no option to prioritise day-to-day economic concerns such as unemployment and decreasing purchasing power, with the result that a previously muted concern for the environment takes centre-stage.
[14]52% support for a European defence policy is recorded in (Eurobarometer 62, 2005: 120), but again with a question which invites this response by classifying the matters at stake as European. See Q40, 'In your opinion, should decisions concerning European defence policy be taken by national governments, by NATO or by the European Union?'

between price rises and the introduction of the euro (Eurobarometer 62, 2005: 26). We are told that attitudes towards the EU tend to correlate positively with those towards 'globalisation' (Eurobarometer 66, 2007: 88), a significant point given the scepticism that can be found towards the latter. Eurobarometer's interpretation of its data on attitudes to globalisation can be rather rosy, and a superficial reading might suggest widespread endorsement. When polled on its contribution to scientific and technological progress, generally a second-order concern, respondents seem willing to give a positive evaluation.[15] However, it seems clear that globalisation is most widely seen as an economic phenomenon, and the assessments voiced of it when framed as such are mixed at best, and on matters of employment downright hostile.[16] Striking, though fully consistent with the findings of the present study, is the observation that on average six out of ten EU citizens believe 'globalisation benefits only companies and not citizens' (Eurobarometer 69 (2), 2008: 5).[17] Insofar as the EU is cast as a symptom of globalisation rather than an exogenous means to cope with it, a positive appraisal of it is unlikely.

These quantitative findings suggest good reason to suppose the conclusions of our study have wider application. Eurobarometer tells us relatively little about the repertoires of understanding through which the EU comes to be interpreted, and is always liable to inflate the EU's importance, given the opinions it assembles are solicited directly. It does, nonetheless, provide some backing for the arguments we have advanced. Particularly interesting, however, is if we turn to a recent piece of qualitative research not dissimilar to our own, whose findings it converges with in several ways.

In this parallel project, a team of researchers based in France, Belgium and Britain convened focus-groups in Paris, Brussels, and Oxford to examine how citizens talk about Europe, and to investigate the kinds of controversy the topic does or does not inspire (Duchesne et al. 2010). The groups were composed with the aim of making cross-class as well as cross-national comparisons. More so than our own

---

[15]See e.g. (Eurobarometer 66, 2007: 89).

[16](Eurobarometer 69 (2), 2008), is devoted to perceptions of globalisation. For respondents' tendency to associate 'globalisation' with economic concerns, notably 'the relocation of some companies to countries where labour is cheaper (41%)', see p.27.

[17]Note of course the possibility that such views are unequally distributed across EU countries: for discussion, see (Eurobarometer 69 (2), 2008: 6).

study, the interviews were organised around Europe-themed questions, but participants could then steer discussion as they wished. Let us highlight just a few of the study's findings as they have been published so far. First, a key observation is that, across the groups, discussion of Europe and the EU appears scarcely separable from discussion of a wider set of political themes. While some groups are clearly more conscious of European integration than others, rarely does it emerge as a distinct topic able to spark debate on its own: it is mainly salient by association rather than intrinsically. Second, it is principally economic issues which bring it to the fore, with motifs of globalisation invariably wrapped into these (Duchesne et al. 2010: 96). Geo-political dimensions are not absent – recurrent links are made to colonialism, again a spatially broad theme – but they are secondary to the economic.

Third, before forces that play out at a global level, the EU, like authority at the national level, is widely considered impotent. 'Even though our participants talk about their daily lives, they locate the main economic actors and processes at the global level. They are convinced of (and truly disappointed by) national failure but they do not put any hope in European agency' (Duchesne et al. 2010: 99). The EU is overshadowed by processes of global change, something which the authors suggest produces in many 'euro-indifference' rather than 'euro-scepticism'. Epiphenomenal to developments elsewhere, it barely appears worthy of rage. Speakers acknowledge the advantages integration provides for mobility – similar to our findings in Chapter 4, there is heightened awareness of EU neighbours and of places of vacation – but this does not amount to anything one might call a 'European identity' (Duchesne et al. 2010: 98). Especially for the French and Belgians, and amongst those lower in the social hierarchy, we are told European integration is 'a fact to which they are resigned', something which 'is there, whether one wishes it or not' (Duchesne et al. 2010: 83). Speakers 'projected sometimes on to the level of Europe a demand for protection, which was translated by the participants into a matter of protection of exchange and jobs, and putting into place a system of solidarity. But the same participants appeared clearly to be sceptical about the possibility that Europe could resolve any of these problems: all consider that the game is global, and that it has overtaken us' (Duchesne et al. 2010: 96). While economic concerns matter to participants, and while, as they acknowledge, the EU matters to the economy, its significance as a source of agency is explicitly downplayed: as a political actor, it matters much less.

That the present study and this parallel one produce these strongly convergent results, despite differences of method and sample, offers further reason to have confidence in the wider significance of our findings. What one can identify in a targeted set of interviews with taxi-drivers seems discernible by other means, and in additional locations. This being so, we may start reflecting on some of the larger implications of what we have said.

Challenges and prospects for a political bond in Europe

In addition to refining the concepts involved, our empirical examination of the scheme outlined in Chapter 1 has highlighted some of the complexities of political allegiance in the contemporary age, as well as some of the obstacles to a political bond supportive of a European polity. Speakers do not fail in the articulation of matters of common concern: they do this with considerable fluidity, and there is little evidence of disengagement from the substance of politics. Moreover, there are indications, modest but appreciable, of a widening of the sense of shared predicament before certain problems, such that their effects are assumed to be felt across a wider-than-national space. Yet at the same time, for the problems discussed in depth, acts of positioning characterised by a transnationalisation of 'us' and a basic tolerance of 'them' are mixed with others more parochial in their inclusion or more hostile in their exclusion. For these same problems, the EU tends not to be invoked as a possible means for their remedy, since expressions of shared predicament rarely follow its contours, and since there is widespread scepticism concerning the very possibility of remedy. More often the EU is treated as yet another manifestation of these problems. Only to a limited extent, and mainly for problems of secondary importance, is the EU 'made sense of' by existing discursive patterns.

It seems clear then from these findings that the kind of collective bond sketched in Chapter 1, one capable of evoking an explicitly political logic for the European polity, is weakly developed as things stand. As the preceding chapters have indicated, the EU's quandary is by no means wholly particular to it, for it replicates – albeit in sharpened form – the uncertain political attachments expressed to the national polity. One instinctively expects the challenge of a multi-level order to be the challenge of divided allegiance, yet the stand-out feature here might better be called *diluted* allegiance, certainly as effects political institutions. While this raises difficulties for political attachment in general, the consequences for the EU would seem especially problematic, given a transnational polity is not only permanently vulnerable to a dissolution into its component parts, but is less able to draw on the additional sources of allegiance associated with the nation-state.

Under such conditions, citizenship in the EU has a hollowed quality. What importantly lacks is not political consent as such – a dubious political good, if it means mere obedience to power – but the kinds of attachment needed for public authority to be regarded as responsive, or at least potentially responsive, to the wills of those it affects. This leaves it dissonant with the idea of collective self-rule. To be sure, if one adheres to a formalistic conception of democracy, centred on the right to participate in free elections, then democracy itself can exist nonetheless, and perhaps is already well established in the EU. But if these institutional structures are not animated by popular commitments, such that citizens recognise them as expressions of their mutual interdependence and their agency, then the principle of collective self-rule that regulates democracy is left out. At a practical level, one can expect diminished levels of political vigilance and participation, for only if citizens have the tools of imagination to see the EU as a possible deliverer of political goods are they likely to seek assurance its policies approximate the standards this requires. Without this necessary basis on which to judge and criticise, the risk will be that the legal and political rights of EU citizenship are neglected, leaving a passive and manipulated citizenry. Furthermore, the feasibility of galvanising support behind political programmes that may require transnational alliances and supranational claims-making – e.g. projects of redistribution or intercultural dialogue – is likely to be weakened also.

It is an open empirical question whether a restoration of ties at the national level represents a more plausible prospect than their strengthening at the transnational level. The variety across domains in the attachments expressed suggests there are no straightforward answers here, although the ongoing pre-eminence of the national seems unmistakeable. An open *normative* question meanwhile is which of these two options would be more desirable – whether a deepening of commitments to the transnational level is preferable to the fostering of more local ties. As it touches on the vexed issue of political boundaries and their relative worth, this is a question beyond our range. But insofar as one takes seriously the European option, it seems plausible to suppose that, with discussion of the EU absorbing motifs present in the appraisal of political matters more widely, any attempt to alter the EU's political reception would necessarily involve simultaneously addressing these broader discursive patterns. It would demand the de-naturalising of various assumptions about the political world in general, and the flagging up of alternative perspectives. Only in this way could one expect the tightening of political allegiances and the maturation of a political bond.

In the remains of this chapter, let us consider in more depth what such changes might involve. Here we enter a more speculative mode of reflection, though our points remain grounded in the material analysed.

When thinking about how new patterns of discursive practice might look, the challenge clearly is not that of imagining an entirely new set of practices for projection onto a *tabula rasa*. It can be taken as axiomatic that, insofar as innovation is possible, it depends not so much on an actor's genius for invention but on their pragmatic ability to make adjustments to existing repertoires of practice, to retrieve older repertoires which have become subordinated, to foster changes of emphasis, and to introduce new resources in ways such that they respond to the patterns which pre-exist them. The extent to which such changes can be engineered will depend on a variety of conjunctural factors, but herein lies the challenge for those 'discursive architects' who would seek to effect a Europe-wide political bond. Existing patterns of discursive practice would constitute both the target to be taken aim at, since certain commonly-made assumptions would need challenging, but also a pool of resources to be utilised, since one could imagine alterations to the speech-act potential of existing formulations, whether achieved by dislodging conventional associations and ascribing new ones, or by extending patterns of usage such that the weight of old formulations is put to new purpose. Rather like the 'innovating ideologists' of the seventeenth century, whose strategies for legitimising the new socio-economic practices of capitalist society Quentin Skinner has discussed, those who would seek to realise a political bond supportive of a European polity would in this sense be 'obliged to march backwards into battle', to keep their eye on the discursive landscape behind them (Skinner 2002: 150).[18] For the same reason, in the section that follows, a certain accent is placed on the way new trends in discursive practice are pre-figured in existing tendencies.

---

[18]Skinner suggests the task of innovating ideologists is 'that of legitimising some form of social behaviour generally agreed to be questionable' (p.148). The scenario is analogous to that of establishing the legitimacy of an emerging polity: there is the need to render acceptable and commonsensical what is new, and which for the very reason it is new seems questionable.

There is of course no guarantee that any such 'discursive architects' who would take it upon themselves to develop alternative repertoires of political understanding would be successful in carrying through their innovations. Like architects, they could design and promote blueprints to be acted upon, but they could not by themselves ensure these came to fruition in everyday practice. Such would be a matter for ongoing political effort. It is worth recalling that many of the discursive practices examined in this study themselves bear the accumulated traces of political campaigning, albeit perhaps at some delay (witness the persistent language of class). As the residue of past political efforts, they are evidence of what initiatives in discursive innovation can achieve, as well as the background conditions for all initiatives to come.[19]

Staying close to the empirical material, we can lay out some of the changes that would seem necessary if a political bond on a European scale were to take shape. Our points in what follows can be related to each of the three dimensions of a political bond: the make-up of the political common, prevalent acts of collective positioning, and assumptions about the worth of political projects. Since the first of these (the political common) is most general in scope, its consideration is postponed until last.

1.   Positioning (I): The opponents as adversaries, not enemies

That opponents of the 'people like us' be accepted as legitimate adversaries to be engaged with (if only to be consistently opposed) is a basic condition of any political bond, whether associated with a European polity or some other political configuration. It has been seen that, for problems to do with *Society and the Law*, this criterion is generally met in the discourse across the sample groups. However, for problems to do with *Relations between Peoples*, it is generally not. Instead, one finds an antagonistic relationship posited between the subjects and their counterparts on the one hand (principally expressed with categories such as 'the West', with certain racial connotations) and their enemies (with particular reference to Arabs/Muslims) on the other. What kinds of discursive change might a democrat hope to see?

One approach to 'taming' the relationship such that it is agonistic rather than antagonistic would be to dislodge some of the characteristics ascribed to the opponents. Instead of them being positioned undifferentiatedly as irrational, aggressive and intransigent, one would

---

[19]See also (White 2010b).

want to see them portrayed as actors rationally advancing their own agenda. To emphasise the irrationality, aggression and intransigence of the other is largely to give up on democratic politics, since these take on the quality of essential attributes unsusceptible to change and inhibiting the possibility of compromise. Surely preferable is when conflict itself is seen as the challenge, not the opponents as such, and when these opponents are held likewise to be seeking ways to resolve it.[20] Reaching such a perspective need not involve counter-arguments which negate the idea of difference to the point of affirming that all people(s) are essentially the same. Opponents would not need to be seen as people like 'us', and assertions of the sort that 'everyone shares the same values' or that 'to be offended by foreign-looking cultural symbols in your neighbourhood is morally wrong' might be unproductive and unwise. However well-intentioned and ostensibly appealing, they would be likely to fall foul of the common criticism that politicians and political parties are too soft in dealing with these problems of conflict, that they wish to paper over them. There are, after all, important debates to be had about the place of religious symbols in public life, the authority of the state to impose a single curriculum on all schools under its jurisdiction, or the course of a country's foreign policy, and there is little reason to expect such debates to be pursued in detached, individualist terms.

The challenge then would not be so much to construct discourses of friendship as to construct discourses of agonism rather than antagonism. Some acknowledgement of the categories of 'them' and 'us' would have its place, provided the dynamic between these two were articulated in a certain way. It will be recalled that at least two major explanatory motifs for inter-people conflict were observed in the discussions, one concerning the supposedly hostile characteristics of opponents, the other concerning the contest for collective power. The first emphasises irrationality (it is a kind of *demonisation*), the second rationality (a form of *rivalrisation*). Insofar as the latter offers the possibility of reasoned compromise whereas the former does not, it may be that one already has a motif available with which to conjure a more agonistic relationship. Rational self-advancement is intelligible and can

---

[20]This perspective is usefully described by Bellamy when laying out the republican ideal of compromise through negotiation: 'Instead of viewing a conflict as a battle to be won or lost, the parties see it as a collective problem to be solved' (Bellamy 1999: 101).

be engaged, whereas irrational self-assertion is beyond explanation: it is tantamount to *evil*, and with evil there can be no compromise. It goes without saying that conflicts for power can 'turn nasty' too, but it may be that the promulgation of this motif provides a better basis for their resolution.

A second approach to taming the hostile dynamic signalled on problems to do with *Relations between Peoples* would involve focusing rather on the formulations used to demarcate the subjects and counterparts. In particular, this might include seeking to diminish the frequency with which the category of 'the West' is adopted, since this generally seems to be used with either racial implications or implications of good sense and peacefulness. While in principle the term could be just a remnant of the Cold War, without an association with any such markers, its deployment in the discussion of current conflicts tends to be more laden. The difficulty, it scarcely needs adding, is not that race is an inherently negative category, but that it is an exclusive and essentialising one which gives any conflict delineated in its terms a sense of permanence and naturalness. Likewise, it is not that 'good sense and peacefulness' should be thought of as negative characteristics: the difficulty is rather that if claimed as intrinsic to the 'people like us' then this will result in those treated as opponents being positioned as deficient in these qualities. *Eradicating* the concept of 'the West' is an implausible and perhaps dubious objective, but there may be some appeal in the promotion of alternative formulations – not least 'Europe' – which can make no claim to embody white-majority countries as a whole.

There is then the question of positioning in the *Economics* domain. The conclusion above was that the opponents here (which include 'the rich', large companies, financial institutions, in some cases those dependent on state welfare, and those 'eastern Europeans' who both compete for jobs and redistributed wealth) are generally positioned as adversaries rather than enemies, but that this remains a precarious condition. Likewise, particularly when discussion is focused on the question of who contributes to and who takes from the EU's finances, the adversaries tend to be demarcated along country lines, a pattern again conducive to resentment of other Europeans. The persistent danger is that the poverty or 'cheapness' which is ascribed to 'them', and which stands as the reason why they are seen to be threatening jobs, wages, earnings and benefits, comes to be regarded as an essential attribute rather than a contingent circumstance. The essentialisation of attributes tends to herald an antagonistic positioning of opponents.

The question therefore arises how any tendencies towards essentialisation might be undermined.

Two possible argumentational strategies stand out. In one of them, the contingency of these attributes would be affirmed by suggesting that inequalities in wealth between western and eastern Europe will level out naturally over time. The argument would be that companies will continue to invest and create jobs in eastern Europe in the short term while wages there are more attractive than in the west, but that this in turn will boost average earnings there to the point that the very economic disparities which make eastern Europe favourable to such companies will no longer exist, prompting those companies to move on, leaving eastern Europe in a similar predicament to 'ours' today. Such an argument serves well to highlight the contingency of wealth inequalities, and implies that the opponents are not fundamentally different from people like 'us'. However, at the same time it works to undermine the credibility of a political project to tackle problems of *Economics*, since it makes the resolution of such problems dependent upon the inclinations of private companies and the market signals to which they respond. It follows the very logic of inevitability and of uncontrollable cycles of good fortune and bad which, as seen in Chapter 5, is precisely the source of a sense of powerlessness towards problems in this domain. It does not respond to the sense that something should be done about these problems; it merely suggests they will go away at some point – and needless to say, is likely to be particularly open to question in times of economic difficulty. A second argumentational strategy, conversely, would involve highlighting the contingency of wealth inequalities by suggesting there are things which can be done about them. Wage competition would be presented not as an eternal and unavoidable fact but as the consequence of, for instance, the absence of a minimum wage and harmonised levels of taxation, or the absence of wealth redistribution from 'the rich' and 'shareholders' (i.e. other adversaries) in western Europe. That a gap exists also in eastern Europe between 'the rich' and 'the little people' would be a fact in need of emphasis, likewise that there too there are 'contributors' as well as 'non-contributors'. The advantage of this approach is that it tempers the idea eastern Europeans might be permanent adversaries without simultaneously putting political agency in question.

As with *Relations between Peoples*, a repositioning of the opponents would depend on undermining or refashioning certain common formulations for the 'people like us'. The frequency with which participants in discussion position only themselves as being 'the ones who contribute' seems problematic, since it can be mobilised to discredit any kind of political project involving state action. The burden – e.g. of taxation or regulation – can be presented as always falling on 'us', and the benefits 'draining away' elsewhere, provoking the misleading conclusion that it is the attempt at democratic control itself which is the problem. Any alternative formulation would do well to preserve the active voice (as one finds with 'the contributors') while avoiding the potential for anti-political manipulation. Maintaining a plural form is also likely to be important, given that individualistic forms can heighten the sense of passive vulnerability before the problems articulated. One strategy that presents itself would be to seek to refashion the subject-position of the 'working people' so as to loosen its association with *contribution* and to play up its association with other economic problems currently linked more strongly to terms such as 'the little people'. Unlike the latter, 'working people' carries overtones of activeness and links better to a sense of the possibilities for action. Such a shift in the term's usage is a considerable task of course, but arguably it has performed this role in the past, in the vocabulary both of trade unions and the revolutionary Left, meaning there is an older pattern of usage to be rediscovered.

Alternatively, as a second strategy, one might accept the emphasis placed on 'us' being contributors, but seek to prevent this leading to the construction of opponents whose legitimate presence in the political community is doubted. For 'eastern Europeans' one would want to substitute a category *not* demarcated in national terms, and therefore one less liable to invite the move to exclude. A deflection of this kind might be achieved with the category of 'the rich' and its cognate terms. As suggested in Chapter 4, when matters of contribution are at stake, 'the rich' tend to be invoked less, and contribution to the tax system tends to be discussed more in simple do-or-don't terms (which draws attention towards the non-contributors 'below' and invites them to be positioned as opponents) rather than in more-or-less terms (which draws attention rather towards those at 'the top' who do contribute, but less than they might). However, the possibility that the contribution motif can be combined with a gaze 'upwards' rather than 'laterally' or 'downwards' is confirmed by this passage from the Kassel discussion:

> H: … The state has always taxed the most those people who have relatively little.
> P: Why? Because the people who have the least have always been the biggest in number. [S: Exactly …] It's quite simple. Why are

the little people – let's say everyone who's sitting here now – why are they paying taxes and why are the big guys not paying taxes like that? The big guys are such a small proportion ... even if they did pay it'd be a drop in the ocean. But us below, because there's a mass of us, there the taxes can really be raked in. But not with those few people at the top.

H: No, no. That's ... when you think that, what is it, 85% of the population has very little money and only 15% of the capital ... how is it, 80% of the capital is managed or held by 15% of the people. And I think, if taxation was done properly ... [D: done properly ...] then that would be quite a considerable amount ... [D: Yeah, absolutely ...]

More of this kind of talk would, one may imagine, enable less of the talk which positions other EU citizens as opponents by virtue of their nationality.

2.   Positioning (II): Other European countries as comparable environments rather than competitive actors, and the wider evocation of counterparts

The demarcation of opponents using the category of nationality is avoided, we have argued, when the member-states that make up the EU are regarded not as unitary actors but as environments in which problems are encountered. It is then that the recognition becomes possible of 'counterparts' outside the home environment who face predicaments similar to those faced by the subjects, and hence the possibility of a deeper understanding of the predicaments faced.

This means in particular the readiness to make transnational comparisons. As we have seen, these already occur with regard to certain problems of *Economics* and *Relations between Peoples*: the decline of industry, wage and price levels, and the conflicts arising from the encounter of different 'peoples' are all problems on which they are made. However, transnational comparisons are conceivable also for problems of *Society and the Law*: commonly-cited problems such as a supposed decline in public-spiritedness, the ineffectiveness of mechanisms of criminal punishment, and the quality of school discipline and education would be plausible candidates in this regard. There is one precedent for this in the interviews: the Erfurt group makes spontaneous reference to the findings of the EU's PISA Study on the relative achievements of different education systems in Europe. Finland's positive evaluation is the source of considerable interest on the grounds that it modelled its school-system on the GDR. Axel expresses scepticism towards the methods of the study – 'for me the PISA Study is a purely statistical thing ... Why do I have to make a European contest out of the knowledge of little children?' – but he, like all the participants, is supportive of the principle that Germany can usefully compare its education system with those of other European countries and perhaps learn from them. This reference, admittedly found only in the one interview, indicates the potential for transnational comparisons in this domain of problems also. More such comparisons would perhaps bring this advantage: awareness that similar problems are replicated elsewhere could serve to undermine the tendency found with regard to some of them – crime and antisocial behaviour especially – to demonise particular individuals in the home environment. It is conceivable that comparisons encourage a more structural rather than actor-based perspective, something which would diminish the tendency to position certain opponents as enemies rather than adversaries.

We have seen that acts of comparison on problems of *Economics* are not uncommon, but generally restricted to a limited range of topics. Further kinds are easily imagined, based on the concerns commonly raised in discussion: comparisons examining the incomes (absolute and relative) of those in different occupations; comparisons examining social-security provision; comparisons examining the structures of different member-state tax regimes and 'who pays what'; comparisons of public spending in different sectors; and comparisons of industrial and manufacturing policies. While currently the knowledge needed for such comparisons may be thinly available – and unlike price levels it can hardly be derived from personal experience – there is no reason why suitable comparative data is inconceivable, should the will to produce it exist.[21] Comparisons for problems to do with *Relations between Peoples* may perhaps be less easily quantifiable but are nonetheless imaginable, e.g. on public opinion regarding decisions to join coalitions for war.

---

[21]That eastern Europe is frequently cast as a 'relevant contrast' for problems of *Economics*, e.g. prices, may not be an insurmountable obstacle to the spatial extension of perceptions of shared predicament, indeed it may be a facilitator: it suggests recognition that the same metric may be applied to both east and west. This is a precondition for counter-arguments suggesting the differences are not so great – as we heard a speaker in the Liberec group make at the beginning of Chapter 4. Conversely, it is those places with which not even *contrasts* are drawn that may be regarded as the most schematically remote.

An interesting feature of the discursive patterns observed is the tendency not only to make occasional comparisons but, for economic problems at least, to express surprise at the extent to which conditions in neighbouring, 'comparable' countries might actually be rather different. Price differences, for example, regularly provoked expressions of bemusement and the sense that things should be more similar than they were. Derek in Reading provides an example of this, to the agreement of Malik: 'Now, we're into Europe, but we don't all have the same rules. You can go to France, it's exactly what you're saying, you buy stuff in France – wine, do the beer trips and the fag trips ... We're into Europe, and you can get on a boat for a pound or whatever it is and come back with a sack load of fags if you want to, you only got to go 20 miles across the Channel ... We're in Europe, but we all got different prices.' Price and wage differences on a *global* scale are not described in these tones – they tend to be treated much more as predictable facts of life. True, this 'surprise' only extends towards conditions in those EU countries treated as broadly comparable: price differences between western and eastern Europe tend to be normalised amongst all the groups. Nonetheless, there is a basis here for an extension of the sense of shared predicament across borders.

Not all kinds of comparison are constructive of a political bond. Comparisons between countries which are based on a competitive principle may instead be corrosive, since they encourage the demarcation of opponents according to nationality, something likely to undermine the plausibility of joint political action. For example, the notion put forward by several German speakers of Germany as the 'tail-light' [*Schlusslicht*] in economic growth evokes a competition along national lines in which some countries must be winners and others losers. It may position those who are the winners as the opponents, something likely to cast doubt on the acceptability of being bound together in the same political community. One sees this in some comments from Peter at Kassel, though the point is contested by Dieter:

> P:　And another thing I can't understand, in Germany we're the tail-light in terms of economic development in Europe.
> S:　We still have very high standards though. [D: Just what I wanted to say ...]
> P:　Yeah but on the one hand we're the tail-light and on the other hand we're the main contributor to the EU. That somehow ... that can't all fit together any more. [D: Yes but ...] And we don't have a single politician who goes to town and says

'That's enough, we need to re-regulate the whole thing.' Just not there.

D: We're talking about two different things. We're the tail-light when it comes to growth. That means for a very long time we were probably out in front ... [P: Gone to sleep, we've gone to sleep ...] No, we've been out in front for a very long time and we were the leaders in development. Now what's happened meanwhile is that, because of EU enlargement, the other states have caught up and naturally their level of development is ... That's the problem. [H: That's the problem ...] That's the problem. It's not that we're worse than the others, it's simply that their development potential ... it's being raised.

P: On the contrary, it's said that we're getting worse. [D: That's rubbish.]

On balance, the idea that other parts of Europe, including the new EU members of the east, represent environments rather than rivals is probably maintained in this passage – Dieter, Sebastian and Hans all adopt this position – but the motif of the 'tail-light' Peter refers to points rather in the contrary direction.

One of the risks of a logic of comparison is that, precisely because it preserves the distinctness of the two or more things compared (X, Y ...), it preserves the possibility that they be portrayed as competitors. Whereas a logic of identity conjures indivisibility ('European workers', for instance, or just 'workers'), a logic of comparison ('workers in Germany' compared with 'workers in France') conjures the discreteness of the two, even when they are recognised as equivalent. This can be the basis for curiosity and enquiry – the affirmation of discreteness promises the possibility of learning something not already known – but it can also be the basis for division. Comparisons can generate not just sympathy towards the comparator but dislike: or put differently, they can evoke opponents as well as counterparts. There are further dangers too: some comparisons may encourage a sense of passive victimhood, for if it is observed that there exist counterparts to 'us' whose situation is no better, this may be taken as a sign of the natural order of things and a further reason to be sceptical about political agency. Comparisons may also provoke the conclusion that 'things could be worse', in the sense that others face predicaments worse than ours, this time with negative implications for the *urgency* as much as the feasibility of tackling the associated grievances. These points remind that it is not just comparative data as such which is influential, but the meanings attached to it. Here again one sees the possibilities for political contestation, over what kinds of data to disseminate, how to present them, and what conclusions to promote.

It was noted in the previous section that accounts of economic problems quite often make reference to the EU and its policies, either as expressions or causes of such problems. The EU's legislation on the free movement of workers and the introduction of the euro are two salient examples. Interestingly, these problems for which a close linkage to the EU is made also attract transnational comparisons with other European countries, as though it were precisely the EU connection which fosters some basic sense of shared predicament. The group in Plzeň for example, while generally indisposed to make comparisons with western Europe on economic issues, shows a fair degree of interest in the experiences of these countries with the euro. Pavel refers to how prices have risen in Germany due to the euro, and to the reluctance of Britain to give up the pound sterling; Michal draws attention to those in Italy who want the country to withdraw from the euro (Pavel and Robert have heard the same, though Robert dismisses them as 'just voices'), and all are willing to extrapolate from these experiences to those that might be felt in the Czech Republic were it too to join. One observes something similar in the Norwich discussion:

Bill: If we've all got the euro, all of Europe including us, then everything's got to be the same prices, like your petrol abroad, your petrol here, your fags, blah blah. And I'm pretty sure, whatever government is in this country would never give up the revenue off cigarettes, beer and fags. So we'd be getting the same wages as our European counterparts but we'd be paying more, so our standard of living would go down yet again. [...]

Les: They've all got mugged on the bloody euro, don't you worry yourself about that. Because you go out to Spain and see how much it bloody costs you.

B: The Dutch don't like it, the Germans are struggling with it.

Malcolm: I tell you who didn't struggle with the euro – financial institutions. They made a packet on it.

The recognition of 'European counterparts' which this specifically European 'problem' invites can be read in at least two ways. In one perspective, it is 'the EU' which is the problem, and any sense of shared predicament it may generate is unconducive to a political bond since a sense of common subjecthood comes at the expense of a sense of the polity's worth. In a second perspective, it is the specific policy (the euro and its manner of introduction) which is the problem, since it has a particularly harmful effect on the subjects and their counterparts (higher prices) while benefiting their adversaries (the 'financial institutions'). In this perspective, a Europe-wide sense of shared predicament could emerge on the back of dissatisfaction with certain kinds of economic policy, and could then contribute to the bond required for a quite different kind of polity pursuing different policies. Fostering a political bond would seem to require resisting the first perspective while promoting something akin to the second. That this is possible in principle seems evident from a passage from the Erfurt discussion. Here one sees how dissatisfaction with a particular problem – in this case, the arrival of workers from abroad working to different conditions – coupled with the idea that 'things should be the same' in economic terms across Europe can result in rejection of the policy combined with affirmation of the idea of the polity:

> Harald: ... If Europe is going to function as a single whole then there can't be one law for Poland, one law for Portugal and whatever, there needs to be one single European law ... [Uli: yeah]. And that applies to all the questions of employment law, questions of tax law ... If it's not done like that then there'll always be this roaming around in Europe and nothing fair will come of it because the cherries will always be picked out for a few individuals who are able to take advantage of it and the bulk of people will be left behind. And it can't function like that. I'm not going to say that I find it all crap, but I do find it crap how it's being executed. It doesn't work. [Axel: I agree] I think if it was done in an orderly way then it'd be a simplification. You can set free so much potential.
>
> Axel: Ok, and then the EU itself would have proper authority ... [H: Yeah, naturally ...] And not like it is at the moment ... [H: Like it is at the moment it doesn't work.]

3. Political projects: New discourses on the possibilities for action

A theme of the empirical findings has been that positive assumptions concerning the possibilities for organised, collective address of the problems of the political common are unevenly distributed across the problem domains, and in some areas quite thin. They are most strongly present as regards *Society and the Law,* but less so as regards *Relations between Peoples* and *Economics,* even though the capacities of 'politicians', 'the government' and 'the state' remain a topic of considerable salience. The deepening of allegiances to a European polity would seem to require two important changes in discursive practice: a multiplication of the frequency with which it is assumed political problems in these second two domains can be addressed; and a multiplication of the frequency with which 'Europe' and the EU are invoked as credible means by which to tackle such problems. Both of these would depend on new discursive repertoires spelling out some of the possibilities for action. It is important not to merge these two points: while transnational political ties do require that problems facing the political subjects and counterparts be treated as amenable to address, they do not require that *all* such problems be treated as in need of address by European-level institutions, nor indeed by governmental authorities at the state level. To say this would be to foreclose in favour of a unitary state what should be a matter for ongoing debate: the distribution of 'competences' amongst different political actors, and the relative balance of government- and society-led approaches. Rather, allegiances at the European level would require only that a plural – though unspecifiable – number of salient problems be treated as plausible *candidates* for address at that level.

There is no strong reason why problems to do with *Society and the Law* should call for a political project specifically European in focus. A broader sense of space based on a greater number of transnational comparisons would arguably be welcome, since it may have a positive effect on the kinds of positioning performed, but this does not imply the necessity of European policy-making in this area. Nor therefore should one necessarily seek new explanatory discourses which challenge the tendency to assume these problems arise primarily from local causes. *Society and the Law* represents just one of the domains of the common, and the assumption of agency here is already quite discernible.

For problems to do with *Relations between Peoples,* on the other hand, the sense that the specifically European context is of no particular relevance is generally coupled with a tendency to doubt whether such problems are amenable to address. Such an assumption weakens political attachments, and new discourses of agency would seem needed. Presumably these would not be ones which simply raised the expectation that opponents can be defeated, e.g. by emphasising 'our' resolve, since this would be likely only to increase the extent to which opponents are positioned as enemies. Rather, as we have said, the focus would need to be on 'conflict' as the problem. Attempts to 'deproblematise' it – for instance, by suggesting that relations between peoples are already harmonious, or by attempting to deconstruct the very idea of 'peoples' – would arguably be utopian and potentially counter-productive, their instinctive appeal notwithstanding. More effective might be to accept such conflict as a problem, and to challenge the view that it is unrelenting by disputing assumptions to do with the irrationality of opponents and by undermining some of the connotations of the prevalent forms of subjecthood. Local instances of conflict in the neighbourhood might then have a more realistic chance of being debated and compromised on in local forums.

The need for new discourses of agency in the *Economics* domain seems quite clear, and given the transnational context readily evoked it would be natural to place emphasis here on the potential for tackling such problems at a European level. Simple assertions of agency without supporting explanatory motifs are unlikely to be credible: what would be needed would be to redescribe the origins of problems, diffusing the sense of mystery that surrounds many and disputing the tendency to explain large numbers of them with reference to distant places of contrast. Narrowing the sense of political space is itself probably conducive to heightening the plausibility of a political project. More specifically, one might see a need to dispute the tendency to attribute causality almost exclusively to the dictates of the global market. For example, it was seen in the analysis of the empirical material that the problem of job losses and the resulting unemployment is repeatedly attributed to the simple fact of cheaper labour costs in eastern Europe and Asia, and thereby given a sense of unavoidability. Possible counter-narratives are easily conceived, and need by no means be of a higher level of complexity. For instance, in many cases, both in manufacturing and the service industry, redundancies can be plausibly attributed to acts of down-sizing which follow takeover deals designed to boost share price. When the cause is presented in these terms, a number of clear, agential responses become available: strong regulations and trade unions are obvious ones, and basically consistent with liberal-economic orthodoxy; wider state ownership of industries, to insulate decision-making from short-term considerations of share price, represent another, more radical possibility.[22] That such policies are best pursued at a European

---

[22]Some of these arguments are explored in (Hutton 2007).

rather than a national level is of course a contention some would challenge, and the purpose here is not to make the case that this is so but to suggest that such is the kind of argument which would need to be made. Such an argument serves at once to weaken the sense of powerlessness before economic problems and to weaken the association made between the EU and the source or the expression of these problems, refashioning it instead as a source of agency.

In thus outlining some of the possibilities for new kinds of discursive practice, the three domains have been treated as largely independent of one another. There has been no implication that by fostering a stronger sense of agency in one domain, or encouraging different acts of positioning therein, this may have automatic positive effects on the same in other domains, nor has any hierarchy been implied such that one domain is in some way more fundamental than the others. A Marxist perspective, while less concerned with ideational issues, and using entirely different terminology, would probably argue just this of course: that the *Economics* domain is more basic than the other two, and that problematisation in the domains of *Society and the Law* and *Relations between Peoples* occurs largely as a consequence of the false appraisal of the economic.

This is a perspective one may be sceptical of partly on the grounds that it derives from a materialist ontology in which economic interests are taken as pre-ideational facts largely determinative of historical (including discursive) action. By reducing the political to the economic in this way – rather like those conceptualising a commercial bond, and analogously to those who conceptualise a cultural bond – this perspective also overlooks that political goals are various and potentially incommensurable. To seek to reduce them to one set of underlying goals is to pursue a coherence probably illusory.[23] Furthermore, it overlooks the normative appeal of a plurality of domains of fairly equal status. As we have seen, the different discursive patterns associated with the domains give rise to different acts of positioning, implying not only multiple forms of exclusion (i.e. ways of positioning as opponents) but also multiple possibilities of inclusion (i.e. ways of positioning as counterparts). Those citizens to whom the motifs of one domain are applied so as to position them as opponents may, according to the logic of another domain, be positioned rather as something much closer to the 'people like us'. It is exactly this absence of one single axis of inclusion and exclusion which works to

---

[23]On incommensurable goods and values, see (Boltanski and Thévenot 2006; Bellamy 1999).

prevent the establishment of hard and impermeable boundaries towards opponents of the kind which might prove destructive of a collective bond.

As was seen in Chapter 4, criteria drawn from the *Economics* domain can be used to position those who are outsiders in some way as being nevertheless 'people like us': it was noted how participants from the Norwich group deploy the argument that 'anybody can come here providing they do their bit,' and Harald in Erfurt expresses his admiration for the immigrant who 'wants to work, he wants to learn. He's not costing anyone else any money.' Axel from the same group points out that 'it'll always be the case that there are foreigners who want to move to another country because the economy there's better. Everyone's done that – the Germans have done that too. [Harald: And it's understandable ...] Because there's a better future to be had there ... [Uli: It's understandable, it's completely normal.]' Motifs from the *Relations between Peoples* domain can also be used for inclusive purposes. Bill in Norwich, for instance, knows of a girl in his area, 'blimey, can't think of the name of the country now, where the Tutsis slaughtered the ... the Tutsis slaughtered ... Rwanda. I mean, she was a genuine ... her family died, they were slaughtered, so I've got no problem ... genuine refugee. Kosovans ... Genuine people like that who were in fear of their lives for political beliefs and like that ...'. 'I've got no problem with that either,' says Malcolm, and a little later continues: 'people should be able to have free speech. If people can't have that free speech and they want to have that free speech, and they've got the bottle to try and do something about it, and in the end if they're going to be killed for it, then come and stay at my house, mate. Eat me food, I don't mind.' Thus the political subjects express the good sense and fair-mindedness that is characteristic of them and extend a kind of honorary status of subject to those non-Westerners who have been victims of conflict and seek peace 'over here'.

It may be objected that a multiplicity of domains carries a risk, which is that by dividing individuals across a series of different subject positions it weakens the possibilities for mobilising them in the name of any one of these. As we have seen, speakers are never confined to just one symbolic category: they may take up the subjecthood of 'the little people' with respect to one set of problems while evoking themselves as 'people who play by the rules' with regard to another. This would seem to increase the porousness of the boundaries of each form of subjecthood. Assuming one can impute some degree of choice on this, the individual always has the possibility of performing a mental shift from one subject position to another, e.g. from low to high status. This is potentially problematic insofar as social psychologists have argued it is exactly the perception of being 'locked' into a certain social category and the experiences associated with it which may prompt the subject to seek remedy of deprivation (Ellemers 1993); or to put it in Hirschman's terms, it is the absence of the 'exit' option which may prompt the subject to seek political 'voice' (Hirschman 1970). The concern would be that this multiplicity emasculates whatever mobilisatory potential for progressive change these subject positions may hold, reducing populations to a myriad of narrow and ineffective forms of subjecthood.[24]

Nothing that has been said however rules out the temporary articulation of links across the domains such that forms of subjecthood are combined with one another and thus given the appearance of indivisible elements in a common political project. Such combinations weaken the subject's capacity to regard the different forms of subjecthood as discrete from each other and thus to seek exit from one into another. Arguably this has been exactly the basis of Left-Right politics – the conjuring of links across different forms of subjecthood, links which are never permanent and which therefore do not threaten the multiplicity of domains (though they may rework the boundaries and content of these).[25] Some ideational formations may also involve the subordination or displacement of certain subject positions and the prioritising of others, at least at given moments, again allowing possibilities for mobilisation. Insofar as the multiplicity of domains persists, rather than blocking these possibilities it provides the opportunity for their excesses to be restrained. It provides a vocabulary with which to oppose those who would evoke an unchanging, single axis of opposition within the political community, underpinned by a fixed distribution of social categories, or cast a minority of citizens as scapegoats for all its ills.[26]

---

[24]An interesting discussion of the dangers of fragmenting forms of collective identification is (Offe 1996: 171ff.). That cross-cutting forms of subjecthood may have potentially de-mobilising effects has been the contention of accounts in the pluralist tradition, some seeing in this a contribution to political stability and tolerance. See e.g. (Lipset 1959: 88ff., 203ff.).

[25]On the translation of disparate societal oppositions into structured but evolving political coalitions, see (Dahl 1966: 379ff.).

[26]As one instance of how the position of minorities becomes especially vulnerable when different domains of problems are elided or cumulated, consider practices of anti-Semitism, which may be read as involving the positioning of 'Jews' as opponents in something like each of the three domains we have examined.

Now, what clearly cannot be established on the basis of examples such as those above is which motifs are preferred in concrete cases when individuals might have to choose whether to extend the status of 'costing no-one else money' (or not) or 'being genuine' (or not) to particular individuals and groups. One cannot infer directly from the discursive practice the other kinds of behavioural practice which might accompany it. One *can* say, however, that a collective bond which incorporates this plurality of domains as a feature of its ideal, rather than emphasising one domain at the expense of the others, offers a greater range of resources for softening the boundaries of inclusion and exclusion. Indeed, it may be that the proper goal is to increase the number of domains rather than reduce them or rank them, i.e. expand the political common.

4.   Expanding the political common

It follows from the definition in Chapter 1 that to 'expand' the political common would be to increase the number of important common problems which are assumed to exist and be in need of address. Its appeal would lie in the further opportunities it offers for collective positioning and the construction of 'people like us' which, if understood at least in some cases in transnational, potentially Europe-wide terms, and if accompanied by expectations of political agency, could advance the degree to which citizenship ties 'make sense' to their holders. While it is usually unwise to speculate on the future course of political contestation, since arguably human freedom is dependent on the substance of politics being resistant to this kind of theorising, nonetheless a few short considerations may be given.

Such expansion of the common could take the form of new problems being articulated in close alignment with the logics of the three domains focused on so far, *Economics, Society and the Law* and *Relations between Peoples*. One could imagine further problematisation of economic inequality for example, or of social atomisation, or of various features of international relations (e.g. justifications for the possession of nuclear weapons). Though this would not in itself advance political allegiances, it would widen the terrain on which the arguments for them could be made. It might also facilitate the development of discourses of agency, if these new acts of problematisation entailed breaking up some of the more abstract existing formulations (such as 'terrorism') into a series of more substantive sub-elements. Expansion of the common could also involve the development of further linkages between these problem domains, such that there is greater facility for the reproblematisation of the problems of one domain according to the logic of another. By promoting the sense that all political problems are linked, that problems to do with *Relations between Peoples* can be treated as problems of *Economics*, that problems of *Economics* can be treated as problems to do with social relations, the significance of multiple resources for inclusion and exclusion would be underscored. At the same time, of course, the danger of one domain achieving a dominant status could thereby increase: one can imagine the disturbing possibility for instance that a large number of problématiques come to be problematised as matters of collective security. There is much to be said for valorising the independence of each domain.

Expansion of the common could also take the form of the development of new domains, i.e. new problematisations which bring with them distinctive acts of positioning and possibilities for agency. The body of articulated but marginalised problems referred to under the loose heading *Quality of Life* would be an appropriate starting-point, particularly given the EU is already cited as a generally positive point of reference for problems of this kind, and since changes in policy do seem to require transnational cooperation to be effective. Pollution and rapid changes to the regional and global environment would have to be treated as more salient problems than they were at the time of interview, and perhaps linked to further issues to do with public health. The kinds of positioning associated with a domain such as this might tend to be globalist, since it can plausibly be argued that the consequences of such problems are evenly spread across all humans, ultimately if not in the short term. A globalist perspective would be questionable if replicated across all domains, since it would undermine the political dynamic and could point towards depoliticised administration. Even if just found in one domain, it might tempt a retreat from those matters of common concern where an adversarial dimension is more prominent. The protection of flora and fauna, for example, represents a cause which most will agree is worthy and on which adversaries tend to be few in number. One can imagine that the reassuring moral certitude this invites – the confidence of being 'on the right side' – might prove all too alluring and divert engagement from other, more contentious, domains. Nonetheless as one strand amongst a plurality of domains, a more universalist positioning of this kind could provide a valuable counterpoint to some of the acts of positioning we have encountered.

Something which is not problematised in any depth in this empirical material, and yet which is clearly a matter of some political significance, is the reliability of the news media. Participants were certainly readers of newspapers and listeners to the radio (see the Appendix), and displayed levels of knowledge and sophistication in their discussions which indicate an active encounter with such news sources (note for instance detailed references to the Middle-East conflict, or to specific cases of corruption in public life). But the reliability of these sources is barely problematised, other than a few very general remarks about how 'you can't trust anything in the newspapers', how editors just want to sell more copies, or how the 'only things you can really be sure about are the girls and the sport'. The reliability of the media is a problématique which does not reduce easily to any of the domains discussed so far, and which might in principle form the basis for a distinctive discursive repertoire. One can imagine formulations for the political subjects as those who 'want to get to the truth of matters', demarcated against those who are thoughtless or who are actively seeking to dupe or mislead. Robert in Plzeň is not the only participant to note that different TV programmes and different newspapers 'narrate things differently', and that one needs to keep an eye on several. Of course, problematisation of this kind would by no means point necessarily towards the worth of a project centred on a European polity to tackle such problems, but one can suppose that transnational comparisons might come naturally in this domain: interest in what the media in other European member-states are saying, and the extent to which they are telling a different story, plus the possibilities available for becoming less reliant on just one set of news sources, would seem fully conceivable. However – and this is a point rarely made in discussions of the possibility of a European public sphere – this widening of the sense of space would seem most likely as an outcome of problematisation, and not simply as a consequence of some general broadening of horizons and widening of the sphere of curiosity.

7
European Integration off the Meter

The empirical study developed over the preceding chapters has high-lighted some of the ways currently-found repertoires of political inter-pretation undermine the extent to which a European polity 'makes sense' to its citizens in the terms proposed in Chapter 1. To recall, our purpose in those opening pages was to sketch a politically desirable perspective on the collective ties needed for political coexistence. While the topic has been a central one in recent discussions of the EU, its handling has been limited in key ways. First, many of the major interventions point towards models of politics and citizenship of dubious appeal, especially in the context of wider trends towards the weakening of the democratic idea of collective self-rule. Second, where contributions to the debate have been empirical, they have tended to rely on a narrow range of methods and data, ones which invite a reductive operationalisation of what political community is. This book has tried to address both shortcomings, elaborating a distinctive per-spective on political allegiance in tandem with an in-depth exploratory study. It has sought to avoid the drawbacks of conceiving the collective in terms of material interests, perceptions of shared culture or values, foregrounding instead the importance of political problems, the lines of opposition they inspire, and the possibilities recognised for their settlement – albeit that the bonds of collectivity as they currently exist may be rather thinner when conceptualised in this way.

Taking seriously the popular dimension of democracy means taking seriously, though not uncritically, the ways people problematise their everyday experiences and the world around them, what it is that causes grievance and that they would like to see changed. These concerns should be central to a conceptualisation of collective ties, for they are elemental to what political community is about. Moreover, the extent to which democratic control can be exercised on these problems is not just a matter of institutional mechanisms and organisation, important and complex enough though these factors are. It is a matter of expectations also – those less quantifiable, 'off-the-meter' dimensions to political integration which will be missed if one looks only at formal arrangements or the opinions consciously formed of them. Language and tacit assumptions are crucial. In the absence of the resources for formulating problems in ways that permit the possibility of meaningful collective action to address them, a political arrangement such as the EU is hardly likely to make sense to its intended audience, hardly likely to be received as an augmentation of self-determination. To explore the idea of a political bond is therefore to study the patterns people draw on when problematising their common experiences.

Talking with taxi-drivers in Britain, Germany and the Czech Republic has given the opportunity to explore these notions in a specific temporal and spatial context. Group discussions are a site where one can study discursive practices in some depth, while the talk of taxi-drivers presents itself a particularly rich site for looking at those which may be distributed more widely. Setting conceptual ideas in a reciprocal relationship with empirical material allows one both to develop those ideas further and to use them for the critical evaluation of what one finds. As was seen in Chapter 3, a wide range of common problems was articulated in these discussions, and in quite similar ways across the interview groups. A *political common* seemed discernible. The importance of accommodating the adversarial dimension in any conceptualisation of the collective bond was borne out in Chapter 4, where the tendency for all formulations of selfhood to be defined in contra-distinction to a set of opponents was noted. Some tendency was observed for 'counterparts' in other countries to be evoked through transnational comparison, suggesting an expanded conception of political space, but it was also seen that such practices were domain-specific, and that they rarely corresponded to the contours of any recognisable European polity. Formulations of selfhood and interpersonal ties were more variegated than conventional notions of national or European identity suggest. In Chapter 5 a connection was drawn between the motifs used to explain problems and the extent to which these problems are assumed susceptible to organised address. It was suggested that the prevalence of localist and globalist motifs, combined with the rarity of more distinctively 'European' ones, served to weaken the credibility of EU-focused *political projects*. Indeed, as was then seen in Chapter 6, rarely was the EU put forward in discussion as a convincing source of political agency. On the contrary, when invoked it was the role of its policies in the generation and expression of problems which tended to be foregrounded.

In the field of EU studies there is an enthusiasm for conceptualising the weaknesses of the EU in terms of 'deficits': notice has been given of the existence of a 'democratic deficit', a 'federal deficit', a 'constitutional deficit' and a 'legitimacy deficit'. Although these are contested terms, they generally point consistently towards institutional factors: to the weak ability of citizens to exert influence on decision-making at the European level, the untransparency of certain EU institutions, or to the unsettled distribution of powers between them. The analysis given here, though not generally incompatible with these, notes that formal opportunities and structures require social practices that consolidate them, and so points to what one might call a deficit of the political imagination. It highlights the dearth of viewpoints from which to see coordinated action at a European level as meaningful and credible, and from which citizens may derive the inspiration to hold the EU accountable for what it does or fails to achieve. Absent a developed political bond, the EU can no doubt endure for some time, just as it may be brought down by factors unrelated. What the strength of these allegiances determines is not the polity's immediate viability, its capacity to exist, but its minimum consistency with the notions of collective self-rule endorsed by almost all political associations since the late-medieval period. These allegiances are a necessary condition of the EU's existence in a normatively appealing form.

There is no doubt a sense in which it is counter-intuitive to conceive a *political* bond in an age many see as characterised by increasing political scepticism and the hollowing of democracy. A whole range of negative trends have been noted by scholars of national democracy, including the decline of ideological cleavages, the weakening of parties, the supposed disengagement of non-elites, and the withering of practices of collective solidarity and organised bargaining. From this perspective, meaningful politics at the national level seems under assault from all sides, leaving the thought that to emphasise political ties for a newly emerging polity is to be severely out of tune with the times. Indeed, some might question whether there was ever a 'golden age' of politics when notions of collective self-rule were practically realised. To an elitist like Schumpeter, such thoughts would have seemed quaint indeed: to imagine 'the people' as anything more than an audience would be misguided and probably dangerous. If popular engagement was never more than a myth, perhaps it is time to 'get real'. Andrew Moravcsik is no doubt just one of a large number of political scientists for whom it is important to separate the *ideal* from the *real* (Moravcsik 2002: 605). Admittedly, such authors can be accused of falling into a version of the naturalist fallacy, of deciding that the real *is* the ideal, or of choosing their ideals such that the status quo confirms them. Such moves risk lending the air of inevitability to what is ultimately a contestable situation, and since even the empiricist is a certain kind of idealist, it is as well to make note of the suppositions embraced. But ultimately, one will wonder, are such authors not right that one should anchor oneself in 'the way things are', and keep one's theorising tightly pegged to reality?

On this they are indeed correct, and it is this concern for 'the real' which inspires an empirical mode of enquiry in this work. If there is a disagreement to be had with the elitist tradition it need not be based on putative idealism versus realism, but on divergent understandings of each. To play the realist for a moment, a brute fact which emerges in this research is the extent to which ordinary people are willing to voice a wide range of common problems about which it is felt something in principle should be done. In no sense do grievances seem to have given way to apathy: they remain strongly present, even in the ostensibly benign economic conditions when these interviews were conducted. Any deepening of these grievances in the years following should be regarded not as a deviation from the norm but the extension of an existing pattern. This, combined with the evident scepticism concerning what can be achieved to improve things through traditional political channels, is what makes the situation potentially critical both for nation-state democracy and the EU. The kind of assumptions we have traced, whereby large numbers of shared problems are articulated yet many prompt feelings of impotence, provide ample grounds for illiberal movements to gain support: the so-called 'right-wing populist' movements found recently in much of Europe may be read as testament to this. Nor can social scientists unmoved by normative concerns afford to dismiss the significance of mass politics for transnational integration. The impact of the 2005 referenda in France and the Netherlands on the Constitutional Treaty demonstrate how far EU politics hinges on the kinds of discursive practice prevalent amongst the voting public. These voters were animated not just (if at all) by the abstract idea of a constitution, but by various associations made between the EU and its policies on the one hand and a whole range of problematised developments on the other, notably the effects of certain economic policies, of increased rates of migration, and the prospect of Turkish membership. To ignore these popular concerns and to focus purely on constitutional politics and elite bargaining, or the technocratic modes of policy-making characteristic of earlier phases of integration, would be idealism of the most unjustifiable kind. Such approaches offer few opportunities for persuading citizens of the worth of the rules developed in their name, and unpersuaded citizens will no doubt seek regular opportunities to oppose or circumvent them.

Furthermore, as these interviews have indicated, the competence of lay people to discuss political issues with sophistication should not be underestimated. We have seen problems elaborated in complex ways, a rich set of links drawn between them, and an evident ability to combine media-inspired messages with personal experiences and local knowledge. Nor is there unredeemed cynicism about public life: while there is useful work to be done by political psychologists on the responses triggered by key words, cynicism – as opposed to pessimism – is not the dominant tone of these discussions. One does not find the major concerns of public life reduced to a small set of problems to do with corruption and 'government waste', as newspaper commentaries sometimes suggest, nor are substantive issues crowded out by the politics of personality and party-branding. Interest in political issues, and the competence to talk about them, is much in evidence, even if accompanied by doubt about the ability to effect change. Importantly, from an objective perspective, there is no reason to consider the problems raised as unavoidable or fabricated, the people who articulate them as whingers. It may be that one wishes to reject the terms in which some are discussed, and it may be one feels certain issues are neglected in discussion, but there is no reason to attribute failings of this kind to incapacity on the part of speakers. Rather, one should see these as reasons to question, contest and expand the set of discursive resources on which speakers are able to draw.

Political parties have, since the nineteenth century at least, been some of the major exponents of political discursive innovation of this kind. They have served both to coin ideas and to project the will to realise them, and as a political form they have several advantages over alternative modes of collective action (White and Ypi 2010). Social movements have played an important auxiliary role, and as influences on parties they may be effective in disseminating political ideas and pressuring parties to keep to them. Small-distribution publications can have the same function, so too think-tanks. Intellectuals have likewise had historical significance in developing forms of political subjecthood and thereby acting as the 'class-producing class' (Bauman 1999: 128). Some media outlets are in a position to amplify such developments to a wider audience, notwithstanding trends in the mainstream media towards the simplification and theatricalising of news and public affairs. Entwined with these, the new digital-based media, in the form of internet blogging or social networks, offer important possibilities for wider influence and cross-national coordination. It is through a variety of activists proceeding in concert that discursive innovation has been and may continue to be led.

Of course, this places a certain burden of imagination on activists themselves, who may also need to shake off some of the patterned ways of seeing the world we have described. Some of the fatalism found in these interviews may be attributable precisely to the failure of parties to develop distinctive programmes indicating the possibilities for political agency, and those conforming to this pattern may exacerbate such tendencies towards scepticism. Yet by the same token those who diverge from it surely have the potential to foster greater conviction of the worth of political agency.

The need to revitalise richer conceptions of citizenship and reaffirm the plausibility of dealing collectively with common problems is not a sufficient argument for a European polity. One can conceptualise the collective in the terms here described in the context of the states inherited from the Westphalian order, and to make a claim for the privileged status of one context is always liable to re-elide the question of the nature of the collective with that of where boundaries should lie. No conceptual scheme can convincingly indicate where lines should be drawn on a pristine, physical map. To be sure, there are good reasons to look to political arrangements on a scale larger than the modern state. Given that a large number of economic practices conditioning life experiences are widely assumed to extend beyond the domestic state realm – assumed, that is, by scholars as much as taxi-drivers – and given there are further processes to do with environmental degradation of which the same may be true, the cultivation of wider horizons of awareness and orientation may be appropriate, and institutional arenas on the continental scale may be a necessary condition of dealing adequately with the problems that arise. Moreover, as this empirical material suggests, collective positioning today is more complex than can be accommodated by the old categories of territorial identity. There is a notable tendency, for some problems in particular, to evoke a political context considerably broader than the Westphalian state, and to the extent there exist doubts about the possibility of political action at a transnational level, these are matched by doubts about the possibilities for agency offered in existing states. Yet ultimately the arguments for looking beyond the political configurations of the modern state system do not apply exclusively to political authority on a European scale, and the concepts developed in this study are relevant beyond the context in which they have been elaborated.

How the EU polity develops in institutional terms will evidently influence in some degree the evolving contours of political allegiance. Institutions cannot themselves establish the sense of the common on which they rely, but they may nonetheless be important to its consolidation. Broadly three lines of future development can be imagined for the EU. In the first, currently seen as unlikely by most observers but advocated by some, the EU regime will come increasingly to resemble a federal Westphalian state on a larger scale, with ultimate decision-making authority located at the European level. From the perspective of citizen ties, the great virtue of such a regime is its simplicity. It has a clear centre, and ultimate political authority and responsibility can quite easily be located, something one may suppose is conducive to generating greater conviction in what political agency can achieve. Insofar as a centred model implies a significant amount of common rule-making – the euro and its attendant policies approximate this – it is also likely to foster awareness of shared experiences and challenges. Conversely, the more legislation takes plural forms, the more notions of counterparts must rely on the comparison of experiences unstructured by the law. The evocation of counterparts is likely to depend also on minimising the number of situations in which EU citizens appear to one another in the guise of competitors – something again for which common rules may be needed, and which may most easily be secured when authority is concentrated.[1] Balancing these points is the fact that the dramatic transfer of powers needed to create a centred regime would presumably require approval in a decisive constitutional moment. Such an approach renders difficult the gradual development of citizen ties and strengthens the prospect of the polity's outright rejection.[2]

---

[1]One thinks for example of minimum wage legislation to prevent situations of wage competition. A Europe-wide system of taxation, with contributions levied according to individual wealth rather than national quota, would presumably weaken nation-based forms of positioning and encourage other European countries to be treated not as competing actors (as in these discussions whenever the finances of the EU were raised) but as environments in which similar economic problems and struggles unfold.

[2]Defending the objective of a pan-EU referendum, see (Habermas 2009).

The second possible trajectory for the EU involves its consolidation as a polycentric or 'compound' regime, in which powers are dispersed and no single branch of government, either at national or European level, has supreme authority over the others (Fabbrini 2005). As a scenario which could emerge incrementally rather than by a one-off transfer of powers, it makes no requirement of the wholesale endorsement of a European polity by its citizens in a given historical moment. It too affords opportunities for the deepening of cross-national allegiances. The characteristic make-up of such a regime – coordinated goal-setting at a European level combined with cross-spatial variety in execution – would seem, at its best, to provide both the necessary degree of commonality for transnational comparisons to be possible and the necessary degree of variation for them to be instructive. It could provide the basis for various forms of collective action, aimed at producing European-level initiatives or widening the frame of reference for those at state level. Admittedly, some visions of a polycentric regime are heavily technocratic and too quick to celebrate the 'governance practices' of today's EU.[3] That such a regime is inherently complicated is another of its challenges. The emergence of partisan lines of divisions spanning different institutional arenas would most likely be needed to simplify it, just as these have simplified the structures of the Westphalian state and offered a means by which to make sense of the political whole.

The third possible scenario for the EU is that it retreats from the status of a self-standing polity, either by reverting to an intergovernmental organisation or by breaking up altogether. Prolonged economic crisis could be one stimulus; a major shift in the geopolitical environment another. How would political allegiance look after European *dis*integration? Clearly the question of social bonds would seem less urgent, and instinctively one would expect few traces of transnationalism amongst citizens. The grounds and opportunities for mutual engagement would be reduced. Yet even in the context of diminishing institutional ties, ties at the popular level might endure or consolidate, whether due to a heightened awareness of things lost – a kind of *Eurostalgie* – or as a function of more general conditions of global interaction. Practices of

---

[3]For a favourable account of 'comitology' and the Open Method of Coordination, see (Sabel and Zeitlin 2007); for a critical assessment (Büchs 2008). Note such models offer limited guarantee that the information resources necessary for political comparison are communicated beyond institutions to the citizenry at large.

cross-national comparison and moves to coordinate political action across borders – the kinds of allegiance explored in this study – would seem to be still plausible under such conditions, and of continuing relevance to peaceful coexistence and the pursuit of progressive goals. Much would no doubt depend on the major narratives through which any putative political retrenchment came to be read: if the dominant perspective relied on nation-based categories, casting break-up as the fault of one or a number of member-states, then the residue of allegiance would surely be thinner than if explanations invoked categories of a non-territorial, e.g. class-based, kind.

Europe's political trajectories remain unresolved at the time of writing, and one imagines likewise at the time of reading. Perhaps the following is the stable observation: that insofar as one takes seriously the idea of a European polity, the question of the collective bond is unavoidable. It seems inadequate to suppose, as some advocates of further integration may, that an acceptable outcome can be secured simply with some adjustments to the Union's institutions. Institutional issues, particularly those in 'distant Brussels', do not tend to be a subject of impassioned discussion amongst Europeans, nor does it seem likely that, simply by offering further opportunities to cast a vote, interest and enthusiasm will emerge spontaneously concerning the possibilities these venues offer. Instead, one would need to prepare the ground over the longer term with clear ideas about what those institutions may be engaged to achieve and why it makes sense to share in them with others. Emphasising the address of common problems presents itself as the most appropriate basis on which to animate a European polity. But this perspective on the common will be without resonance if one overlooks the ways the political world is interpreted more generally. Any reconstruction of political allegiance must start with those routine acts of positioning and unquestioned assumptions that structure people's expectations of what should and can be achieved.

Methodological Appendix

Taxi-driving is a job that mixes bursts of activity with a fair bit of killing of time. Some hours are busier than others, varying according to the city, the rank, and the customers catered to. For those who tend to work at a railway-station, the busy times coincide with the arrival of long-distance and peak-time commuter trains: early mornings especially can be heavy. For those who tend to work a rank in the town-centre, the busy times tend to follow shopping hours: early mornings can be quiet, but work picks up towards the lunchtime rush. Those who work nights will probably mix lonely hours mid-week with considerable activity at weekends. A Munich taxi-driver – in a conversation separate from the body of this research – reported that, with people increasingly saving on luxuries (the euro had made everyone poorer), the only times when custom was reliable were Friday and Saturday nights between 1am and 6am.[1] Whatever the variations in individual routine, most drivers can expect quite considerable periods of hanging around, especially when a job has been recently completed and the driver returns to the back of the rank, turns off the engine and waits for those in front to take customers.

Such time is spent in various ways. A few drivers install televisions in their vehicles, but for the majority it is the radio or newspaper. 'I think a lot of the guys read the paper,' Malik in Reading told me. 'Half the time they don't move up in their queue because they're reading the bloody paper, or nattering away to somebody ...'. Local and tabloid-style newspapers are much in evidence on the rank, and were the most commonly cited when participants were asked how they passed their spare time. Bill in Norwich reads 'any sort of newspaper, always got an interest in the newspapers. I listen to the radio all day so I've got the news on, and I do watch Sky News at night, flip it on, keep an eye on what's going on in the world.' In some cities, e.g. Swansea, reading the local newspaper meant exposure to very local, city-based stories; in others the coverage could be much wider: the *Main Post*, cited by Ulrich in Würzburg, carried international as well as local news. That significant time is spent with the newspaper and radio is evident from the frequency with which they were cited in discussion. Headlines, or something 'just heard on the radio', crop up regularly, though sometimes in unexpected ways: when Bill in Norwich refers to a photograph in yesterday's *Evening News* featuring a group of mothers and children, he focuses not on the paedophile they were protesting against but the fact that they all seemed to be single mothers, and hence probably unemployed. One also finds in the interviews pieces of information, e.g. to do with conflict in Rwanda or the sale of weapons to China, that would be difficult to account for other than as a result of exposure to media sources (on or off the job). At the same time, many drivers were keen to trivialise the time they spent with newspapers: Malik in Reading was emphatic that he is 'never that much up to date' with the news,

---

[1] Private conversation, Munich (Schwabing), Sunday 17th April 2005, 5am.

229

'about ten years behind', and direct questioning about newspapers (as opposed to their spontaneous mention) would reliably lead to jokes about topless women. For Zbyněk at Ostrava, the only really credible thing in the newspapers is 'the sex': 'no-one's going to deceive me on that. They can write what they want but that's something I know about, I know how that functions.' No doubt the sport sections are read in a similar spirit.

These daily pastimes have to be easily interruptible. Not only is there the need to move up on the rank but for many drivers there is the prospect of being greeted by colleagues. Jochen in Lübeck explains: 'you can't really read the *Frankfurter Allgemeine* [i.e. a serious newspaper] here on the rank ... there's always someone coming past your door, "come on, let's go for coffee," you can hardly read even one article in peace. I really don't understand how some of our colleagues can read a book in the car – really big books sometimes ... [Niklas & Werner: yeah, yeah ...].' Except for when it is raining or cold, drivers near the back of the rank will often be outside their vehicles, talking in small groups. On larger ranks, like that at Würzburg station, they may also have a hut to go to. Apart from at peak times, one rarely sees a whole rank of drivers sitting alone in their vehicles: conversations are a common way of whiling away the quieter moments. Where the drivers are employed by a firm and more than one firm works the same rank, these social relations seem to take place mainly amongst those working for the same firm. The more lonely periods are likely to be the night shifts, not least because fewer drivers do these. But in the daytime, most ranks are fairly social places and the job generates plenty of group contexts, aside from those with customers.

My arrival at the taxi-rank was timed to coincide with low customer demand – generally sometime after 9am or 2pm. The interviews were not arranged in advance: I simply selected the largest of the city ranks and recruited directly. I styled myself as what I was: a student doing research. Wearing jeans and a jacket and carrying a folder of papers under my arm, I tried to appear both young and serious. Just as I did not want to look too casual, I wanted to avoid the impression of formality or officialdom: the fraud inspector represents an ominous figure for many taxi-drivers, and anyone asking questions at the rank does well to ensure they are not mistaken. Also, the image of the student, with what I assumed to be connotations of someone reliant on a favour, perhaps a little naïve in the ways of the world and in need of having things explained, was one I thought might benefit the research both during recruitment and during the discussions themselves.

Several methodological considerations must be borne in mind when adopting group discussions as a research method. Important decisions need to be made about the size of the groups, the degree to which they are to be 'natural' (in part a matter of whether participants will be acquaintances or strangers), and the degree to which they are to be homogeneous (as evaluated by any number of criteria, including ethnic and socio-economic make-up). Much of the earlier writing on this research method was connected to commercial market research, where 'focus groups' were intended to provide insights into the reception of brands and advertising. For this purpose, the recommendations were that groups should be fairly large (six to eight people), that participants should be strangers to one another, and often that they should be drawn from diverse backgrounds. Such groups would allow the researcher speedily to gather responses from a broad section of society to whatever stimuli the client wanted tested. My purposes were different, and like much of the later, academic applications of this method I felt able to reject some of these stipulations (Bloor et al. 2001; Morgan 1997; Millward 2000; Puchta and Potter 2004; Ritchie and Lewis 2004; Kitzinger and Barbour 1999).[2] With taxi-drivers often in conversation when I approached them, and familiar with most of the rank, an attempt to recruit groups of strangers would have been impractical and perverse. I was interested not in the short, impulsive responses of individuals (like marketing research) but in how discussions were built up collectively and pursued in depth. Also, I had chosen taxi-drivers as people for whom the discussion would not represent a major upheaval in their schedule, and this would be truer where the participants were already in conversation. Furthermore, individuals are more likely to participate if their peers do, so the success of the recruitment process can generally be improved by taking advantage of existing social relations.

The groups I assembled were 'natural' in the sense that the core was often drawn from a pre-existing conversation. Not all participants knew each other in advance, but there were always at least a couple familiar with everyone, and perhaps a general expectation that drivers on the rank had some degree of mutual acquaintanceship. 'It's like a little institute,' was how Les in Norwich described the rank. When, during recruitment in Würzburg, Oskar suggested to Ralf enlisting the participation of Ulrich, Ralf seemed not to know him, but Oskar still felt it realistic to try to jog his memory: 'you know, the guy who plays the piano.' Ralf himself was identifiable to several drivers on the rank by way of his hobby – running marathons. Many of the discussions also featured cross-references to conversations participants had had on prior occasions. Admittedly, this degree of mutual familiarity carried dangers: where drivers were helping with recruitment, they might be inclined to 'invite up', as Gamson has put it (Gamson 1992: 190) – i.e. encourage those whom they considered better-educated or more thoughtful to participate while dismissing the candidacy of others – or they might lose enthusiasm if someone they disliked looked ready to participate. At Kassel, Dieter asked me whether he should single out some 'sensible' drivers to take part (I said it was unimportant), while in Swansea one driver confidentially made their participation conditional on another individual not taking part, a condition made irrelevant when the latter departed with a customer. Even once the discussions were underway, what was said or not said might be influenced by past conversations in ways I would be unable to appreciate. These dangers, however, seemed outweighed by the likelihood that 'political talk' occurs more naturally amongst acquaintances than strangers (Conover et al. 2002).

With a concern for depth of discussion, I wanted relatively small groups: most were composed of four participants, three comprised three. Groups of this size facilitate contributions from all participants rather than a dominant few, and reduce the likelihood of fragmentation into multiple discussions which are difficult to transcribe. For the same reasons, groups of three to four participants can be moderated with a light touch (Morgan 1997: 42–3). Equally practically,

---

[2]The terms 'group discussion' or 'group interview' have been preferred in this work to 'focus group', but cf. (Morgan 1997: 5ff.).

assembling more than four participants would have been a challenge. At ranks where turnover was fast, one was always liable to lose those who had pledged participation if one lingered for more: the arrival of one or two customers could force withdrawals, in turn generating scepticism amongst those remaining about the likelihood of the exercise going ahead. Also, while most cities had a principal taxi-rank – usually by the train station or in the town centre – some would have a series of smaller ranks equal in size, perhaps with no more than five vehicles. A few rejections on a small rank could produce 'negative inertia', whereby other drivers would quickly reject participation too. This happened in Plzeň, and after several hours I settled for just three drivers – more would have been unrealistic. In Ostrava, the problem was not that the taxis were divided between ranks: it was simply that there were not many taxis anywhere. Although the largest city I interviewed in, it was also the poorest. A couple of vehicles waited at the railway station, but too few to justify an approach. In the city centre, the square where taxis would normally park was being dug up. I was lucky to discover a taxi-hut still manned on the square, and when the three drivers inside expressed enthusiasm I decided to proceed with the interview.

The question of homogeneity is always an elusive one, given the range of criteria by which it can be assessed and the uncertainty surrounding which ones are relevant. One never knows how far the standard criteria – e.g. class, gender, ethnicity – are likely to influence the kind of discourse produced, and the danger is that once one starts making assumptions about their relevance one reverts to a determinist perspective whereby what people say is accounted for by 'who they are'. Such a perspective, while perhaps appealing to the traditional sociologist, can be objectionable from a political-theoretical perspective, and the resultant dilemma is typical of those faced when one works at the interface of two disciplines, each with its own body of concerns. The difficulty cannot be evaded by seeking to include in the sample variation on all possible criteria, such that no prior assumptions are made, since there will always be more criteria than one can address. Attempting to control methodically for the heterogeneity or homogeneity of the groups would also disrupt any naturalness achieved in the selection of participants on the rank. Moreover, how one isolates variables in this case is by no means obvious. For example, one might wish to introduce variation according to income levels, an objective which – given the reticence of drivers about their earnings – one would probably operationalise indirectly by interviewing night-drivers (whose earnings are generally higher) as well as day-drivers. Night-drivers, however, are also more likely to be single, since their hours combine badly with a family. One would therefore be introducing variation according to marital status too, something potentially just as significant. And the variables proliferate. Night-drivers are likely to spend less time in each other's company than day-drivers; night-drivers will spend less time reading newspapers (because they are more busy, and because it is dark) but will spend more time listening to the radio; the content of night-time radio tends to differ from that of day-time radio, and so on.

For these reasons, recruitment was guided by quite simple criteria. I was not interested in questions to do with the causal significance of particular variables, and therefore the statistical representativity of my sample was not a great concern. Age-balance was sought for each interview, with the youngest driver in his 20s to 30s and the oldest in his 50s to 60s. Where ethnic minorities were strongly visible on the rank the sample was chosen to reflect this (three of the four participants in Reading were of first- or second-generation Asian background, though all had been living in the city for at least a decade).[3] Female drivers were rare in the cities studied, and while no effort was made to exclude them they did not feature in the sample.

The nature of group interviews makes issues of composition, particularly statistical representativity, difficult to control even should one wish to. Unlike taking part in a short survey questionnaire, a two-hour interview represents a major commitment of time and energy even for those in the most flexible of occupations, and well-intentioned sampling procedures can easily be undone by low response rates and last-minute withdrawals. Gamson reports that his attempts to follow a statistical procedure had to be abandoned because typically only 10% of those selected for participation would follow through (Gamson 1992: 190). Self-selection is virtually impossible to eliminate. Even once the interview is underway, there are plenty of opportunities for the unexpected. At Erfurt, I decided to conduct the interview with three drivers due to the low numbers available on the rank. We settled down as a group in a *Kneipe* opposite the station, alongside tables of elderly men having their first beer of the morning, and went through the card exercise with which each interview began. Just as we finished and were poised to open out the discussion, Harald's mobile phone rang: it was the boss calling, asking them to move their taxis as they were blocking the rank. A short intermission followed while Harald, Uli and Matthias went off to resolve this, leaving me playing with my place-mat and wondering whether I needed to be assertive in some way. Several minutes later, they returned with the good news that new parking spots had been found and accompanied, by the way, by a fourth driver interested in joining us, Axel. After making a quick assessment of Axel's level of good will, and bringing him up to date on the card exercise, I restarted the discussion and we continued for a further two, highly productive hours. In the face of this kind of unpredictability, an inflexible stance would not have served me well. Disallowing the participation of Axel because I had not selected him myself, or declaring the interview void due to the few minutes of interruption, would not only have cost me a very rich amount of data but would probably have so alienated the three existing participants that the chances of recruiting a new set of drivers later in the day would have been slim.

While my sample makes no claim to statistical representativeness, it remains important to ask what kinds of factor might have informed the self-selection process such that some drivers agreed to participate while others declined. In almost all cities (Ostrava was the exception) I encountered at least some drivers unwilling to take part, and in the cases of Swansea, Würzburg and Plzeň it was several hours before a willing team was assembled. Significant remuneration was on offer, set at a rate above waiting-time and intended to represent a sound return on two hours' work for most drivers (though it was never so high that a driver might not, in principle, have made the same amount in the same time on

---

[3]There was only one other non-white participant in the study: Hamid, a first-generation Iranian immigrant, who took part in the discussion in Lübeck.

the job).[4] But the money was clearly not the sole factor in determining the success of recruitment, and my impression is that the decision to accept was rarely based principally on an assessment of the interview's financial worth. Certainly it was made universally clear to me that no-one was going to give up their time for free, and a few drivers needed reassuring that I really did possess the money I was claiming to offer.[5] But the majority of participants and non-participants who were approached expressed the opinion that the sum on offer was favourable. Some drivers who declined participation did state inadequate remuneration as their reason, but there were doubts as to whether this was their 'real reason' – other drivers would often intervene with comments like 'you'll be lucky if you make that in the next two hours.' Drivers who had rejected the offer could often be seen inert on the rank for long periods thereafter, earning no money at all. If one can fairly say the level of remuneration was more often an excuse than a reason for non-participation, it is worth then considering what other motivations there may have been for rejection. Moments where the research seemed to be 'failing', with an absence of volunteers and a number of refusals, provided a good opportunity to explore the likely nature of my sample, and by asking those who declined for their reasons I made sure they too were a part of the study.

Some reasons for non-participation were straightforward (though hard to confirm). Drivers might have regular bookings that needed to be honoured – in Swansea, large numbers were unavailable mid-afternoon because they were committed to taking children home from school. The weather was another practical constraint: not only might an outbreak of rain significantly increase the supply of customers, thereby thinning the rank and reducing the appeal of my offer, it would also keep the drivers who remained on the rank inside their taxis. This would remove the possibility of approaching pre-existing groups, meaning I would have to convince drivers one by one. This was always a more difficult approach – groups tended to be more willing to 'hear me out', perhaps because the individuals involved would feel less trapped than when cornered alone.

A third practical obstacle to participation derived from the fact that most ranks contained a mixture of employed and self-employed drivers. The latter had considerably more flexibility than the former, who might be required to produce records to their boss to account for their earnings. Several drivers expressed the concern their boss would raise awkward questions if they agreed to take part, even if (or indeed especially if) they were to set their meter to run on waiting-time for two hours. This was a reason for reluctance frequently cited in Würzburg, and was considered fully credible by Ralf, an eventual participant. In Plzeň, another city where recruitment was difficult, some of the taxi firms were quite small, and by engaging four drivers at once I would have taken that firm off the road for two hours, again

---

[4] In Britain and Germany the rates were €60–70 per head; in the Czech Republic c. €40. These rates would have been more or less appealing according to the time of day: at peak times (which I tried to avoid) they might have represented a loss on expected earnings, and therefore would have been insufficient to attract any but the most curious. Likewise, for drivers at the front of the rank, for whom a new fare was likely to be imminent, these figures would have been less attractive than for those at the back, on whom I concentrated my energies.
[5] Only in Plzeň did participants insist on being paid before the interview began.

something to displease the boss. Generally, in order to participate it seemed that drivers would have either to be self-employed or, if not, to enjoy decent relations with their boss (as Ralf said he did) or to be indifferent to potential complications of that sort, and perhaps to be attached to a firm large enough to accommodate their absence without disruption. Whilst these were not especially demanding hurdles – even a sceptical boss could probably later be convinced that worthwhile money had been gained – they were nonetheless enough to rule out some.

However, rejections also came from those for whom these practical difficulties would not have arisen. General scepticism towards unusual propositions, especially when voiced by outsiders, might have accounted for a number of refusals. This was a reason sometimes cited by drivers who were sympathetic to my project, or who had committed to participate themselves, to explain the reluctance of colleagues. In Swansea I was told by one such driver that 'people are very suspicious around here', and a driver in Plzeň implied something similar with 'that's Plzeň for you.' In Würzburg, I was told the problem was that this was 'a small, pretty little town' and that people were generally wary of outsiders. 'They just want to go to and fro from the station, no distractions,' said one driver. Ralf drew a comparison with another occasion when a stranger had approached the rank offering €50 to whichever driver would lend him a hand in putting up a sign: 'no-one was willing to do it but me, I thought I couldn't be hearing right, what was wrong with them?' Aversion to commercial polling and advertising also seemed evident – a non-participant in Swansea told me he was 'sick of people ringing up to ask questions', and my insistence that I was from a university rather than a private company seemed of little relevance. This diffuse scepticism towards the unknown, what one might call an hostility towards intrusion, was no doubt compounded when drivers saw others declining my offer: negative inertia could build quickly in these circumstances, and there was a danger I could develop the reputation of a pest. (This was starting to happen in Plzeň, before Pavel took up my case and lent some legitimacy to my requests.) In Britain, mixed in with these concerns was probably the more specific one that I might be an inspector from the fraud office wanting to take a look at the accounts.

How the researcher is perceived by potential participants can be crucial in this type of research. As someone who grew up in London, I could have passed for a local in the two cities in southern England where I interviewed, Norwich and Reading. Indeed, in Reading the participants assumed I was from Reading University. But in Swansea I would have been clearly classifiable as English rather than Welsh, and in the cities in Germany and the Czech Republic I would have been fairly easy to place as English or British, even had I not introduced myself as such.[6]

---

[6]For the German and Czech interviews I considered taking a local assistant, but decided against. The production of qualitative data tends to require considerable exercise of judgement, especially where interviews are used. While a local moderator might have created functional equivalence on nationality, it would have disrupted continuity in the exercise of judgement. Different, or more frequent, interventions can change the tone and direction of the discussion. It would also have changed the number of researchers involved. The diminutive presence I was able to achieve on my own, which I sensed served me well in allowing drivers to deal confidently with me and with little awareness of an audience, would have been lost.

Generally I had no reason to believe this was adversely affecting the recruitment process (for consideration of how it might have affected the interviews themselves, see below). However, in Würzburg it may well have been significant. This is a city that was heavily bombed by the British RAF at the end of World War II, and where an association might readily be made between an historical event, a broader set of national antagonisms, and a modern-day visitor who seemed to be looking for favours. I asked Ralf during the interview why he thought I had had difficulty in recruiting participants that morning: 'well I spoke to one of them, Fritz ... [now to Ulrich and Oskar:] Fritz Biedermann, the one who drives 16.2. I've always assumed he was a very reasonable person so I was a bit surprised when he reacted like that. But it was something to do with the British ... your country, the World War II context. I don't know ... whether ... he didn't say anything more concrete, but perhaps it was to do with the bombing here in Würzburg.' All participants predictably suggested this was inappropriate of Fritz, but they seemed to take Ralf's explanation as credible. Hostility of this kind was not something I was aware of while recruiting: indeed, several non-participants tried to assist me. In particular, Fritz himself had given me the slightly different – but equally plausible – explanation that he felt it was not possible for him to express the kind of opinions he wanted to in public. 'If I say what I want to say they'd put me in prison,' was his remark. Another driver claimed his own views were 'not allowed' in today's Germany. A counter-reading to Ralf's account would therefore be that Fritz, and others like him, declined to participate not because of any targeted hostility but because of a perception that certain opinions could not be expressed – perhaps especially in the presence of an outsider. This is a reason for non-participation which one could summarise as the feeling of 'unmentionability'.

Unmentionability might have been of special significance in the Würzburg case. The day before the interview, then-Chancellor Schröder had given a speech to commemorate the sixtieth anniversary of the liberation of the concentration camp Buchenwald, and had spoken of the special responsibility of Germans to ensure anti-Semitism and racism did not re-emerge. The speech was reported and head-lined in the newspapers many drivers were reading the following morning as I was recruiting. It is quite possible that certain drivers were hostile to the speech, with its emphasis on German war-guilt, and were unwilling to discuss their hostility in a public place, perhaps all the more so in my presence as a British person. One non-participant, who spoke to me on political issues for about five minutes from behind the wheel, was certainly quick to raise this subject, and spoke indignantly of how 'you can't say what you want to in Germany. You're not allowed to be proud to be German, if you ever criticise the Jews they say "he's anti-Semitic!" and they immediately bring up the Holocaust.'

Assuming this problem of 'unmentionability' did affect his decision to decline participation – and on these cognitive questions there can be little certainty – this suggests my research method was likely to generate a sample which excluded those inclined to say certain things: that it might, loosely speaking, contain a 'liberal bias'. But there are reasons to think this was not a major problem, not least the fact that the German discussions (Würzburg included) covered in considerable detail precisely the issues which it was being suggested here were unmentionable. While some non-participating drivers might take pleasure in positioning themselves as no-nonsense types whose common-sense wisdom was too painful and truthful to be aired, other participating drivers were quite able to bring these concerns with them to the table. In other words, while some drivers might use these discursive motifs as reasons to exclude themselves from the discussion, this did not mean that the motifs themselves were excluded: they were simply supplied by others.

A largely similar argument can be made with regard to a final reason for non-participation cited by some: that 'politics' did not interest them and that they had nothing to say on the subject. This was a reaction I had anticipated, and when recruiting I tried to avoid using the word 'politics' on the assumption it might carry associations rather narrower than I intended. Given current everyday usage of the term, 'politics' might be taken to mean no more than a certain set of individuals and institutions, without regard for the substantive issues these might address, and maybe with connotations of self-indulgent, empty talk. Cramer Walsh describes how, for the 'Old Timers' whose coffeeshop conversations she would listen to, 'politics is about impasse and petty griping,' 'controversy and the stuff of people who lack common sense ...' (Cramer Walsh 2004: 38, 39). I wanted to be able to recruit those who might 'talk politics' even without knowing or intending it. I wanted to avoid reactions like that of one non-participant in Würzburg, who – having given me five minutes of opinions on the euro, the state of German society and the problem of imported goods – rejected participation on the grounds that 'politicians are liars, the politicians shit on me and I shit on them.' Moreover, I wanted to avoid presenting the proposed discussion as something akin to a knowledge test: to declare that I was looking for 'opinions on politics' would maximise the risk that drivers felt unqualified to take part.

Instead, I used vaguer phrases such as 'your thoughts on problems in public life', 'the kind of problems people encounter in daily life', and 'positive and negative developments in society', hoping to allow potential participants to fill this ambiguity with their own expectations. To some extent this worked, as could be observed when enthusiastic drivers were trying to convince colleagues to take part: a wide range of descriptions was produced, including 'he's interested in our views about everyday problems ... the way society's going ... political views ... opinions about the times we live in,' or as Ralf in Würzburg put it, '*Weltanschauungen*'. For many drivers, this was quite enough information to be getting on with. 'Right, God, where do I start?' or 'yeah, I'll give him a few views' were typical responses, with each of us acting as though we fully knew what the other had in mind. However, there were a number of instances when I was pressed for further details – 'what is it you're looking for *exactly*?' – and on these occasions I would make some kind of reference to 'politics' since with further vagueness I would probably lose the listener's attention. There is therefore undoubtedly the possibility that some drivers refused participation because they heard a word they did not like. What are the implications? Does the sample contain a 'politico bias'? This would only be the case if those who participated could be classed as unusually enthusiastic about politics, marked out from their colleagues in this regard. There does not seem to be much grounds for believing this: indeed, participants could express considerable disillusionment with political institutions, individuals and processes, as we saw in the analysis. Perhaps particularly striking is a comment which Oskar made at the end of the Würzburg interview when asked about where he got his news from: he did not read much in the newspapers, he said, because he was generally 'cynical about politics'! Thus Oskar, who had contributed fully and with considerable sophistication throughout the course of the two-hour discussion, was moved to say something little different in tone from the non-participant on the rank who, as well as 'talking politics' for a while, had denounced all politicians as liars. Clearly, a self-declared aversion to 'politics' understood narrowly did not indicate a lack of competence to speak about substantive issues, and while this aversion may have induced some drivers not to participate, other drivers who also voiced it were nonetheless willing to do so.

These points provide further basis for the arguments made in Chapter 2 concerning the constitution of research cases. For if one wanted to treat the discourse produced in interviews such as these as indicative of the dispositions of a particular social group, one would certainly be concerned about the extent to which members of that group chose not to involve themselves. Noting the recurrence of self-selection, one would probably conclude that a certain 'type' of person was missing, leaving a hole in the sample. Yet if one treats the cases as providing access to a discursive field, there is significantly less reason for concern. For what matters then is that those who *did* participate provided a suitably rich and varied set of data, taking in the discursive patterns non-participants might have contributed had they been present.

Once three or four participants had been secured, we proceeded directly to the pub, bar or café in which the discussion would take place. Although sometimes the drivers themselves had a place in mind, and were encouraged to follow their preference, often the choice was left to me. For obvious reasons to do with the recording, a fairly quiet location was required. Upstairs cafés, away from swinging doors and the noise of the street, tended to be best where available; pubs (and their German and Czech equivalents) could be suitable in the hours before lunchtime, when generally there were few customers and no music; hotel bars were also a reliable option. A location which was deathly quiet on the other hand would be one to avoid, since I did not want participants feeling they might be overheard, either by neighbouring tables or staff. Operating without an assistant and in ten different cities, it would have been difficult to secure in each case the kind of setting described in certain focus-group manuals: a private room laid out with jugs of orange-juice, pots of coffee and a selection of biscuits, observable through a one-way mirror. Such an approach requires considerable preparation for dubious advantage. I wanted, in particular, a location the participants might plausibly have chosen to spend time in themselves, one in which they would feel, as one puts it, 'at home'. Particularly favourable was if the proposed location was visible from the taxi-rank, since this could be used during recruitment to heighten the immediacy of the exercise and to diminish any sense of mystery ('we'll just be going to that place over there'), plus to convince drivers they would not be abandoning their taxis and that after the discussion they would be able to return quickly to work. The small risk associated with such locations was that some drivers might be reluctant to associate themselves with a place serving alcohol, either on professional or religious/cultural grounds. This was not a protest I encountered however, and participants themselves seemed content simply not to order alcohol, or to order a small amount.

Once the group was seated around a table, we made some brief introductions and I laid out some of the usual rules associated with group interviews (e.g. that participants should avoid speaking at the same time, and should not treat me as someone directing the discussion). I requested permission to make an audio recording, a request which never met objection and which had no appreciable impact on the participants' style of interaction.[7] I then reiterated my interest in 'problems in public life' before feeding directly into the card exercise. There was no pre-interview questionnaire. While this might have produced some interesting bio-graphical data, it would have atomised the group – extended silence is a bad way to begin a discussion – and would have taken up valuable time better devoted to collective rather than individual activities. Also, questionnaires can be tedious and can create an exam-hall atmosphere. Luke in Swansea was one driver to make his participation conditional on there not being 'any forms to fill out'.

In contrast, the card exercise provided an engaging way to initiate the session. Aside from the theoretical rationale outlined in Chapter 3, it was intended to 'warm up' the participants so that the transition to a free discussion would be smooth. In this respect it was successful, and there were generally no indications that it was received either as patronising or dull; overall, there was confirmation of the pos-itive experiences other researchers have reported when using this method (Coxon 1999; Meinhof 2004).[8] Two participants from the group in Kassel displayed some frustration about the difficulty of sorting the cards into piles, arguing it was poss-ible to link all of the themes displayed to one another, but momentum was main-tained by the other two participants. The images and captions chosen for display on the cards can be seen at the end of the Appendix. The intention was to assem-ble a series of thematically-related visual prompts which could be read in multiple ways. German and Czech versions were used where appropriate, and all translations were discussed in depth with native-speakers of those languages (who were also social scientists). Originally the plan was to conduct two exercises with these cards, one at the beginning of the discussion – as outlined in Chapter 3 – and one in the later stages, in which participants would be invited to arrange them according to what kind of political institution (if any) should be in charge of developing policies for the redress of the problems articulated. The aim here would have been to explore how readily institutions other than the national government were invoked, parti-cularly the EU. Having attempted this second exercise during the Reading discus-sion, I decided to abandon it. It was clear it would involve unnecessary repetition of the material which had already arisen spontaneously in discussion, plus the ques-tion seemed hard to convey to participants – perhaps precisely because a problem-rather than institution-oriented approach was one that resonated better. Also, at a practical level, a second exercise at this point in the interview, when the dis-cussion was mature, would have been disruptive of the flow and might have led to digressions.

The discussions lasted between 90 minutes and two hours. In some cases (e.g. Erfurt and Würzburg) the discussion could usefully have continued longer, and

---

[7]The use of a video camera, on the other hand, might well have generated a degree of self-consciousness, and would have diminished the anonymity that a couple of the drivers requested. Furthermore, the early phase of a group interview requires establishing a certain rapport with participants and conveying a sense of purpose. In the absence of an assistant, it would have been unwise for me to spend those early moments absorbed in the adjustment of technical equipment. Cf. (Gamson 1992: 194; Morgan 1997: 56).

[8]For the use instead of vignettes and imagined scenarios as means to prompt group discussion, see (Gamson 1992; Perrin 2006).

participants continued to say interesting things after the capacity of my recorder had been exhausted (at which point I switched to hand-written notes, though none of these have been cited as quotations). In Swansea and Plzeň, it would have been difficult to extend the discussion much beyond ninety minutes, since repetition was starting to occur.

Relations between myself and the groups were, from my perspective, generally positive. Eliasoph describes how the people she talked to for her ethnographic research tended to find her project rather 'quaint' (Eliasoph 1998: 273); while I did encounter an avuncular manner from some drivers, the most common reaction was a fair degree of seriousness about the project, expressed in the sentiment that it was about time people took the views of 'people like us' seriously and that it was perfectly appropriate for a student to be expressing his interest. In the Czech Republic, particularly at Ostrava, there was a sense that it was rather commendable that someone had come all the way from London to talk to them. Several participants asked why I chose to speak to taxi-drivers; such questions I postponed until the end of the interview (arguing I did not want to run out of recording time), and then made general remarks about their depth of experience and good connections, remarks which drew approval. Only from one participant, in Plzeň, did I sense animosity towards me: this driver, younger than me, seemed keen to test my credentials for interviewing him, and went to some lengths to work out which university I was from, whether such a university existed, and what my informed opinion was on the problems under discussion. Fortunately the other two participants were supportive of my desire to keep questions about myself to the end. This experience was quite exceptional however: almost all drivers seemed to be little interested in me and my personal biography, and much more interested in making sure that their fellow participants and I were listening to what they had to say.

In much ethnographic work there is the need to avoid, or at least to reflect on, the possibility of 'going native' in the course of one's field-work. Although this is a somewhat ambiguous idea, one takes it to mean the danger of developing emotional attachments to one's subject-matter, in particular to individual persons, which then alter the conclusions drawn. In the context of two-hour interviews, prefaced by a generally short period of recruitment, such a consideration is minor. Naturally I warmed to those drivers who helped me to recruit on the rank, and to all those who spoke thoughtfully in discussion, but there was little opportunity for such evaluations to feed back into the data-collection. Likewise, when participants expressed views which in other contexts I might have objected to – for example, that excessive reproduction in the Third World might be tackled by a policy of castration – I was quite able in the brief context of these interviews to react with indifference, using the same news-receipts ('right ...', 'hmmm ...' or a repetition of words) that I used throughout. While the danger remains that judgements of this kind might affect my choice of passages for analysis and quotation, it should be clear from the empirical chapters that no attempt has been made to launder the material in this way.

When it came to transcribing the interviews, the names were changed, partly to preserve anonymity (though few drivers insisted on this) and partly to avoid confusion, since some names recurred. Following Gamson, the transcript style was kept simple, without recourse to the subtleties employed in linguistic conversation-analysis, which are both time-consuming to honour and difficult for the uninitiated reader to follow (Gamson 1992: 194). Preliminary coding analysis of the transcripts was carried out using WinMax software. As will have been evident in the analysis, while numbers are used to give an approximate indication of the relative frequency of certain motifs, statistics have not been applied. This decision is directly related to the observations made above concerning the ambiguity of the universe from which the sample was taken, due to the element of self-selection in recruitment. Only if the interviewees were taken to be statistically representative of a well-defined broader population would it make sense to take a statistical approach to the motifs evident in their conversation. Such a claim, always a bold one, is one that has been avoided here.

Interview Topic Guide

<u>*Declaration of research interest*</u> – *issues in public life and the **possibilities** for* **dealing** *with them.* **Not necessarily just** *attitudes towards current* **government** *and its policies ...* **broader** *than that.*

Introductions ... names
... seating arrangement:

- **Here are 17 index cards** – relating to different issues in public life. Spend 2 mins thinking to yourself about what **issues 'go together naturally'.** Then **move** cards. No right / wrong way, whatever **natural**; some can be left single. **Think aloud.**

  [Probe on organising **criteria** being used. Note the **first pairs** and **physical proximity** on the table.]

  Then: decide on a **name** for each card grouping. [Write name on small card; read out for recorder.]

  Any issue areas need **adding** to these? [Create new cards if necessary.]
  [c. 20 mins]

- So got **card piles**. Let's **talk** in **more** depth about the **important/pressing stuff**. Start wherever. Perhaps you can give **examples** of the **problems** which can arise ... things personally encountered or heard about?

  [Where a number of problems/experiences cited, and pursued by more than one participant:]

– How do you **explain** that? – Anyone to **blame**: – Who **affected/not affected**? – **Winners** and **losers**? – Who praise for success?	– Can **anything** be done about that? – If so, **what**? – **Authorities: right ones** in charge? [If not: how change?] Probe on **transnational** dimension if raised.	What **specific** **examples** thinking of/what experiences of these problems have had?
Opinions of people: – **general** – fellow **nationals** – fellow **professionals**	What **news sources** used? Probe on: – newspaper/TV news – trade unions/professional gatherings – new technologies	[c. 70 mins]

[Probe on any **neglected card piles** before continuing.]

- [If not already mentioned (if so, probe when mentioned):] the **EU.** How does it **fit in** to all this?
  Can it **help** somehow? ... Yes – **how**? ... No – **why**?
  [c. 20 mins]

The Interview Prompt Cards

THE LEGAL SYSTEM

MARKETS·PRODUCTION

POLICING

MONEY + PRICES

WORK

HEALTH + SAFETY STANDARDS

OVERSEAS AID

TRANSPORT

The Interview Prompt Cards – continued

TREATMENT OF OUTSIDERS

CORRUPTION

PEACE + WAR

PURCHASE OF PROPERTY

EDUCATION + TRAINING

MEDICAL CARE

SCIENCE + RESEARCH

TAXATION

THE ENVIRONMENT

Cards/ Groups	Money/ Prices	Markets/ Prod.	Purchase of Prop.	Work	Taxation	Educ. & Train.	Corrup.	Legal System	Policing	Treat. of Outs.	Peace & War	Overseas Aid	Environ.	Science/ Research	Transp.	Medic. Care	Health/ Safety
Reading	Money	Money	Money	Money	Money	Law & Order	Law & Order	Law & Order	Law & Order	Conflict	Conflict	Conflict	General Environ.	General Environ.	General Environ.	Care	Care
Swansea	Money & Work	Money & Work	Money & Work	Money & Work	Money & Work	Educat.	Justice/ Law	Justice/ Law	Justice/ Law	Immigrants	Immigrants	Immigrants	(sep.)	Educat.	(sep.)	(sep.)	Money/ Work
Norwich	Everyday	Everyday	Everyday	Everyday	Britain	Britain	Britain	Britain	Britain	The World	The World	The World	The Future	The Future	Everyday	(sep.)	Everyday
Lübeck	Economy & Occupat.	Economy & Occupat.	(sep.)	Economy &Occupat.	Economy & Occupat.	Economy & Occupat.	Domest. Security	Domest. Security	Domest. Security	Domest. Security	Foreign Policy	Foreign Policy	Environ. & Transpt.	Economy & Occupat.	Environ. & Transpt.	Health	Health
Kassel	Political Economy	Political Economy	Political Economy	Political Economy	Political Economy	Develop-ment	Pol Econ and Legal Sy	Legal System	Legal System	Legal System	Internat. Relations	Internat. Relations	Develop-ment	Develop-ment	Develop-ment	Health	Health
Erfurt	'Every-where'	Capitalism	Capitalism	Educat. & Future	Capitalism	Educat. & Future	Legal System	Legal System	Legal System	Foreign Policy	Foreign Policy	Foreign Policy	Quality of Life	Educat. & Future	Quality of Life	Quality of Life	Quality of Life
Würz'burg	Economy & Finances	Economy & Finances	Economy & Finances	Social Surroun-dings	Economy & Finances	Social Surroun-dings	'Every-where'	Legal System	Legal System	Legal System	Foreign Policy	Foreign Policy	Quality of Life	Social Surroun-dings	Quality of Life	Quality of Life	Social Surroun-dings
Liberec	Financial Situation	Financial Situation	Financial Situation	Financial Situation	Financial Situation	Educat.	State Services	State Services	State Services	Security	Security	Aid	Aid	Educat.	State Services	State Services	Financial Situation
Plzeň	Finances	Finances	Finances	Finances	Finances	Educat.	Law	Law	Law	Educat.	Educat.	Aid	Educat.	Educat.	Finances	Aid	Finances
Ostrava	Everyday	State Sector	Educat. & Laws	Everyday	Everyday	Educat. & Laws	Educat. & Laws	Educat. & Laws	Everyday	Everyday	Global	Global	Global	State Sector	State Sector	State Sector	Everyday

Summary of Card Arrangements
Words indicate the headings given to card piles. '(Sep.)' refers to cards which were not placed in piles but kept separate. For each row, shadings generally correspond to card piles, but override these in cases where subsequent discussion suggests to do so. Across the rows, shadings correspond approximately to the domains *Economics, Society and the Law* and *Relations between Peoples*, and the 'Quality of Life' set.

A Note on Transcription and Translation

Extracts from the interview transcripts have been presented using a simple notation style, the key features of which are as follows. '...' indicates a break in the speaker's delivery, or the transition from one speaker to the next where there is no pause between the two. Where there is just a short pause, and the first speaker's intervention was grammatically complete, this is marked by a full stop. Where there is a longer pause, and again the first speaker's intervention was grammatically complete, this is marked by a full stop followed by '[pause]'. Where there is a longer pause, and the first speaker's intervention tailed off, this is marked by '... [pause]'. Short interventions that affirm what a speaker is saying without significantly adding to it are included in the body of that speaker's text and marked by square brackets. Abridgements of the text are marked by '[...]'.

All translations from German and Czech are the work of the author. For the occasional word or phrase which is difficult to translate, or which has an idiomatic sense that would be lost in translation, the original is included in square brackets.

Bibliography

Abizadeh, Arash (2005) 'Does Collective Identity Presuppose an Other? On the Alleged Incoherence of Global Solidarity', *American Political Science Review*, 99 (1).

Anderson, Benedict (1991) *Imagined Communities: Reflections on the Origin and Spread of Nationalism* (London: Verso).

Anderson, Christopher (1998) 'When in Doubt, Use Proxies: Attitudes Toward Domestic Politics and Support for European Integration', *Comparative Political Studies*, 31 (5).

Antaki, Charles (1988) 'Explanations, Communication and Social Cognition', in Charles Antaki (ed.) *Analysing Everyday Explanation: A Casebook of Methods* (London: Sage).

—— (1994) *Explaining and Arguing: The Social Organization of Accounts* (London: Sage).

—— (1998) 'Identity as an Achievement and as a Tool', in Charles Antaki and Sue Widdicombe (eds) *Identities in Talk* (London: Sage).

Archibugi, Daniele (2008) *The Global Commonwealth of Citizens: Toward Cosmopolitan Democracy* (Princeton N.J.: Princeton UP).

Barnes, Barry (1995) *The Elements of Social Theory* (London: UCL Press).

—— (2001) 'Practice as Collective Action', in Theodore R. Schatzki, Karin Knorr Cetina and Eike von Savigny (eds) *The Practice Turn in Contemporary Theory* (London: Routledge).

Bauman, Zygmunt (1999) *In Search of Politics* (Cambridge: Polity).

—— (2004) 'From Social State to Security State', in Zygmunt Bauman (ed.) *Europe: An Unfinished Adventure* (Cambridge: Polity).

Beck, Ulrich (1997) *World Risk Society* (Oxford: Blackwell).

—— (2007) 'The Cosmopolitan Condition: Why Methodological Nationalism Fails', *Theory, Culture & Society*, 24 (7–8).

Bellamy, Richard (1999) *Liberalism and Pluralism: Towards a Politics of Compromise* (London: Routledge).

Bellamy, Richard and Castiglione, Dario (1998) 'The Normative Challenge of a European Polity: Cosmopolitan and Communitarian Models Compared, Criticised and Combined', in Andreas Follesdal and Peter Koslowski (eds) *Democracy and the European Union* (Berlin: Springer-Verlag).

Benhabib, Seyla, Shapiro, Ian and Petranović, Danilo (2007) *Identities, Affiliations, and Allegiances* (Cambridge: CUP).

Billig, Michael (1991) *Ideology and Opinions* (London: Sage).

Bloor, Michael, Frankland, Jane, Thomas, Michelle and Robson, Kate (2001) *Focus Groups in Social Research* (London: Sage).

Boltanski, Luc and Thévenot, Laurent (1999) 'The Sociology of Critical Capacity', *European Journal of Social Theory*, 2 (3).

—— (2006) *On Justification: Economies of Worth* (Princeton: Princeton UP).

Brown, Rupert and Haeger, Gabi (1999) '"Compared to What?" Comparison Choice in an International Context', *European Journal of Social Psychology*, 29 (1).

Brubaker, Rogers (2004) *Ethnicity Without Groups* (Cambridge Mass.: Harvard UP).

Brubaker, Rogers and Cooper, Frederick (2000) 'Beyond "Identity"', *Theory and Society*, 29 (1).

Bruter, Michael (2005) *Citizens of Europe? The Emergence of a Mass European Identity* (Basingstoke: Palgrave Macmillan).

Büchs, Milena (2008) 'How Legitimate is the Open Method of Co-ordination?', *Journal of Common Market Studies*, 46 (4).

Canovan, Margaret (1996) *Nationhood and Political Theory* (Cheltenham: Edwin Elgar).

—— (2005) *The People* (Cambridge: Polity).

Carey, Sean (2002) 'Undivided Loyalties: Is National Identity an Obstacle to European Integration?', *European Union Politics*, 3 (4).

Checkel, Jeffrey T. and Katzenstein, Peter J. (eds) (2009) *European Identity* (Cambridge: CUP).

Chernilo, Daniel (2006) 'Social Theory's Methodological Nationalism: Myth and Reality', *European Journal of Social Theory*, 9 (1).

Choudhry, Sujit (2001) 'Citizenship and Federations: Some Preliminary Reflections', in Kalypso Nicolaidis and Robert Howse (eds) *The Federal Vision: Legitimacy and Levels of Governance in the United States and the European Union* (Oxford: OUP).

Cobb, Roger W. and Rochefort, David A. (eds) (1994) *The Politics of Problem Definition: Shaping the Policy Agenda* (Lawrence, Kansas: University Press of Kansas).

Connolly, William E. (1974) 'On Interests in Politics', in William E. Connolly (ed.) *Social Structure and Political Theory* (Lexington MA: Heath & Co).

—— (1995) *The Ethos of Pluralization* (Minneapolis MN: University of Minnesota Press).

Conover, Pamela, Searing, Donald D. and Crewe, Ivor (2002) 'The Deliberative Potential of Discussion', *British Journal of Political Science*, 32 (1).

Coxon, Anthony (1999) *Sorting Data: Collection and Analysis* (London: Sage).

Cramer Walsh, Katherine (2004) *Talking about Politics: Informal Groups and Social Identity in American Life* (London: University of Chicago Press).

Crompton, Rosemary (1998) *Class and Stratification: An Introduction to Current Debates* (Cambridge: Polity).

Cronin, Ciaran (2003) 'Democracy and Collective Identity: In Defence of Constitutional Patriotism', *European Journal of Philosophy*, 11 (1).

Dahl, Robert (1966) 'Some Explanations', in Robert Dahl (ed.) *Political Oppositions in Western Democracies* (New Haven: Yale UP), 348–86.

—— (1990) *After the Revolution? Authority in a Good Society* (Revised edn; New Haven: Yale UP).

Davies, Bronwyn and Harré, Rom (1990) 'Positioning: The Discursive Production of Selves', *Journal for the Theory of Social Behaviour*, 20 (1).

Delanty, Gerard (2002) 'Models of European Identity: Reconciling Universalism and Particularism', *Perspectives on European Politics and Society*, 3 (3).

Delanty, Gerard and Rumford, Chris (2005) *Rethinking Europe: Social Theory and the Implications of Europeanisation* (London: Routledge).

Delhey, Jan and Kohler, Ulrich (2006) 'From Nationally Bounded to Pan-European Inequalities? On the Importance of Foreign Countries as Reference Groups', *European Sociological Review*, 22 (2).

Delli Carpini, Michael X. and Keeter, Scott (1996) *What Americans Know about Politics and Why It Matters* (New Haven, Conn.: Yale UP).

Díez Medrano, Juan (2003) *Framing Europe: Attitudes to European Integration in Germany, Spain, and the United Kingdom* (Princeton N.J.: Princeton UP).

Downs, Anthony (1957) *An Economic Theory of Democracy* (New York: Harper).

Draper, Stephen W. (1988) 'What's Going On in Everyday Explanation?', in Charles Antaki (ed.) *Analysing Everyday Explanation: A Casebook of Methods* (London: Sage).

Duchesne, Sophie (2008) 'Waiting for a European Identity ... Reflections on the Process of Identification with Europe', *Perspectives on European Politics and Society*, 9 (4).

Duchesne, Sophie and Haegel, Florence (2007) 'Avoiding or Accepting Conflict in Public Talk', *British Journal of Political Science*, 37 (1).

Duchesne, Sophie, Haegel, Florence, Frazer, Elizabeth, van Ingelgom, Virginie, Garcia, Guillaume and Frognier, André-Paul (2010) 'Europe between Integration and Globalisation: Social Differences and National Frames in the Analysis of Focus Groups Conducted in France, Francophone Belgium and the UK', *Politique Européénne*, 30 (Spring), pp.67–106.

Duckitt, John (2003) 'Prejudice and Intergroup Hostility', in David O. Sears, Leonie Huddy and Robert Jervis (eds) *Oxford Handbook of Political Psychology* (Oxford: OUP).

Dyer, Richard (2000) 'The Matter of Whiteness', in Les Back and John Solomos (eds) *Theories of Race and Racism: A Reader* (London: Routledge).

Eder, Klaus (1995) 'Does Social Class Matter in the Study of Social Movements? A Theory of Middle Class Radicalism', in Louis Maheu (ed.) *Social Movements and Social Classes* (London: Sage).

Eder, Klaus and Kantner, Cathleen (2000) 'Transnationale Resonanzstrukturen in Europa. Eine Kritik der Rede vom Öffentlichkeitsdefizit', in Maurizio Bach (ed.) *Die Europäisierung nationaler Gesellschaften. Sonderheft 40 der Kölner Zeitschrift für Soziologie und Sozialpsychologie* (Wiesbaden: Westdeutscher Verlag).

Eliasoph, Nina (1990) 'Political Culture and the Presentation of a Political "Self"', *Theory and Society*, 19 (4).

—— (1998) *Avoiding Politics: How Americans Produce Apathy in Everyday Life* (Cambridge: CUP).

Elkin, Stephen L. and Soltan, Karol Edward (eds) (1999) *Citizen Competence and Democratic Institutions* (University Park, PA: Penn State UP).

Ellemers, Naomi (1993) 'The Influence of Social Structural Variables on Identity Management Strategies', *European Review of Social Psychology*, 4.

Elster, Jon (1986) 'The Market and the Forum: Three Varieties of Political Theory', in Jon Elster and Aanund Hylland (eds) *Foundations of Social Choice Theory* (Cambridge: CUP).

Eriksen, Erik O. (2005) 'Reflexive Integration in Europe', in Erik O. Eriksen (ed.) *Making the European Polity: Reflexive Integration in the EU* (London: Routledge).

Ester, Peter, Halman, Loek and de Moor, Ruud (eds) (1993) *The Individualizing Society: Value Change in Europe and North America* (Tilburg: Tilburg UP).

European Commission (2010) Eurobarometer 71, 'Public Opinion in the EU' and 'The Future of Europe' (Brussels: European Commission).

—— (2008) Eurobarometer 69 (3), Standard Eurobarometer, 'Europeans' State of Mind' (Brussels: European Commission).

—— (2008) Eurobarometer 69 (2), Standard Eurobarometer, 'The Europeans and Globalisation' (Brussels: European Commission).

—— (2007) Eurobarometer 67, Standard Eurobarometer, Full Report (Brussels: European Commission).

—— (2007) Eurobarometer 66, Standard Eurobarometer, Full Report (Brussels: European Commission).

—— (2005) Eurobarometer 63, Standard Eurobarometer, Full Report (Brussels: European Commission).

—— (2005) Eurobarometer 62, Standard Eurobarometer, Full Report (Brussels: European Commission).

Fabbrini, Sergio (2005) 'Madison in Brussels: The EU and the US as Compound Democracies', *European Political Science*, 4.

Favell, Adrian (2007) *Eurostars and Eurocities: Free Moving Urban Professionals in an Integrating Europe* (London: Blackwell).

Feinberg, Joel (1974) 'Non-Comparative Justice', *The Philosophical Review*, 83.

Fligstein, Neil (2008) *Euroclash: The EU, European Identity, and the Future of Europe* (Oxford: OUP).

Føllesdal, Andreas (2006) 'Survey Article: The Legitimacy Deficits of the European Union', *Journal of Political Philosophy*, 14 (4).

Føllesdal, Andreas and Hix, Simon (2006) 'Why There is a Democratic Deficit in the EU: A Response to Majone and Moravcsik', *Journal of Common Market Studies*, 44 (3).

Forst, Rainer (2001) 'The Rule of Reasons: Three Models of Deliberative Democracy', *Ratio Juris*, 14 (4).

Fuchs, Dieter and Klingemann, Hans-Dieter (2000) 'Eastward Enlargement of the European Union and the Identity of Europe', in Peter Mair and Jan Zielonka (eds) *The Enlarged European Union: Diversity and Adaptation* (London: Frank Cass).

Gabel, Matthew and Palmer, Harvey D. (1995) 'Understanding Variation in Public Support for European Integration', *European Journal of Political Research*, 27 (1).

Gambetta, Diego and Hamill, Heather (2005) *Streetwise: How Taxi Drivers Establish their Customers' Trustworthiness* (New York: Russell Sage).

Gamson, William (1992) *Talking Politics* (Cambridge: CUP).

Gellner, Ernest (1983) *Nations and Nationalism* (Oxford: Blackwell).

Gerhards, Jürgen (2002) 'Das Öffentlichkeitsdefizit der EU im Horizont normativer Öffentlichkeitstheorien', in Hartmut Kaelble, Martin Kirsch and Alexander Schmidt-Gernig (eds) *Transnationale Öffentlichkeiten und Identitäten im 20. Jahrhundert* (Frankfurt/Main: Campus).

Gerhards, Jürgen and Holscher, Michael (2005) *Kulturelle Unterschiede in der Europäischen Union: ein Vergleich zwischen Mitgliedsländern, Beitrittskandidaten und der Türkei* (Wiesbaden: Verlag für Sozialwissenschaften).

Giddens, Anthony (1984) *The Constitution of Society: Outline of the Theory of Structuration* (Cambridge: Polity).

—— (1994) *Beyond Left and Right* (Cambridge: Polity).

Gieryn, Thomas F. (1983) 'Boundary-Work and the Demarcation of Science from Non-Science: Strains and Interests in Professional Ideologies of Scientists', *American Sociological Review*, 48 (6).

Goodin, Robert E. (2007) 'Enfranchising All Affected Interests, and Its Alternatives', *Philosophy and Public Affairs*, 15 (1).

Grice, H. Paul (1975) 'Logic and Conversation', in Peter Cole and Jerry L. Morgan (eds) *Syntax and Semantics, Vol. 3, Speech Acts* (New York: Academic).

Grimm, Dieter (1995) 'Does Europe Need a Constitution?', *European Law Journal*, 1 (3).

Guimond, Serge (ed.) (2006) *Social Comparison and Social Psychology: Understanding Cognition, Intergroup Relations and Culture* (Cambridge: CUP).

Habermas, Jürgen (1984) *The Theory of Communicative Action* (Boston: Beacon).

—— (1992) 'Citizenship and National Identity', *Praxis International*, 12 (1).

—— (2001) 'Why Europe Needs a Constitution', *New Left Review* (September/October).

—— (2006) 'Is the Development of a European Identity Necessary, and Is It Possible?', in Ciaran Cronin (ed.) *The Divided West* (Cambridge: Polity).

—— (2009) 'European Politics at an Impasse: A Plea for a Policy of Graduated Integration', *Europe: The Faltering Project* (Cambridge: Polity).

Harré, Rom (2002) 'Material Objects in Social Worlds', *Theory, Culture and Society*, 19 (5/6).

Harré, Rom and van Langenhove, Luk (eds) (1999) *Positioning Theory* (Oxford: Blackwell).

Hay, Colin (2007) *Why We Hate Politics* (Cambridge: Polity).

Hayek, Friedrich A. (1939/1948) 'The Economic Conditions of Interstate Federalism', *Individualism and Economic Order* (London: Routledge).

Held, David (2003) 'Cosmopolitanism: Globalisation Tamed?', *Review of International Studies*, 29 (4).

Herrmann, Richard K. and Brewer, Marilynn B. (2004) 'Identities and Institutions: Becoming European in the EU', in Richard K. Herrmann, Thomas Risse and Marilynn B. Brewer (eds) *Transnational Identities: Becoming European in the EU* (Oxford: Rowman & Littlefield).

Hibbing, John R. and Theiss-Morse, Elizabeth (2002) *Stealth Democracy: Americans' Beliefs about How Government Should Work* (Cambridge: CUP).

Hirschman, Albert O. (1970) *Exit, Voice and Loyalty: Responses to Decline in Firms, Organizations, and States* (Cambridge MA: Harvard UP).

—— (1996) *The Passions and the Interests: Political Arguments for Capitalism Before Its Triumph* (Princeton N.J.: Princeton UP).

Hobolt, Sara Binzer and Klemmemsen, Robert (2005) 'Responsive Government? Public Opinion and Government Policy Preferences in Britain and Denmark', *Political Studies*, 53 (2).

Hobsbawm, Eric (1989) *The Age of Empire, 1875–1914* (New York: Vintage).

—— (1991) *Nations and Nationalism since 1780* (Cambridge: CUP).

Hollis, Martin (1994) *The Philosophy of Social Science: An Introduction* (Cambridge: CUP).

Hooghe, Liesbet and Marks, Gary (2005a) 'The Neofunctionalists Were (Almost) Right: Politicization and European Integration', *Constitutionalism Web-Papers. ConWEB*, 5 (05).

—— (2005b) 'Calculation, Community and Cues: Public Opinion on European Integration', *European Union Politics*, 6 (4).

Howarth, David and Torfing, Jacob (2005) *Discourse Theory in European Politics: Identity, Policy and Governance* (Basingstoke: Palgrave Macmillan).

Hutton, Will (2007) *The Writing on the Wall: China and the West in the 21st Century* (London: Little, Brown).

Imig, Doug and Tarrow, Sidney (2000) 'Political Contention in a Europeanising Polity', *West European Politics*, 23 (4).

Kalra, Virinder S. (2000) *From Textile Mills to Taxi Ranks: Experiences of Migration, Labour and Social Change* (Aldershot: Ashgate).

Karolewski, Ireneusz Pawel (2009) *Citizenship and Collective Identity in Europe* (London: Routledge).

Kitzinger, Jenny and Barbour, Rosaline S. (1999) 'The Challenge and Promise of Focus Groups', in Jenny Kitzinger and Rosaline S. Barbour (eds) *Developing Focus Group Research: Politics, Theory and Practice* (London: Sage).

Kohli, Martin (2000) 'The Battlegrounds of European Identity', *European Societies*, 2 (2).

Kraus, Peter (2008) *A Union of Diversity* (Cambridge: CUP).

Kundera, Milan (1984) 'The Tragedy of Central Europe', *New York Review of Books*, 31 (7).

Lamont, Michèle (2000) *The Dignity of Working Men: Morality and the Boundaries of Race, Class and Immigration* (Cambridge MA: Harvard UP).

Lamont, Michèle and Molnár, Virág (2002) 'The Study of Boundaries in the Social Sciences', *Annual Review of Sociology*, 28.

Lamont, Michèle and Thévenot, Laurent (eds) (2000) *Rethinking Comparative Cultural Sociology* (Cambridge: CUP).

Lefort, Claude (1988) 'The Question of Democracy', *Democracy and Political Theory* (Minneapolis: University of Minnesota).

Lipset, Seymour (1959) *Political Man* (London: Heinemann).

Loriaux, Michael (2008) *European Union and the Deconstruction of the Rhineland Frontier* (Cambridge: CUP).

Maguire, Eleanor A., Woollett, Katherine and Spiers, Hugo J. (2006) 'London Taxi Drivers and Bus Drivers: A Structural MRI and Neuropsychological Analysis', *Hippocampus*, 16 (12).

Mair, Peter (2006) 'Ruling the Void? The Hollowing of Western Democracy', *New Left Review*, 42 (Nov/Dec).

Majone, Giandomenico (1996) *Regulating Europe* (London: Routledge).

—— (1999) 'The Regulatory State and its Legitimacy Problems', *West European Politics*, 22 (1).

—— (2001) 'Nonmajoritarian Institutions and the Limits of Democratic Governance: A Political Transaction-Cost Approach', *Journal of Institutional and Theoretical Economics*, 157 (1).

Markell, Patchen (2000) 'Making Affect Safe for Democracy?: On "Constitutional Patriotism"', *Political Theory*, 28 (1).

Mason, Andrew (2000) *Community, Solidarity, and Belonging: Levels of Community and Their Normative Significance* (Cambridge: CUP).

McLaren, Lauren (2002) 'Public Support for the European Union: Cost/ Benefit Analysis or Perceived Cultural Threat?', *The Journal of Politics*, 64 (2).

—— (2006) *Identity, Interests and Attitudes to European Integration* (Basingstoke: Palgrave).

Meinhof, Ulrike Hanna (2004) 'Europe Viewed from Below: Agents, Victims, and the Threat of the Other', in Richard K. Herrmann, Thomas Risse and Marilynn B. Brewer (eds) *Transnational Identities: Becoming European in the EU* (Oxford: Rowman & Littlefield).

Merton, Robert (1957) 'Contributions to the Theory of Reference Group Behavior (with Alice Kitt Rossi)/Continuities in the Theory of Reference Groups and Social Structure', *Social Theory and Social Structure* (Glencoe Ill: Free).

Mill, John Stuart (1975) 'Considerations on Representative Government', *Three Essays* (Oxford: OUP).

Miller, David (2000) 'In Defence of Nationality', in David Miller (ed.) *Citizenship and National Identity* (Cambridge: Polity).

Millward, Lynne J. (2000) 'Focus Groups', in Glynis M. Breakwell, Sean Hammond and Chris Fife-Schaw (eds) *Research Methods in Psychology* (London: Sage).

Monnet, Jean (1963) 'A Ferment of Change', *Journal of Common Market Studies*, 1 (3).

Moravcsik, Andrew (2002) 'In Defence of the "Democratic Deficit": Reassessing Legitimacy in the European Union', *Journal of Common Market Studies*, 40 (4).

Morgan, David L. (1997) *Focus Groups as Qualitative Research* (Qualitative Research Methods Series 16; London: Sage).

Morgan, Glyn (2005) *The Idea of a European Superstate: Public Justification and European Integration* (Princeton: Princeton UP).

Mouffe, Chantal (1993) *The Return of the Political* (London: Verso).

—— (2005) *On the Political* (London: Verso).

Müller, Jan-Werner (2007) *Constitutional Patriotism* (Princeton: Princeton UP).

Nicolaidis, Kalypso (2001) 'Conclusion: The Federal Vision Beyond the Federal State', in Kalypso Nicolaidis and Robert Howse (eds) *The Federal Vision: Legitimacy and Levels of Governance in the United States and the European Union* (Oxford: OUP).

Nicolaidis, Kalypso and Lacroix, Justine (2003) 'Order and Justice Beyond the Nation-State: Europe's Competing Paradigms', in Rosemary Foot, John Gaddis and Andrew Hurrell (eds) *Order and Justice in International Relations* (Oxford: OUP).

Niedermayer, Oskar (1995) 'Trust and Sense of Community', in Oskar Niedermayer and Richard Sinnott (eds) *Public Opinion and Internationalized Governance* (Oxford: OUP).

Offe, Claus (1996) 'Democracy Against the Welfare State?', *Modernity and the State: East and West* (Cambridge: Polity), 147–82.

—— (2000) 'The Democratic Welfare State: A European Regime under the Strain of European Integration', *Political Science Series, Institute for Advanced Studies, Vienna*, 68.

OPTEM (2006) 'The European Citizens and the Future of Europe: A Qualitative Study in the 25 Member States' (Eurobarometer).

Parekh, Bhikhu (1995) 'Politics of Nationhood', in Keebet von Benda-Beckman and Maykel Verkuyten (eds) *Nationalism, Ethnicity and Cultural Identity in Europe* (Utrecht: ERCOMER).

Perrin, Andrew J. (2006) *Citizen Speak: The Democratic Imagination in American Life* (Chicago IL: University of Chicago).

Polanyi, Michael (1966) *The Tacit Dimension* (London: Routledge & Kegan Paul).

Potter, Jonathan and Wetherell, Margaret (1987) *Discourse and Social Psychology: Beyond Attitudes and Behaviour* (London: Sage).

Puchta, Claudia and Potter, Jonathan (2004) *Focus Group Practice* (London: Sage).

Reckwitz, Andreas (2002) 'Towards a Theory of Social Practices: A Development in Culturalist Theorising', *European Journal of Social Theory*, 5 (2).

Risse, Thomas (2010) *A Community of Europeans? Transnational Identities and Public Spheres* (Ithaca NY: Cornell UP).

Ritchie, Jane and Lewis, Jane (2004) *Qualitative Research Practice: A Guide for Social Science Students and Researchers* (London: Sage).

Robyn, Richard (ed.) (2005) *The Changing Face of European Identity* (London: Routledge).

Sabel, Charles F. and Zeitlin, Jonathan (2007) 'Learning from Difference: The New Architecture of Experimentalist Governance in the EU', in Charles F. Sabel and Jonathan Zeitlin (eds) *Experimentalist Governance in the European Union: Towards a New Architecture* (Oxford: OUP).

Sanders, Lynn M. (1997) 'Against Deliberation', *Political Theory*, 25 (3).

Scharpf, Fritz (1999) *Governing in Europe: Effective and Democratic?* (Oxford: OUP).

Schatzki, Theodore R. (1996) *Social Practices: A Wittgensteinian Approach to Human Activity and the Social* (Cambridge: CUP).

—— (2002) *The Site of the Social: A Philosophical Account of the Constitution of Social Life and Change* (University Park: Pennsylvania State UP).

Scheuer, Angelika and Schmitt, Hermann (2007) 'Dynamics in European Political Identity', in Michael Marsh, Slava Mikhaylov and Hermann Schmitt (eds) *European Elections after Eastern Enlargement: Preliminary Results from the European Election Study 2004* (Mannheim: CONNEX Report Series No. 1).

Schumpeter, Joseph (1943) *Capitalism, Socialism, and Democracy* (London: Allen & Unwin).

Sewell, William H. (1992) 'A Theory of Structure: Duality, Agency, and Transformation', *American Journal of Sociology*, 98 (1).

Shibutani, Tamotsu (1955) 'Reference Groups as Perspectives', *American Journal of Sociology*, 60 (6).

Shore, Cris (2000) *Building Europe: The Cultural Politics of European Integration* (London: Routledge).

Siedentop, Larry (2000) *Democracy in Europe* (London: Allen Lane).

Silber, Ilana Friedrich (2003) 'Pragmatic Sociology as Cultural Sociology: Beyond Repertoire Theory?', *European Journal of Social Theory*, 6 (4).

Singer, Brian C. J. (1996) 'Cultural versus Contractual Nations: Rethinking Their Opposition', *History and Theory*, 35 (3).

Skinner, Quentin (2002) 'Moral Principles and Social Change', in Quentin Skinner (ed.) *Visions of Politics, vol. 1: Regarding Method* (Cambridge: CUP).

Smith, Adam (1990) *An Inquiry into the Nature and Causes of the Wealth of Nations* (London: Encyclopaedia Britannica).

Smith, Anthony (1992) 'National Identity and the Idea of European Unity', *International Affairs*, 68 (1).

—— (1998) *Nationalism and Modernism: A Critical Survey of Recent Theories of Nations and Nationalism* (London: Routledge).

Smith, Rogers M. (2003) *Stories of Peoplehood: The Politics and Morals of Political Membership* (Cambridge: CUP).

Sniderman, Paul M., Brody, Richard A. and Tetlock, Philip E. (1991) *Reasoning and Choice: Explorations in Political Psychology* (New York: CUP).

Stråth, Bo (2002) 'A European Identity: To the Historical Limits of a Concept', *European Journal of Social Theory*, 5 (4).

Suls, Jerry, Martin, René and Wheeler, Ladd (2002) 'Social Comparison: Why, With Whom, and With What Effect?', *Current Directions in Psychological Science*, 11 (5).

Sunstein, Cass (1991) 'Preferences and Politics', *Philosophy and Public Affairs*, 20 (1).

Swidler, Ann (1986) 'Culture in Action', *American Sociological Review*, 51 (2).

—— (2001) *Talk of Love: How Culture Matters* (Chicago IL: University of Chicago Press).

Tajfel, Henri (1981) *Human Groups and Social Categories: Studies in Social Psychology* (Cambridge: CUP).

Tajfel, Henri and Turner, John (1986) 'The Social Identity Theory of Inter-Group Behavior', in Stephen Worchel and William G. Austin (eds) *Psychology of Intergroup Relations* (Chicago: Nelson-Hall).

Taylor, Charles (1971) 'Interpretation and the Sciences of Man', *Review of Metaphysics*, 25 (1).

Thomassen, Jacques (2007) 'European Citizenship and Identity', in Michael Marsh, Slava Mikhaylov and Hermann Schmitt (eds) *European Elections after Eastern Enlargement: Preliminary Results from the European Election Study 2004* (Mannheim: CONNEX Report Series No. 1).

—— (ed.) (2009) *The Legitimacy of the European Union After Enlargement* (Oxford: OUP).

Tilly, Charles (2002) *Stories, Identities and Political Change* (Oxford: Rowman & Littlefield).

Todorova, Maria (2009) *Imagining the Balkans* (Oxford: OUP).

Tönnies, Ferdinand (2001) *Community and Civil Society* (Cambridge: CUP).

Toulmin, Stephen (1958) *The Uses of Argument* (Cambridge: CUP).

Tully, James (2002) 'The Unfreedom of the Moderns in Comparison to Their Ideals of Constitutional Democracy', *The Modern Law Review*, 65 (2).

Wagner, Peter (1996) 'Crises of Modernity: Political Sociology in Historical Contexts', in Stephen Turner (ed.) *Social Theory and Sociology: The Classics and Beyond* (Oxford: Blackwell).

—— (2001) *A History and Theory of the Social Sciences: Not All that is Solid Melts into Air* (London: Sage).

Wagner, Peter and Friese, Heidrun (2002) 'Survey Article: The Nascent Political Philosophy of the European Polity', *Journal of Political Philosophy*, 10 (3).

Wedeen, Lisa (2002) 'Conceptualising Culture: Possibilities for Political Science', *American Political Science Review*, 96 (4).

Weiler, J. H. H. (1999) 'To Be a European Citizen', *The Constitution of Europe: Do the New Clothes have an Emperor? and Other Essays on European Integration* (Cambridge: CUP).

Whelan, Frederick G. (1983) 'Democratic Theory and the Boundary Problem', in J. Roland Pennock and John W. Chapman (eds) *Nomos XXV: Liberal Democracy* (New York: NYUP).

White, Jonathan (2009a) 'The Social Theory of Mass Politics', *Journal of Politics*, 71 (1).

—— (2009b) 'Thematization and Collective Positioning in Everyday Political Talk', *British Journal of Political Science*, 39 (4).

—— (2010a) 'Europe and the Common', *Political Studies*, 58 (1).

—— (2010b) 'European Integration by Daylight', *Comparative European Politics*, 8 (1).

—— (2010c) 'Europe in the Political Imagination', *Journal of Common Market Studies*, 48 (4).

White, Jonathan and Ypi, Lea (2010) 'Rethinking the Modern Prince: Partisanship and the Democratic Ethos', *Political Studies*, 58 (4).

Wittgenstein, Ludwig (1976) *Philosophical Investigations*, trans. G. E. M. Anscombe (Oxford: Blackwell).

Wlezien, Christopher (2005) 'On the Salience of Political Issues: The Problem with "Most Important Problem"', *Electoral Studies*, 24.

Yack, Bernard (2001) 'Popular Sovereignty and Nationalism', *Political Theory*, 29 (4).

Zaller, John R. (1992) *The Nature and Origins of Mass Opinion* (Cambridge: CUP).

Zielonka, Jan (2006) *Europe as Empire: The Nature of the Enlarged European Union* (Oxford: OUP).

Index